THE CASTLE OF PERSEVERANCE

Edited by
David N. Klausner

TEAMS • Middle English Texts Series

MEDIEVAL INSTITUTE PUBLICATIONS
Western Michigan University
Kalamazoo

Library of Congress Cataloging-in-Publication Data

The castle of perseverance / edited by David N. Klausner.
     p. cm. -- (Middle English texts series)
  "Published for TEAMS (The Consortium for the Teaching of the Middle Ages) in association with the University of Rochester."
  Includes bibliographical references.
  Summary: The play deals allegorically with the life of man and his struggle against sin, and the structure is for the most part based on a sequence of temptation, fall and redemption. The play describes the whole ontology of man, opening before his birth and ending after his death and his judgment before the throne of God. The volume includes an introduction, textual and explanatory notes, a bibliography and a glossary.
  ISBN 978-1-58044-149-0 (pbk. : alk. paper)
  1. Fall of man--Drama. 2. Theological anthropology--Christianity--Drama. 3. Moralities, English. 4. English drama--To 1500. I. Klausner, David N.
  PR1261.C3 2010
  822'.2--dc22

                        201001660

ISBN 978-1-58044-149-0

P 5 4 3 2 1

CONTENTS

❧ ACKNOWLEDGMENTS

I have the *felix labor* of thanking several people for their help in producing this edition. My first debt is to the late David Parry who, in the process of editing the text for his dissertation at the Graduate Centre for Study of Drama in the University of Toronto and directing it for the 1979 production by Poculi Ludique Societas, first sparked my interest in the play. More recently, Russell Peck has been a continual source of support and advice during the editorial process and contributed substantially to the glosses and notes, while John H. Chandler, Sandy Johnston, and Alan Lupack read and commented on the whole volume. The complex task of formatting the volume was in the hands of Leah Haught; thanks are due to Patricia Hollahan and her staff at Medieval Institute Publications for shepherding it through the press. I am grateful to the librarian of the Folger Library for permission to publish this part of the text of the Macro Manuscript, and for supplying the photograph of the manuscript's stage plan. Finally, it is a pleasure to acknowledge the generous support given to the Middle English Texts Series by the University of Rochester, the National Endowment for the Humanities, and TEAMS.

❧ Introduction

THE MORALITY PLAYS

The surviving morality plays, or moral interludes, as they were generally known to their contemporaries, comprise a group of five texts dating from the late fourteenth to the early sixteenth centuries: *The Pride of Life*, *The Castle of Perseverance*, *Mankind*, *Wisdom*, and *Everyman*.[1] Each of these plays deals allegorically with the life of man and his struggle against sin, and their structure is for the most part based on a sequence of temptation, fall, and redemption. Scholars have been hesitant to call this group of plays a genre, since each play differs from the others in substantial ways. *The Castle of Perseverance* describes the whole ontology of man, opening before his birth and ending after his death and his judgment before the throne of God. *Everyman*, in contrast, deals only with the final journey towards death. The group of plays is held together, however, by their consistent use of allegorical figures, by their use (in most cases) of a central representative human figure (variously called Mankind, Everyman, or Humanum Genus), and by their personification of the forces of good and evil which act upon him. Some of the plays (*Mankind*, *Wisdom*) require either considerable theatrical resources and skill sufficient to imply that they may have been intended for professional performance; *The Castle of Perseverance*, on the other hand, with its large cast of thirty-three players (plus two heralds), is unlikely to have been intended entirely for professional players, but may well have been performed by a mixed group of professionals and nonprofessionals.[2]

The background to these plays lies in part in the allegorization of good and evil which found its earliest expression in the *Psychomachia* of the late fourth-century poet Aurelius Clemens Prudentius. This poem describes a battle for the soul of man in which seven evil characteristics (Idolatry, Lust, Wrath, Pride, Indulgence, Greed, Discord) are pitted against seven virtues (Faith, Chastity, Patience, Humility, Sobriety, Good Works, Concord).[3] Since the battle takes place within the mind of man, there is no representative human figure. Prudentius' allegorical mode was immensely popular throughout the Middle Ages, and became one of the primary models for the allegorization of human characteristics, leading eventually to such texts as the *Roman de la Rose* of Guillaume de Lorris and Jean de Meun, as well as Robert Grosseteste's *Chateau d'Amour*. A second impetus behind the morality plays can be seen in the canon *Omnius utriusque sexus* of the Fourth Lateran Council (1215), which confirmed and elaborated earlier legislation and tradition requiring annual confession of all

---

[1] Scholarly argument over the appropriateness of the word "morality" continues. See Bawcutt, "Note on the Term 'Morality.'"

[2] On the possible use of mixed professional/nonprofessional casts for large plays, see Johnston, "Parish Playmaking," pp. 326–27.

[3] A useful translation of the *Psychomachia* is found in Isbell, *Last Poets of Imperial Rome*, pp. 127–52.

Christians, thus laying the groundwork for one of the most extensive educational programs in the history of the world. Faced with the necessity not only of educating the priesthood in the technical aspects and methodology of confession and penance but also of explaining to the laity the taxonomy of sins, allegory — the personification of individual sins, virtues, personal characteristics, or abstract qualities — was quickly adopted as an effective tool.

It is easy, however, to overestimate the importance of both these influences. The *Psychomachia* provided only the most general model of an allegorical battle, while the nature of sin as presented in these plays was both well-known and orthodox, so the plays' purpose is less educational, more, as Pamela King describes it, "to confirm and to celebrate rather than to argue."[4] From the late fifteenth century, the form and structure of the morality play was adapted in a variety of new directions, giving rise to a genre now most commonly known as the "Tudor interlude."[5] Where the morality play takes as its subject the whole moral life of man, the Tudor interludes focus on specific aspects of this life: political (Skelton's *Magnyfycence*, Bale's *King Johan*), educational (*Wyt and Science*), or social (*Youth*, *Hick Scorner*).

The frequent use in the morality plays of a "Vice" figure distinguished from the allegorized sins, such as Backbiter in *The Castle of Perseverance*, Mischief and the three Worldlings in *Mankind*, and Lucifer in *Wisdom*, has been seen as influencing Shakespeare's Falstaff and Iago as well as Marlowe's Mephistopheles. Indeed, for many years this possible influence on the canonical plays of the Elizabethan theater represented the sole interest in the morality plays. Those days are now in the past, and performances of all of these plays (with the exception of the fragmentary *Pride of Life*) have shown them to be highly effective vehicles for moral thought based on a keen understanding of the potential of allegory as a technique for the concrete representation of abstract ideas.

THE CASTLE OF PERSEVERANCE

The most comprehensive of the five surviving English morality plays, *The Castle of Perseverance* begins before the birth of Mankind (or Humanum Genus, as he is called in the speech headings) and concludes after his death with his ultimate salvation. The play opens with a sequence of "banns," the announcement of a forthcoming performance intended to be delivered as advertisement a week earlier. Blanks are left in lines 134, 145, and 148 for the insertion of the name of the town in which the play would be performed. This does not necessarily mean that the play was intended for touring, which (given its size) seems unlikely. Alexandra F. Johnston has argued that the text would likely have been used for performance at a chosen site, the name of which would then be inserted in the banns. The performance, probably involving the resources of a number of parishes, would have remained stationary, with the banns drawing in audiences from the surrounding countryside.[6] That this performance situation could recur in a different location at a different time is suggested by the options for the construction of the ditch given on the stage plan. Variations between the banns and the playtext (the appearance of Conscience in the banns but not in the play; the intercession of the Virgin Mary at the conclusion, rather than the Four Daughters of God) would seem to indicate that the play was revised at some point, without the banns being brought up to date.

---

[4] King, "Morality Plays," p. 243.

[5] See especially Craik, *Tudor Interlude*, and Happé and Hüsken, *Interludes and Early Modern Society*.

[6] See Johnston, "Parish Playmaking," pp. 326–27.

The play proper opens with boasting speeches (bringing to mind the ranting of Herod in the biblical plays) by Mankind's traditional three enemies, the World, the Flesh, and the Devil. Each of these speaks from his own scaffold, introducing his followers, the Seven Deadly Sins. World points out his chief henchman, Greed (Avarice, or Covetousness), whose central importance in the seduction of Mankind is signaled by his placement on his own scaffold. Flesh is accompanied by Sloth, Gluttony, and Lechery; the Devil by Pride, Wrath, and Envy. Mankind is born, perhaps from the bed which lies at the base of the castle. He points out his ignorance and helplessness, asking for God's grace; he introduces his two companions, the Good and Bad Angels, noting that every man has such a pair of advisors, one good and one evil. The two angels present their cases for the proper mode of life, and Mankind opts for the pleasures of the World. Introduced to the World by the Bad Angel, Mankind is dressed in fine clothes by the World's servants, Pleasure (Lust-liking) and Folly, and is sent with the help of the vice Backbiter to meet with Greed. Greed introduces him to the other Sins, who are called from the scaffolds of Flesh and the Devil, and Mankind takes his seat with them on Greed's scaffold.

Called by the Good Angel, Confession and Penitence invite Mankind to leave Greed; his initial reluctance disappears when he is pricked by the sharp lance of Penitence. He leaves Greed's clutches, and is invited by the Good Angel to take up residence in the Castle of Perseverance, where he will be protected by the seven cardinal virtues, Meekness (Humility), Abstinence, Chastity, Charity, Patience, Generosity, and Busyness (Industry). Once Mankind is ensconced in the castle, Backbiter begins to stir up trouble, by pressing the World, the Flesh, and the Devil to punish their attendant sins for losing Mankind's allegiance and then by assembling all the forces of evil to mount a siege of the castle. Each of the sins fights with its opposite virtue, and after a substantial onstage battle (including the Devil's appearance with fireworks, as described on the stage plan), the sins are defeated by the virtues with a shower of red roses, symbols of the Passion. But the battle is not over. During the fight, Mankind has grown old, and as the virtues triumph, Greed quietly approaches the castle and suggests to Mankind that now, in his old age, it would be appropriate to take some comfort in the world and enjoy his remaining days. Greed's arguments are persuasive, and to the virtues' dismay, Mankind leaves the castle to follow Greed. But his pleasure in his newfound wealth is interrupted by the figure of Death, who stabs Mankind with his lance. As Mankind lies dying, the World sends a young man who is to be known only as "I-Don't-Know-Who" to take away Mankind's riches. With his last words Mankind places himself in God's mercy.

At the moment of Mankind's death (presumably on the castle bed, where he was born), his Soul emerges from under the bed. Since Mankind died in a state of sin, the Good Angel is unable to help his Soul, and the Bad Angel carries it off to the Devil. But Mankind's last request for mercy has summoned the Four Daughters of God — Truth, Justice, Peace, and Mercy — who approach God's scaffold to plead the case for and against Mankind's salvation. With God sitting in judgment, Truth and Justice present the details of Mankind's sins, claiming that his deathbed repentance is insufficient for his salvation. Peace and Mercy present the case for Mankind, that to his repentance must be added Christ's sacrifice. God judges in favor of Mankind, and directs the Daughters to remove the Soul from Hell (the Devil's scaffold) and bring it to the seat of judgment, where the Soul is received into Heaven through God's mercy. Finally, to end the play, the actor playing God steps out of character and invites the audience to draw the proper moral conclusion, that from the beginning of our lives we should consider our endings.

STAGING

The Castle of Perseverance is unique among English medieval plays in its provision in the manuscript of a stage plan. Such drawings are known from plays on the continent, but no other English play includes such a wealth of information on the intended physical layout of the stage locations mentioned in the text and the stage directions.[7] The stage plan and a transcription of its text appear on pp. 8–9. Some aspects of this drawing are unambiguous. Situated at the outskirts of the playing-place (*platea*) are five "scaffolds," four of them at the compass points, each assigned to a major character in the play: God in the east, the World in the west, Flesh in the south, and the Devil in the north. The fifth scaffold, for Greed, is placed in the north-east between the scaffolds of God and the Devil, perhaps implying that money in itself is morally neutral and can be used either for good (almsgiving) or ill (overindulgence in the things of the world). The stage plan gives no indication of the structure of these scaffolds, but other illustrations, primarily continental, suggest that they were simply platforms with one or more sets of steps for access and seating for at least the scaffold's primary resident.[8] Painted backdrops would certainly have been a possibility.

The placement of the crenellated castle at the center of the acting area is also clear, as is the provision for Mankind's bed under the castle. To the right and left of the castle the position of Greed's "copbord" is given, and although it is not entirely clear what "at the ende of the castel" means, "be the beddys feet" would suggest its placement. The castle clearly stands on legs so that the bed beneath it is visible, with the upper part of the castle enclosed by stonework, perhaps painted on canvas. The castle must have room for nine people: the seven cardinal virtues, Mankind, and the Good Angel. Since they all speak, they must all be visible, and the virtues' throwing of roses (a symbol of the Passion) to defeat the sins would suggest that they must be on a higher level than the ground. The castle, therefore, likely had an upper level allowing its residents to appear above the crenellations. The bottom of the stage-plan page includes costume details for the Devil and for the Four Daughters of God.

Beyond this we begin to tread on less firm ground, though it is important to bear in mind that the stage plan is not a scale drawing, and that the physical relationship between its elements may be governed by the necessities of text placement. The principal problem in interpreting the stage plan has been the position of the ditch which surrounds the castle. Richard Southern thought it would have lain around the outside of the *platea* (following the plan's description that the water is "abowte the place"), and would have been a means of separating a paying audience.[9] This interpretation has been followed by many, such as Michael R. Kelley, although we have no evidence elsewhere in the fifteenth century of provisions taken for the separation of audience, nor for advance payment (the audience is asked to pay to see the devil Titivillus in *Mankind*, but only during the play).[10] More recent readings of the stage

---

[7] See Mills, "Diagrams for Staging Plays," and Fifield, "Arena Theatres."

[8] See, for example, the well-known miniature of the martyrdom of St. Apollonia by Jean Fouquet. A good copy can be found at <http://gallery.euroweb.hu/html/f/fouquet/bookhour/miniatu7.html>.

[9] Southern, *Medieval Theatre in the Round*. See, in particular, his reconstruction of the stage, pp. 123–42. Southern's interpretation assumes that "abowte" must mean "surrounding," but the word's meaning in the fifteenth century was quite broad enough to encompass both "surrounding" and simply "in" (see *Oxford English Dictionary* "about," 2).

[10] Kelley, *Flamboyant Drama*, p. 32.

plan take the ditch as encircling the castle itself and interpret its distance from the castle on the drawing as the scribe's recognition that he would need space to write a significant amount of explanatory text. By this reading, the ditch would form a moat around the castle, and might well be the ditch from which Sloth empties the water of grace at line 2329. This is not a perfect solution, since the stage plan's description of the ditch allows that the space "be strongly barryd al abowt" as an alternative to digging a ditch, and it is difficult to see how such a fence or wall could be used dramatically for the water of grace.[11] All of these aspects of the manuscript's stage plan were tested in practice in the full production of the play at the University of Toronto in 1979, under the direction of David Parry. That production was videotaped, and has been highly influential in demonstrating the likelihood that the ditch is intended to encircle the castle itself, not the entire acting area.[12]

THE MANUSCRIPT

The Castle of Perseverance is found uniquely in the so-called Macro Manuscript, named for a previous owner of the manuscript, the Reverend Cox Macro (1683–1767) of Bury St. Edmunds, Norfolk. Now housed in the Folger Library, Washington, DC, as MS V.a.354, the volume presently contains *Wisdom* and *Mankind* as well as *Castle*, and these three plays are commonly known as the "Macro plays" or the "Macro moralities." The volume does not represent a single manuscript; the three plays in their separate manuscripts were first bound together along with three other manuscripts in 1819, and then in the following year were rebound in a volume containing only the three plays. *The Castle of Perseverance* is now the third play in the volume, occupying folios 154–191. Two leaves are missing from the text, after line 1601 and line 3029. Since the scribe normally wrote about forty-eight lines to the page, each of these missing passages must have been about 100 lines long. An error in binding has put two sheets out of place, but the text is clear at these points and the proper order can easily be reconstructed.

The text was copied by a single scribe around 1440, and he was without question working from a previous manuscript. The pointed shoes which Pride recommends to Mankind had gone out of fashion by around 1425, so the most likely dating for the composition of the play (as opposed to its surviving manuscript) is sometime in the first quarter of the fifteenth century.

VERSE

Most of the play is written in a variant of the "bob and wheel" stanza familiar from such alliterative texts as *Sir Gawain and the Green Knight*, though the playwright also uses rhyme consistently and alliteration frequently but irregularly. About three-quarters of the stanzas are thirteen lines long, consisting of two quatrains (most commonly rhyming *abababab*) followed by the "bob and wheel" of five lines, rhyming *cdddc*. Most of the remaining stanzas are of nine lines, beginning with one rather than two quatrains. There has been consider-

---

[11] See Schmitt, "Was There a Medieval Theatre in the Round?" and Belsey, "Stage Plan of *The Castle of Perseverance*." The various arguments are summarized by Tydeman, *English Medieval Theatre 1400–1500*, pp. 78–85.

[12] The complete videotape of the production, as well as a one-hour "overview" of the play are produced by the University of Toronto's Information Commons, and are available both for purchase and rental from <http://www.utoronto.ca/ic/mediadistribution/videocollection/mediev.html>.

able discussion over the possibility of multiple authorship; Jacob Bennett argued that three authors were likely involved, one composing the Banns (lines 1–156), one the bulk of the play from line 157 to the appearance of the Soul (line 3120), and a third author (perhaps revising an earlier ending) adding the colloquy of the Four Daughters of God (from line 3021 to the end). Considering the style of writing and the vocabulary of the various parts of the play, the argument in favor of more than one author for the play itself is not strong, though a good case can be made for a different author for the Banns.

The playwright's use of alliteration frequently leads him to end a line with a phrase used more as a tag or filler than for its meaning. This is especially common as the Three Enemies or the Seven Sins describe the extent of their influence by means of a phrase whose real meaning is "everywhere." The bulk of these tag lines are made up of a pair of prepositional phrases with a contrasting but alliterating pair of nouns as their objects; among these would be such phrases as "be dykys and be denne," "be fen and flode," "be strete and stalle," "be strete and stye," "be sompe and syke," "be downe and dyche," etc.

THE BANNS

Introductory banns ("proclamations, announcements") appear in several other plays, including *The Pride of Life*, the Croxton *Play of the Sacrament*, and the N-Town Plays, and were likely a common mode of publicizing an upcoming performance. The usual format of the banns involves a summary of the action of the play and an invitation to attend a performance. This invitation is sometimes locally specific (as in both *Castle* and the N-Town Plays), with a blank space or place-marker left to allow the speaker to insert the name of the town in which the performance will take place (see lines 134, 145, and 148). The time for the performance is usually made clear: *Castle* will take place "this day sevenenyt" — a week hence. The speaker(s) of the banns are often styled as "vexillators" (heralds or standard-bearers), from Latin "*vexilla*" (banner).

EXTRA-METRICAL LATIN LINES

An unusual problem in the text of *Castle* is the frequent appearance in the manuscript of single lines of Latin (often scriptural quotations) which are clearly not a part of the metrical structure of the stanza. In some cases, the content of these lines also appears in English as a part of the stanza, although, as David Parry points out, the sense of the Latin does not always correspond to the English, and some of the scriptural quotations seem more like reflective comments on the playtext.[13] Some of these lines are written in the manuscript as though they were part of the playtext, some of them appear as glosses in the margin. Parry's 1983 dissertation concluded, I think rightly, that these lines were not intended as part of the play.[14] It is most likely that they were added to an earlier manuscript of the play as marginal or interlinear glosses on the English passages which translate them, and either in the present manuscript or a close ancestor of it were mistakenly incorporated into the text of the play. Parry concludes that of the forty-six extra-metrical Latin lines, seven do make sense as part of the playtext. These are the single line of Mercy at 3313a and the six lines of God after 3562.[15]

---

[13] Parry, "Margin of Error," pp. 42–50.

[14] Parry, "Margin of Error."

[15] Parry, "Margin of Error," pp. 54–56.

I have followed Eccles' practice of printing the lines where they occur in the manuscript but not including them in the line numbering. In performance it is very likely that these lines should not be spoken, though it should also be noted that there are also in the play lines of Latin (see, for example, lines 3271–73 and 3284–86) which are a part of the metrical structure of the stanza and should be spoken.

THIS EDITION

The present edition is based on a fresh transcription of the manuscript from David Bevington's facsimile edition.[16] The text has been lightly modernized: manuscript thorn (þ) has been replaced by *th* ("þis">"this") and yogh (ȝ) by *y* ("ȝet">"yet") or *g* ("ȝive">"give") as appropriate. The manuscript's interchangeability of *u* and *v* (and sometimes *w*) to indicate *v* ("euery">"every") has been rationalized; *w* has been left when it indicates *u* ("abowt"). Ampersands (&) have been expanded to "and." Manuscript spelling is relatively consistent: "se" is used for the verb of vision, "see" for a large body of water. Since the scribe uses "the" both as the definite article and as the second person oblique pronoun, the latter is adjusted to "thee" in the text. Final *e* which must be pronounced in polysyllabic words is indicated by an acute accent ("chastité"). Where appropriate *i* has been replaced by *j* ("iustice">"justice"); initial *ff* has been replaced by *F*. Unambiguous scribal errors and passages damaged in the manuscript have been silently corrected; details of such corrections can be found in the textual notes. Major emendations are indicated with square brackets. For purely practical reasons, I have adopted Eccles' division of the play into twenty-three scenes. These divisions are generally quite clear in the action of the play, but there is no manuscript justification for them.

The manuscript indicates the metrical scheme of each stanza with brackets, placing the first and last lines of the "wheel" to the right of the bracket enclosing the rest of the lines; as an indication of this manuscript distinction, the lines written to the right of the brackets are indented.

MANUSCRIPT

Indexed as item 917 in Boffey and Edwards, eds., *New Index of Middle English Verse*:

• Folger Shakespeare Library MS. V.a.354 (the Macro Manuscript)

EDITIONS AND FACSIMILES

Bevington, David, ed. *The Macro Plays: A Facsimile Edition with Facing Transcription*. New York: Johnson Reprint, 1972. Pp. 1–154.

———. *Medieval Drama*. Boston: Houghton Mifflin Company, 1975. Pp. 796–900.

Eccles, Mark, ed. *The Macro Plays*. EETS o.s. 262. London: Oxford University Press, 1969. Pp. 1–112.

Furnivall, F. J., and A. W. Pollard, eds. *The Macro Plays*. EETS e.s. 91. London: Oxford University Press, 1904. Pp. 75–188.

Happé, Peter, ed. *Four Morality Plays*. Harmondsworth: Penguin Books, 1979. Pp. 75–210.

Schell, Edgar T., and J. D. Schuchter, eds. *English Morality Plays and Moral Interludes*. New York: Holt, Rinehart and Winston, 1969. Pp. 1–110.

---

[16] Bevington, *Macro Plays*.

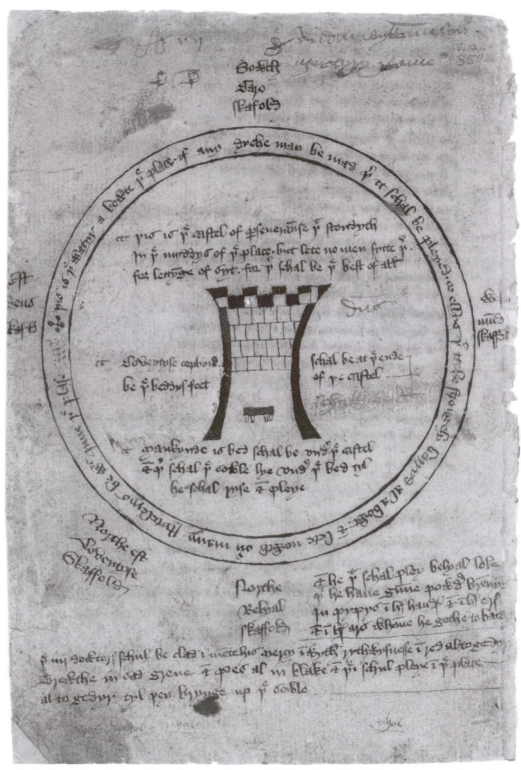

Stage Plan for *Castle of Perseverance*. Folger MS V.a.354, fol. 191v. By permission of the Folger Library, Washington, D.C.

THE CASTLE OF PERSEVERANCE

> Sowth
> Caro (Flesh)
> Skafold

This is the watyr abowte the place, if any dyche may be mad ther it schal be pleyed, or ellys that it be strongely barryd al abowt, and lete nowth ovyrmany stytelerys (marshalls) be wythinne the plase.

> This is the castel of perseveraunse that stondyth
> in the myddys of the place, but lete no men sytte ther,
> for lettynge (blocking) of syt (sight), for ther schal be the best of all.

Est	Coveytyse (Greed's) copbord be the beddys feet /	West
Deus (God)	schal be at the ende of the castel.	Mundus (World)
Skafold		Skaffold

> Mankynde is bed schal be undyr the castel
> and ther schal the sowle lye undyr the bed tyl
> he schal ryse and pleye.

Northe est	Northe	And he that schal pley Belyal loke
Coveytyse (Greed)	Belyal (Devil)	that he have gunnepowdyr brennynge
Skaffold	Skaffold	in pypys in hys handys and in hys erys
		and in hys ars whanne he gothe to batayl.

The iiij dowterys schul be clad in mentelys, Mercy in wyth, Rythwysnesse[1]
in red altogedyr, Trewthe in sad (somber) grene, and Pes al in blake, and thei schul
pleye in the place altogedyr tyl they brynge up the sowle.

THE CASTLE OF PERSEVERANCE

> Hec sunt nomina ludentium.
In primis ij vexillatores.

---

[1] *The four daughters will be clad in mantles, Mercy in white, Righteousness*

Mundus et cum eo Voluptas, Stulticia, et Garcio.
Belyal et cum eo Superbia, Ira, et Invidia.
Caro et cum eo Gula, Luxuria, et Accidia.
Humanum Genus et cum eo Bonus Angelus et Malus Angelus.
Auaricia, Detraccio.
Confessio, Penitencia.
Humilitas, Paciencia, Caritas, Abstinencia, Castitas, Solicitudo, et Largitas.
Mors.
Anima.
Misericordia, Veritas, Justicia, et Pax.
Pater sedens in trono.
  Summa xxxvj ludentium.

  [These are the names of the players.
First, two standard-bearers.
World and with him Pleasure, Folly, and the Boy.
Devil and with him Pride, Anger, and Envy.
Flesh and with him Gluttony, Lechery, and Sloth.
Mankind and with him Good Angel and Bad Angel.
Greed, Backbiter.
Confession, Penance.
Meekness, Patience, Charity, Abstinence, Chastity, Industry, and Generosity.
Death.
The Soul.
Mercy, Truth, Justice, and Peace.
The Father sitting in his throne.
  In total 36 players.]

THE BANNS

PRIMUS VEXILLATOR Glorious God, in all degres lord most of myth,[1]	
That Hevene and erthe made of nowth, bothe se and lond,	*nought; sea*
The aungelys in Hevene hym to serve bryth	*bright*
And mankynde in mydylerd he made wyth hys hond,	*on earth*
5 And our lofly Lady, that lanterne is of lyth,	*Lady full of love; light*
Save oure lege lord the kynge, the leder of this londe,	*liege; leader*
And all the ryall of this rewme and rede hem the ryth,[2]	
And all the goode comowns of this towne that beforn us stonde	*common people*
In this place.	
10 We mustyr you wyth menschepe,	*summon; honor*

---

[1] *FIRST STANDARD-BEARER Glorious God, in all degrees lord of most might*

[2] *And all the nobles of this realm, and advise them the right (way)*

And freyne you of frely frenchepe.[1]
Cryst safe you all fro schenchepe   *save; harm*
    That knowyn wyl our case.   *theme*

SECUNDUS VEXILLATOR The case of oure comynge you to declare *SECOND STANDARD-BEARER*
15   Every man in hymself for sothe he it may fynde: *as a truth*
Whou Mankynde into this werld born is ful bare   *How; naked*
And bare schal beryed be at hys last ende.   *buried*
God hym gevyth to aungelys ful yep and ful yare,   *two; alert; quick*
The Goode Aungel and the Badde to hym for to lende.   *with him; dwell*
20   The Goode techyth hym goodnesse, the Badde synne and sare.   *misery*
Whanne the ton hath the victory, the tothyr goth behende   *one; other goes behind*
    Be skyll.   *According to [one's] desire (choice)*
The Goode Aungel coveytyth evermore Mans salvacion   *yearns for*
And the Badde bysytyth hym evere to hys dampnacion.   *besets (harasses)*
25   And God hathe govyn Man fre arbritracion   *given; free will*
    Whethyr he wyl hymself save or hys soule spyll.   *destroy*

PRIMUS VEXILLATOR Spylt is Man spetously whanne he to synne asent.[2]
The Bad Aungel thanne bryngyth hym thre enmys so stout: *enemies; strong*
The Werlde, the Fende, the fowl Flesche so joly and jent;   *Devil; comely; elegant*
30   Thei ledyn hym ful lustyly wyth synnys al abowt.   *lead*
Pyth wyth Pride and Coveytyse, to the Werld is he went,   *Furnished; gone*
To meynten hys manhod all men to hym lout.   *maintain his reputation; bow*
Aftyr Ire and Envye the Fend hath to hym lent,   *Anger; Devil*
Bakbytynge and endytynge wyth all men for to route,[3]
35   Ful evyn.   *Completely*
But the fowle Flesch, homlyest of all,   *most familiar*
Slawth, Lust and Leccherye gun to hym call,   *Sloth; begin*
Glotony and othyr synnys bothe grete and small.
    Thus Mans soule is soylyd wyth synnys moo thanne sevyn.   *more*

SECUNDUS VEXILLATOR Whanne Mans sowle is soylyd wyth synne and wyth sore, *misery*
41   Thanne the Goode Aungyl makyth mykyl mornynge   *much*
That the lofty lyknesse of God schulde be lore   *lost*
Thorwe the Badde Aungellys fals entysynge.
He sendyth to hym Concyens, pryckyd ful pore,   *dressed very poorly*
45   And clere Confescyon wyth Penauns-doynge.
Thei mevyn Man to mendement that he mysdyd before.   *move; reform that which*
Thus thei callyn hym to clennesse and to good levynge,
    Wythoutyn dystaunce.   *disagreement*
Mekenesse, Pacyense, and Charyté,

---

[1] *And ask generous friendship of you*

[2] *Destroyed is mankind cruelly when he to sin agrees*

[3] *Slandering and accusing against all men to stir up trouble*

50	Sobyrnesse, Besynesse, and Chastyté,	*Abstinence, Industry*
	And Largyté, vertuys of good degré,	*Generosity*
	Man callyth to the Castel of Good Perseveraunce.	

PRIMUS VEXILLATOR   The Castel of Perseverauns wanne Mankynde hath tan,[1]

	Wel armyd wyth vertus and ovyrcome all vycys,	
55	There the Good Aungyl makyth ful mery thanne	
	That Mankynde hath ovyrcome hys gostly enmiis.	*spiritual enemies*
	The Badde Aungyl mornyth that he hath myssyd Man.	*mourns; lost*
	He callyth the Werld, the Fende, and the foule Flesch, iwys,	*Devil; truly*
	And all the sevene synnys to do that they canne	
60	To brynge Mankynd ageyn to bale out of blys,	*harm*
	With wronge.	
	Pride asayleth Meknesse wyth all hys myth,	*might*
	Ire ageyns Paciensse ful fast ganne he fyth,	*Wrath; fight*
	Envye ageyn Charyté stryvyth ful ryth,	*against; strives fiercely*
65	But Covytyse ageyns Largyté fytyth ovyrlonge.	*fights*

SECUNDUS VEXILLATOR   Coveytyse Mankynd evere coveytyth for to qwell.   *desires to destroy*

	He gaderyth to hym Glotony ageyns Sobyrnesse,	*Abstinence*
	Leccherye wyth Chastyté fyteth ful fell	*fights cruelly*
	And Slawthe in Goddys servyse ageyns Besynesse.	*Sloth; Industry*
70	Thus vycys ageyns vertues fytyn ful snelle.	*fight; vigorously*
	Every buskyth to brynge Man to dystresse.	*Each one strives*
	But Penaunce and Confescion wyth Mankynd wyl melle,	*Unless; intervene*
	The vycys arn ful lyckely the vertues to opresse,	*likely*
	Saun dowte.	*Without*
75	Thus in the Castel of Good Perseverance	
	Mankynd is maskeryd wyth mekyl varyaunce.	*confused; much contention*
	The Good Aungyl and the Badde be evere at dystaunce;	*in opposition*
	The Goode holdyth hym inne, the Badde wold brynge hym owte.	

PRIMUS VEXILLATOR   Owt of Good Perseveraunce whanne Mankynde wyl not come,

80	Yyt the Badde Aungyl wyth Coveytyse hym gan asayle,	*attack*
	Fyndende hym in poverté and penaunce so benome,	*Finding; numbed*
	And bryngyth hym in beleve in defaute for to fayle.[2]	
	Thanne he profyrth hym good and gold so gret a sowme,	*offers him goods; sum*
	That if he wyl come ageyn and wyth the Werld dayle,	*dally*
85	The Badde Aungyl to the Werld tollyth hym downe	*entices*
	The Castel of Perseveraunce to fle fro the vayle	*flee; benefit*
	And blysse.	
	Thanne the Werld begynnyth hym to restore.	
	Have he nevere so mykyl, yyt he wold have more;	*much*

---

[1] *When Mankind has taken possession of the Castle of Perseverance*

[2] *And causes him to believe he will suffer need through poverty*

THE CASTLE OF PERSEVERANCE

90   Thus the Badde Aungyl leryth hym hys lore.   *teaches; lesson*
           The more a man agyth, the harder he is.   *ages; more miserly*

SECUNDUS VEXILLATOR   Hard a man is in age and covetouse be kynde.   *by nature*
           Whanne all othyr synnys Man hath forsake,
           Evere the more that he hath the more is in hys mynde
95   To gadyr and to gete good wyth woo and wyth wrake.   *gather; harm*
           Thus the Goode Aungyl caste is behynde
           And the Badde Aungyl Man to hym takyth,
           That wryngyth hym wrenchys to hys laste ende   *deceives him with tricks*
           Tyl Deth comyth ful dolfully and loggyth hym in a lake   *lodges*
100   Ful lowe.
           Thanne is Man on molde maskeryd in mynde.   *on earth confused*
           He sendyth afftyr hys sekkatours, ful fekyl to fynde,   *executors, untrustworthy*
           And hys eyr aftyrward comyth evere behynde,   *heir*
           I-Wot-Not-Who is hys name, for he hym nowt knowe.   *I-Don't-Know-Who; not at all*

PRIMUS VEXILLATOR   Man knowe not who schal be hys eyr and governe hys good.   *heir*
106   He caryth more for hys catel thanne for hys cursyd synne.   *possessions*
           To putte hys good in governaunce he mengyth hys mod,[1]
           He wolde that it were scyfftyd amongys hys ny kynne.   *divided; near kin*
           But ther schal com a lythyr ladde wyth a torne hod,   *rascal; hood*
110   I-Wot-Nevere-Who schal be hys name, hys clothis be ful thynne, *I-Know-Never-Who*
           Schal eryth the erytage that nevere was of hys blod,   *inherit; heritage; in his family*
           Whanne al hys lyfe is lytyd upon a lytyl pynne   *reduced to*
               At the laste.
           On lyve whanne he may no lenger lende,   *Alive; remain*
115   Mercy he callyth at hys laste ende:
           "Mercy, God! Be now myn frende!"
               Wyth that Mans spyryt is paste.   *departed*

SECUNDUS VEXILLATOR   Whanne Manys spyryt is past, the Badde Aungyl ful fell *very cruel*
           Cleymyth that for covetyse Mans sowle schuld ben hys   *Claims; greed*
120   And for to bere it ful boystowsly wyth hym into Hell.   *violently*
           The Good Aungyl seyth nay, the spyryt schal to blys
           For at hys laste ende of mercy he gan spell   *Because; he spoke*
           And therfore of mercy schal he nowth mysse,   *not*
           And oure lofly Ladi if sche wyl for hym mell,   *Lady full of love; intercede*
125   Be mercy and be menys in Purgatory he is,   *Through; mediation*
               In ful byttyr place.   *very*
           Thus mowthys confession   *oral*
           And hys hertys contricion   *heart's*
           Schal save Man fro dampnacion
130   Be Goddys mercy and grace.

---

[1] *To put his goods in the control [of others] troubles his mind*

PRIMUS VEXILLATOR   Grace if God wyl graunte us of hys mykyl myth   *great power*
   These parcellys in propyrtés we purpose us to playe[1]
   This day sevenenyt before you in syth   *a week from tonight; sight*
   At _____ on the grene in ryal aray.   *royal*
135 Ye, haste you thanne thedyrward, syrys, hendly in hyth,   *Yes; very graciously*
   All goode neyborys ful specyaly we you pray,
   And loke that ye be there betyme, luffely and lyth,   *early, willingly and ready*
   For we schul be onward be underne of the day,   *ready by midmorning (ca. 9 a.m.)*
    Dere frendys.
140 We thanke you of all good dalyaunce   *pleasant company*
   And of all youre specyal sportaunce   *entertainment*
   And preye you of good contynuaunce   *continuing [of your favor]*
   To oure lyvys endys.

SECUNDUS VEXILLATOR   Os oure lyvys we love you, thus takande oure leve.   *As; taking*
145 Ye manly men of _____, ther Crist save you all!
   He maynten youre myrthys and kepe you fro greve   *[May] he; pleasures; from grief*
   That born was of Mary myld in an ox stall.
   Now mery be all _____, and wel mote ye cheve,   *may you thrive*
   All oure feythful frendys, ther fayre mote ye fall!   *may good luck befall you*
150 Ya, and welcum be ye, whanne ye com prys for to preve   *to test our worth*
   And worthi to be worchepyd in bowre and in hall   *honored; chamber; hall*
    And in every place.
   Farewel, fayre frendys,
   That lofly wyl lystyn and lendys.   *graciously; give ear*
155 Cryste kepe you fro fendys!
   Trumpe up and lete us pace.   *Blow the trumpet; pass*

[Scene i]
MUNDUS   Worthy wytys in al this werld wyde,   *THE WORLD; persons*
   Be wylde wode wonys and every weye-went,   *forest dwellings; pathway*
   Precyous prinse, prekyd in pride,   *adorned with*
160 Thorwe this propyr pleyn place in pes be ye bent!   *fine open; silence; submissive*
   Buske you, bolde bachelerys, undyr my baner to abyde   *Prepare yourselves; young men*
   Where bryth basnetys be bateryd and backys ar schent.   *bright helmets; broken*
   Ye, syrys semly, all same syttyth on syde,   *all [who] sit together*
   For bothe be see and be londe my sondys I have sent,   *sea; messengers*
165   Al the world myn name is ment.   *[Through] all; spoken*
   Al abowtyn my bane is blowe,   *summons is announced*
   In every cost I am knowe,   *land; known*
   I do men rawyn on ryche rowe   *I make men act madly in a rich procession*
    Tyl thei be dyth to dethys dent.   *put to death's blow*

---

[1] *We intend to play these parts with stage properties*

170	Assarye, Acaye, and Almayne, — *Assyria, Achaia (Greece); Germany*
	Cavadoyse, Capadoyse, and Cananee, — *Calvados, Cappadocia; Canaan*
	Babyloyne, Brabon, Burgoyne, and Bretayne, — *Brabant, Burgundy; Brittany*
	Grece, Galys, and to the Gryckysch See, — *Galicia (Spain); Aegean Sea*
	I meve also Masadoyne in my mykyl mayne, — *control; Macedonia; great power*
175	Frauns, Flaundrys, and Freslonde, and also Normandé, — *Friesland*
	Pyncecras, Parys, and longe Pygmayne,[1]
	And every toun in Trage, evyn to the Dreye Tre, — *Thrace(?); Dry Tree*
	Rodys and ryche Rome. — *Rhodes*
	All these londys at myn avyse — *direction*
180	Arn castyn to my werldly wyse. — *placed in; manner*
	My tresorer, Syr Covetyse, — *treasurer*
	Hath sesyd hem holy to me. — *given; entirely*
	Therfor my game and my gle growe ful glad. — *sport; pleasure*
	Ther is no wythe in this werld that my wytte wyl me warne. — *creature; wisdom; refuse*
185	Every ryche rengne rapyth hym ful rad — *powerful kingdom hastens quickly*
	In lustys and in lykyngys my lawys to lerne. — *desires; pleasures*
	Wyth fayre folke in the felde freschly I am fadde. — *gaily; fed*
	I dawnse doun as a doo be dalys ful derne. — *doe; valleys very dark*
	What boy bedyth batayl or debatyth wyth blad, — *offers; contends; sword*
190	Hym were betyr to ben hangyn hye in Hell herne — *a corner of Hell*
	Or brent on lyth levene. — *burned with bright lightning*
	Whoso spekyth ageyn the Werld
	In a presun he schal be sperd. — *prison; confined*
	Myn hest is holdyn and herd — *command is obeyed and heard*
195	Into hyye Hevene. — *As far as*

[Scene ii]

BELYAL	Now I sytte, Satanas, in my sad synne, — *steadfast*
	As devyl dowty, in draf as a drake. — *brave; filth; dragon*
	I champe and I chafe, I chocke on my chynne, — *gnash my teeth; thrust out*
	I am boystous and bold, as Belyal the blake. — *violent; black*
200	What folk that I grope thei gapyn and grenne, — *grasp; gape; gnash teeth*
	Iwys, fro Carlylle into Kent my carpynge thei take,[2]
	Bothe the bak and the buttoke brestyth al on brenne, — *burst; burning*
	Wyth werkys of wreche I werke hem mykyl wrake. — *vengeance; do them much harm*
	In woo is al my wenne. — *pleasure*
205	In care I am cloyed — *sorrow; burdened*
	And fowle I am anoyed — *foully; offended*
	But Mankynde be stroyed — *Unless; destroyed*
	Be dykys and be denne. — *ditches; valleys (i.e., everywhere)*

---

[1] *Pincenarii (Thrace), Paris, and the land of the Pygmies*

[2] *Truly, from Carlisle into Kent they receive my rebuke (i.e., all of England — see note)*

	Pryde is my prince in perlys ipyth;	*decorated*
210	Wretthe, this wrecche, wyth me schal wawe;	*Wrath; go*
	Envye into werre wyth me schal walkyn wyth;	*war; walk nimbly*
	Wyth these faytourys I am fedde, in feyth I am fawe.	*deceivers; fed; happy*
	As a dyngne devyl in my dene I am dyth.	*worthy; den; placed*
	Pryde, Wretthe, and Envye, I sey in my sawe,	*speech*
215	Kyngys, kayserys, and kempys, and many a kene knyth,[1]	
	These lovely lordys han lernyd hem my lawe.	*have taught them*
	To my dene thei wyl drawe.	*den; come*
	Al holy Mankynne	*Entirely*
	To Helle but I wynne,	*unless; entice*
220	In bale is my bynne	*torment; bin (confinement)*
	And schent undyr schawe.	*confounded; forest (grove, thicket)*

	On Mankynde is my trost, in contré iknowe,	*expectation; known*
	Wyth my tyre and wyth my tayl tytly to tene.	*attire; quickly to harm*
	Thorwe Flaundris and Freslonde faste I gan flowe,	*Friesland quickly; move*
225	Fele folke on a flokke to flappyn and to flene.	*Many; beat; flay*
	Where I graspe on the grounde, grym ther schal growe.	*Wherever I touch; strife*
	Gadyr you togedyr, ye boyis, on this grene!	
	In this brode bugyl a blast wanne I blowe,	
	Al this werld schal be wood, iwys, as I wene	*mad; think*
230	And to my byddynge bende.	*obey*
	Wythly on syde	*Quickly*
	On benche wyl I byde	
	To tene, this tyde,	*harm; time*
	Al holy Mankende.	*Entirely*

[Scene iii]

CARO	I byde as a brod brustun-gutte abovyn on these tourys.	*FLESH; dwell; bursting gut*
236	Every body is the betyr that to myn byddynge is bent.	*obedient*
	I am Mankyndys fayre Flesch, florchyd in flowrys.	*adorned with*
	My lyfe is wyth lustys and lykynge ilent.	*pleasure set*
	Wyth tapytys of tafata I tymbyr my towrys.	*tapestries; decorate*
240	In myrthe and in melodye my mende is iment.	*thought is disposed*
	Thou I be clay and clad, clappyd undir clowrys,	*clod, thrust under ground*
	Yyt wolde I that my wyll in the werld went,	*desire*
	Ful trew I you behyth.	*promise*
	I love wel myn ese,	
245	In lustys me to plese;	
	Thou synne my sowle sese	*Although; possess*
	I geve not a myth.	*mite*

---

[1] *Kings, emperors, soldiers, and many a brave knight*

        In Glotony gracyous now am I growe;   *grown*

        Therfore he syttyth semly here be my syde.   *handsomely*

250   In Lechery and Lykynge lent am I lowe   *Pleasure; placed*

        And Slawth, my swete sone, is bent to abyde.   *Sloth; inclined*

        These three are nobyl, trewly I trowe,   *believe*

        Mankynde to tenyn and trecchyn a tyde.   *harm; trick at times*

        Wyth many berdys in bowre my blastys are blowe,   *maidens in bowers; blown*

255   Be weys and be wodys, thorwe this werld wyde,

            The sothe for to seyne.   *truth*

        But if mans Flesch fare wel   *Unless; succeed*

        Bothe at mete and at mele,   *food*

        Dyth I am in gret del   *Put; sorrow*

260   And browt into peyne.

        And aftyr good fare in feyth thou I fell,   *meal; though I die*

        Thou I dryve to dust, in drosse for to drepe,   *Although; turn; dirt; drop*

        Thow my sely sowle were haryed to Hell,   *Although; miserable; harrowed*

        Woso wyl do these werkys, iwys he schal wepe   *Whoso; truly*

265   Evyr wythowtyn ende.

        Behold the Werld, the Devyl, and me!

        Wyth all oure mythis we kyngys three   *powers*

        Nyth and day besy we be   *Night*

            For to distroy Mankende

270   If that we may.

        Therfor on hylle

        Syttyth all stylle   *Sit*

        And seth wyth good wylle   *see*

            Oure ryche aray.   *display*

[Scene iv]

HUMANUS GENUS   Aftyr oure forme-faderys kende   *MANKIND; forefather's nature*

276   This nyth I was of my modyr born.   *night*

        Fro my modyr I walke, I wende,   *go*

        Ful feynt and febyl I fare you beforn.   *feeble; go before you*

        I am nakyd of lym and lende   *loin*

280   As Mankynde is schapyn and schorn.   *shaped and fashioned*

        I not wedyr to gon ne to lende   *I do not know where; stay*

        To helpe myself mydday nyn morn.   *nor*

            For schame I stonde and schende.   *am confounded*

        I was born this nyth in blody ble   *night; condition*

285   And nakyd I am, as ye may se.

        A, Lord God in Trinité,

            Whow Mankende is unthende!   *How; feeble*

        Whereto I was to this werld browth   *Why; brought*

        I ne wot, but to woo and wepynge   *don't know, except*

290   I am born and have ryth nowth   *nothing at all*

To helpe myself in no doynge.   *anything I do*
I stonde and stodye al ful of thowth.   *am confused; anxiety*
Bare and pore is my clothynge.
A sely crysme myn hed hath cawth   *little chrisom; caught*
295   That I tok at myn crystenynge.
          Certys I have no more.
Of erthe I cam, I wot ryth wele,   *know right well*
And as erthe I stande this sele.   *at this time*
Of Mankende it is gret dele.   *pity*
300   Lord God, I crye thyne ore!   *beg your grace*

To aungels bene asynyd to me: *Two; assigned*
The ton techyth me to goode;   *The one urges me toward*
On my ryth syde ye may hym se;   *right*
He cam fro Criste that deyed on Rode.   *Cross*
305   Anothyr is ordeynyd here to be
That is my foo, be fen and flode;   *by fen and stream (everywhere)*
He is about in every degré   *constantly*
To drawe me to tho devylys wode   *those fierce devils*
          That in Helle be thycke.
310   Swyche to hath every man on lyve   *Such two; alive*
To rewlyn hym and hys wyttys fyve.   *rule*
Whanne man doth evyl, the ton wolde schryve,   *one will absolve him*
          The tothyr drawyth to wycke.   *other entices; wickedness*

But syn these aungelys be to me falle,   *since; are alloted to me*
315   Lord Jhesu, to you I bydde a bone   *ask a boon*
That I may folwe, be strete and stalle,   *street; dwelling (i.e., everywhere)*
The aungyl that cam fro Hevene trone.   *Heaven's throne*
Now, Lord Jhesu in Hevene halle,
Here whane I make my mone.   *Hear [me] when; complaint*
320   Coryows Criste, to you I calle.   *Caring*
As a grysly gost I grucche and grone,   *frightful spirit; complain*
          I wene, ryth ful of thowth.   *think; anxiety*
A, Lord Jhesu, wedyr may I goo?   *where*
A crysyme I have and no moo.   *chrisom*
325   Alas, men may be wondyr woo   *very woeful*
          Whanne thei be fyrst forth browth.   *brought*

BONUS ANGELUS   Ya forsothe, and that is wel sene,   *GOOD ANGEL; truly; appropriate*
Of woful wo man may synge!
For iche creature helpyth hymself bedene   *fends for himself immediately*
330   Save only man at hys comynge.   *Except; birth*
Nevyrthelesse turne thee fro tene   *harm*
And serve Jhesu, Hevene kynge,
And thou shalt, be grevys grene,   *groves*
Fare wel in all thynge.   *Succeed*

335   That Lord thi lyfe hath lante.   *lent*
      Have hym alwey in thi mynde
      That deyed on Rode for mankynde   *died; Cross*
      And serve hym to thi lyfes ende
        And sertys thou schalt not wante.   *certainly*

MALUS ANGELUS Pes, aungel, thi wordys are not wyse. *BAD ANGEL; Peace*
341   Thou counselyst hym not aryth!   *properly*
      He schal hym drawyn to the Werldys servyse *take himself*
      To dwelle wyth caysere, kynge, and knyth, *emperor; knight*
        That in londe be hym non lyche. *So that there will be no one like him in the world*
345   Cum on wyth me, stylle as ston.
      Thou and I to the World schul goon   *go*
      And thanne thou schalt sen anon   *see*
        Whow sone thou schalt be ryche.   *How soon*

BONUS ANGELUS A, pes, aungel, thou spekyst folye.   *peace*
350   Why schuld he coveyt werldys goode,
      Syn Criste in erthe and hys meynye   *followers*
      All in povert here thei stode?   *poverty; lived*
      Werldys wele, be strete and stye, *wealth; path (i.e., everywhere)*
      Faylyth and fadyth as fysch in flode,   *stream*
355   But Heveneryche is good and trye, *kingdom of Heaven; worthy*
      Ther Criste syttyth bryth as blode,   *bright*
        Wythoutyn any dystresse.
      To the World wolde he not flyt   *run*
      But forsok it every whytt.   *completely*
360   Example I fynde in holy wryt,
        He wyl bere me wytnesse.

    Divicias et paupertates ne dederis michi, Domine.[1]

MALUS ANGELUS Ya, ya, man, leve hym nowth,   *believe; not*
      But cum wyth me, be stye and strete. *path (i.e., everywhere)*
      Have thou a gobet of the werld cawth, *[Once] you have a taste; caught*
365   Thou schalt fynde it good and swete.
      A fayre lady thee schal be tawth   *given*
      That in bowre thi bale schal bete. *chamber your sorrow will be remedied*
      Wyth ryche rentys thou schalt be frawth, *income; furnished*
      Wyth sylke sendel to syttyn in sete. *clothing; seat*
370   I rede, late bedys be. *advise, let prayer beads alone*
      If thou wylt have wel thyn hele   *health*
      And faryn wel at mete and mele,   *fare; meal*

---

[1] *Give me neither wealth nor poverty, Lord* (see Proverbs 30:8)

Wyth Goddys servyse may thou not dele	*be concerned*
But cum and folwe me.	

HUMANUM GENUS   Whom to folwe wetyn I ne may.   *I do not know*
376   I stonde and stodye and gynne to rave.   *am confused; begin*
        I wolde be ryche in gret aray   *fine clothes*
        And fayn I wolde my sowle save.   *gladly*
            As wynde in watyr I wave.   *waver*
380   Thou woldyst to the World I me toke,   *myself*
        And he wolde that I it forsoke.
        Now so God me helpe and the holy boke
            I not wyche I may have.   *do not know*

MALUS ANGELUS   Cum on, man, whereof hast thou care?
385   Go we to the Werld, I rede thee, blyve,   *advise; quickly*
        For ther thou schalt mow ryth wel fare,   *be able to fare very well*
        In case if thou thynke for to thryve,
            No lord schal be thee lyche.   *equal*
        Take the Werld to thine entent   *purpose (desire)*
390   And late thi love be theron lent.   *let; fixed*
        Wyth gold and sylvyr and ryche rent   *revenues*
            Anone thou schalt be ryche.   *Soon*

HUMANUM GENUS   Now syn thou hast behetyn me so,   *since; promised*
        I wyl go wyth thee and asay.   *try it*
395   I ne lette, for frende ner fo,   *will not stop; nor*
        But wyth the Werld I wyl go play,
            Certys a lytyl throwe.   *Certainly; while*
        In this World is al my trust
        To lyvyn in lykyng and in lust.   *indulgence; pleasure*
400   Have he and I onys cust,   *once kissed*
            We schal not part, I trowe.   *believe*

BONUS ANGELUS   A, nay, man, for Cristys blod,
        Cum agayn be strete and style.   *stile (i.e., every way)*
        The Werld is wyckyd and ful wod   *mad*
405   And thou shalt levyn but a whyle.   *live*
            What coveytyst thou to wynne?
        Man, thynke on thyn endynge day
        Whanne thou schalt be closyd undyr clay,
        And if thou thenke of that aray,   *condition (plight)*
410   Certys thou schalt not synne.

Homo, memento finis et in eternum non peccabis.[1]

---

[1] *Man, remember your ending, and you will never sin* (see Ecclesiasticus 7:40)

MALUS ANGELUS   Ya, on thi sowle thou schalt thynke al betyme.   *Nonsense; soon enough*
      Cum forth, man, and take non hede,   *heed*
      Cum on, and thou schalt holdyn hym inne.   *restrain him (the disruptive Good Angel)*
      Thi flesch thou schalt foster and fede
415   Wyth lofly lyvys fode.   *delicious food of life*
      Wyth the Werld thou mayst be bold
      Tyl thou be sexty wyntyr hold.   *old*
      Wanne thi nose waxit cold,   *When; becomes*
        Thanne mayst thou drawe to goode.   *turn*

HUMANUM GENUS   I vow to God, and so I may
421   Make mery a ful gret throwe.   *time*
      I may levyn many a day;   *live*
      I am but yonge, as I trowe,
        For to do that I schulde.
425   Myth I ryde be sompe and syke   *I can; by swamps and streams (i.e., everywhere)*
      And be ryche and lordlyke,
      Certys thanne schulde I be fryke   *Certainly; eager (hearty)*
        And a mery man on molde.   *earth*

MALUS ANGELUS   Yys, be my feyth, thou schalt be a lord,
430   And ellys hange me be the hals!   *Or; neck*
      But thou must be at myn acord.   *in agreement with me*
      Othyrwhyle thou muste be fals   *Sometimes*
        Amonge kythe and kynne.
      Now go we forth swythe anon,   *very quickly*
435   To the Werld us must gon,
      And bere thee manly evere among   *always*
        Whanne thou comyst out or inne.

HUMANUM GENUS   Yys, and ellys have thou my necke,
      But I be manly be downe and dyche;   *Unless; hill and ditch (i.e., everywhere)*
440   And thou I be fals, I ne recke,   *I do not care*
      Wyth so that I be lordlyche.   *As long as*
        I folwe thee as I can.
      Thou schalt be my bote of bale,   *remedy for sorrow*
      For were I ryche of holt and hale   *woods; hall*
445   Thanne wolde I geve nevere tale   *pay no heed*
        Of God ne of good man.

BONUS ANGELUS   I weyle and wrynge and make mone.   *wail; moan*
      This man wyth woo schal be pylt.   *distressed*
      I sye sore and grysly grone   *sigh; groan*
450   For hys folye schal make hym spylt.   *destroyed*
        I not wedyr to gone.   *do not know where to go*
      Mankynde hath forsakyn me.
      Alas, man, for love of thee!

| | Ya, for this gamyn and this gle | *sport; pleasure* |
| 455 | Thou schalt grocchyn and grone. | *complain; groan* |

Pipe up musyk

[Scene v]

MUNDUS	Now I sytte in my semly sale;	*WORLD; fine hall*
	I trotte and tremle in my trew trone;	*move about; thrill with pleasure; throne*
	As a hawke I hoppe in my hende hale;	*splendid hall*
	Kyng, knyth, and kayser to me makyn mone.	*knight; emperor; petition*
460	Of God ne of good man gyf I nevere tale.	*I pay no attention*
	As a lykynge lord I leyke here alone.	*pleasure-loving; play*
	Woso brawle any boste, be downe or be dale,	*[would] brag; hill; valley (i.e., everywhere)*
	Tho gadlyngys schal be gastyd and gryslych grone	*Those rascals; frightened; pitiably*
	Iwys.	*Truly*
465	Lust, Foly, and Veynglory,	
	All these arn in myn memory.	
	Thus begynnyth the nobyl story	
	Of this werldys blys.	

	Lust-Lykyng and Foly,	*Pleasure*
470	Comly knytys of renoun,	*knights*
	Belyve thorwe this londe do crye	*Quickly; make a proclamation*
	Al abowtyn in toure and toun.	*tower and town (everywhere)*
	If any man be fer or nye	*distant or near*
	That to my servyse wyl buske hym boun,	*make himself ready*
475	If he wyl be trost and trye	*steadfast; true*
	He schal be kyng and were the croun	*wear*
	Wyth rycchest robys in res.	*very soon*
	Woso to the Werld wyl drawe	
	Of God ne of good man gevyt he not a hawe,	*hawthorn berry (trifle)*
480	Syche a man, be londys lawe,	*the law of the land*
	Schal syttyn on my dees.	*dais*

VOLUPTAS	Lo, me here redy, lord, to faryn and to fle,	*PLEASURE; go; run*
	To sekyn thee a servaunt dynge and dere.	*worthy and dear*
	Whoso wyl wyth foly rewlyd be	*ruled*
485	He is worthy to be a servaunt here	
	That drawyth to synnys sevene.	*Who betakes himself to*
	Whoso wyl be fals and covetouse	*greedy*
	Wyth this werld he schal have lond and house.	
	This werldys wysdom gevyth not a louse	
490	Of God nyn of hye Hevene.	*nor; high*

Tunc descendit in placeam pariter.[1]

Pes, pepyl, of pes we you pray.	*Peace (Silence)*
Syth and sethe wel to my sawe.	*Sit; pay attention; speech*
Whoso wyl be ryche and in gret aray	*fine clothes*
Toward the Werld he schal drawe.	*take himself*
495 Whoso wyl be fals al that he may,	*can*
Of God hymself he hath non awe,	
And lyvyn in lustys nyth and day	*lives in pleasure night*
The Werld of hym wyl be ryth fawe	*very happy*
Do dwelle in his howse.	*To have [him]*
500 Whoso wyl wyth the Werld have hys dwellynge	
And ben a lord of hys clothynge	*livery*
He muste nedys, ovyr al thynge,	
Everemore be covetowse.	*covetous (greedy)*

Non est in mundo dives qui dicit, "habundo."[2]

STULTICIA Ya, covetouse he must be		*FOLLY*
505 And me, Foly, muste have in mende,		*mind*
For whoso wyl alwey foly fle		*flee from*
In this werld schal ben unthende.		*unsuccessful*
Thorwe werldys wysdom of gret degré		
Schal nevcre man in werld moun wende		*be able to succeed*
510 But he have help of me		*Unless*
That am Foly, fer and hende.		*fair; handsome*
He muste hangyn on my hoke.		*hook*
Werldly wyt was nevere nout		*never amounted to anything*
But wyth foly it were frawt.		*Unless; combined*
515 Thus the wysman hath tawt		*taught*
Abotyn in his boke.		*About*

Sapiencia penes Domini.[3]

VOLUPTAS Now all the men that in this werld wold thryve,		*PLEASURE*
For to rydyn on hors ful hye,		*ride; high*
Cum speke wyth Lust-and-Lykynge belyve		*quickly*
520 And hys felaw, yonge Foly.		
Late se whoso wyl us knowe.		*Let see*
Whoso wyl drawe to Lykynge-and-Luste		
And as a fole in Foly ruste,		*fool; waste away*

---

[1] *Then he descends together [with Folly] into the platea*

[2] *There is no rich man in the world who says, "Enough"*

[3] *Wisdom is with the Lord (see Ecclesiasticus 1:1)*

| | On us to he may truste | *two* |
| 525 | And levyn lovely, I trowe. | *live splendidly, I believe* |

MALUS ANGELUS	How, Lust-Lykyng, and Folye,	*Pleasure; Folly*
	Take to me good entent!	*Pay devoted attention to me*
	I have browth, be downys drye,	*brought; barren hills*
	To the Werld a gret present.	
530	I have gylyd hym ful qweyntly,	*tricked; craftily*
	For syn he was born I have hym blent.	*since; blinded*
	He schal be servaunt good and try,	*true*
	Amonge you his wyl is lent,	*fixed*
	To the Werld he wyl hym take.	*betake himself*
535	For syn he cowde wyt, I undirstonde,	*since he could comprehend*
	I have hym tysyd in every londe.	*enticed*
	Hys Good Aungel, be strete and stronde,	*shore (i.e., everywhere)*
	I have don hym forsake.	*made him*

	Therfor, Lust, my trewe fere,	*Pleasure; companion*
540	Thou art redy alwey iwys	*truly*
	Of worldly lawys thou hym lere	*teach him*
	That he were browth in werldly blys.	*So that; brought*
	Loke he be ryche, the sothe to tell.	*See to it; truth*
	Help hym, fast he gunne to thryve,	*quickly he'll begin*
545	And whanne he wenyth best to lyve	*thinks*
	Thanne schal he deye and not be schryve	*die; absolved*
	And goo wyth us to Hell.	

VOLUPTAS	Be Satan, thou art a nobyl knave	*By*
	To techyn men fyrst fro goode.	*guide; away from*
550	Lust-and-Lykynge he schal have,	*Pleasure*
	Lechery schal ben hys fode,	*sustenance*
	Metys and drynkys he schal have trye.	*rich*
	Wyth a lykynge lady of lofte	*pleasure-loving; high degree*
	He schal syttyn in sendel softe	*silk*
555	To cachen hym to Helle crofte	*trap; Hell's prison*
	That day that he schal deye.	*die*

STULTICIA	Wyth ryche rentys I schal hym blynde	*revenues*
	Wyth the Werld tyl he be pytte,	*fixed (entrapped)*
	And thanne schal I, longe or hys ende,	*before*
560	Make that caytyfe to be knytte	*rascal; bound*
	On the Werld whanne he is set sore.	*To; sorely beset*
	Cum on, man, thou schalt not rewe	*regret*
	For thou wylt be to us trewe.	
	Thou schalt be clad in clothys newe	
565	And be ryche everemore.	

HUMANUM GENUS   Mary, felaw, gramercy!   *many thanks*
            I wolde be ryche and of gret renoun.
            Of God I geve no tale trewly   *pay no attention*
            So that I be lord of toure and toun,   *As long as; tower*
570   Be buskys and bankys broun.   *bushes (i.e., everywhere)*
            Syn that thou wylt make me
            Bothe ryche of gold and fee,   *income*
            Goo forthe, for I wyl folow thee
                And ladys lovely be dale and every towne.   *valley (i.e., everywhere)*

Trumpe up. Tunc ibunt Voluptas et Stulticia, Malus Angelus et Humanum Genus ad
Mundum, et dicet:[1]

VOLUPTAS   How, lord, loke owt! for we have browth   *brought*
576   A servant of nobyl fame.
            Of worldly good is al hys thouth,   *thought*
            Of lust and folye he hath no schame.
                He wolde be gret of name.
580   He wolde be at gret honour   *in*
            For to rewle town and toure.   *rule*
            He wolde have to hys paramoure   *lover*
                Sum lovely dynge dame.   *noble lady*

MUNDUS   Welcum, syr, semly in syth!   *handsome in sight*
585   Thou art welcum to worthy wede.   *clothes*
            For thou wylt be my servaunt day and nyth,   *night*
            Wyth my servyse I schal thee foster and fede.   *feed*
            Thi bak schal be betyn wyth besawntys bryth,   *adorned; bright bezants (coins)*
            Thou shalt have byggyngys be bankys brede,   *buildings along the bank's breadth*
590   To thi cors schal knele kayser and knyth   *body; emperor; knight*
            Where that thou walke, be sty or be strete,   *path (i.e., everywhere)*
                And ladys lovely on lere.   *face*
            But Goddys servyse thou must forsake
            And holy to the Werld thee take   *entirely*
595   And thanne a man I schal thee make
                That non schal be thi pere.   *So that; peer*

HUMANUM GENUS   Yys, Werld, and therto here myn honde   *hand*
            To forsake God and hys servyse.
            To medys thou geve me howse and londe   *In return*
600   That I regne rychely at myn enprise.   *So that; will*
            So that I fare wel be strete and stronde
            Whyl I dwelle here in werldly wyse,

---

[1] *The trumpet sounds. Then Pleasure and Folly, the Bad Angel and Mankind go to the World, and he*
[Pleasure] says

I recke nevere of Hevene wonde   *I care not; Heaven's punishment*
Nor of Jhesu, that jentyl justyse.
605   Of my sowle I have non rewthe.   *concern*
What schulde I recknen of Domysday   *care at Judgment Day*
So that I be ryche and of gret aray?   *So long as; fine clothes*
I schal make mery whyl I may,
         And therto here my trewthe.   *pledge*

MUNDUS   Now sertys, syr, thou seyst wel.   *indeed*
611   I holde thee trewe fro top to the too.   *toes*
But thou were ryche it were gret del   *Unless; pity*
And all men that wyl fare soo.   *will do so*
Cum up, my servaunt trew as stel.   *steel*

         Tunc ascendet Humanum Genus ad Mundum.   Then Mankind ascends the World's platform

615   Thou schalt be ryche, whereso thou goo.
Men schul servyn thee at mel   *meals*
Wyth mynstralsye and bemys blo,   *blowing of trumpets*
         Wyth metys and drynkys trye.   *rich*
Lust-and-Lykynge schal be thin ese.   *Pleasure; ease*
620   Lovely ladys thee schal plese.
Whoso do thee any disesse   *harm*
         He schal ben hangyn hye.   *high*

Lykynge, belyve   *Pleasure, quickly*
Late clothe hym swythe   *Have him clothed speedily*
625   In robys ryve   *ample*
         Wyth ryche aray.   *decor*
Folye, thou fonde,   *fool*
Be strete and stronde,
Serve hym at honde   *close by*
630   Bothe nyth and day.   *night*

VOLUPTAS   Trostyly,   *Faithfully*
         Lord, redy,
         Je vous pry,   *I beg you [come this way]*
         Syr, I say.
635   In lyckynge and lust   *pleasure*
He schal rust   *waste away (deteriorate)*
Tyl dethys dust
Do hym to day.   *Causes him to die*

STULTICIA   And I, Folye,
640   Schal hyen hym hye   *lift; high*
Tyl sum enmye   *enemy*
Hym ovyrgoo.   *overcome*

	In worldys wyt	*wisdom*
	That in Foly syt	*That [one] who sits*
645	I thynke yyt	*intend yet*
	Hys sowle to sloo.	*kill*

[Scene vi] *Trumpe up.*

DETRACCIO All thyngys I crye agayn the pes   *BACKBITER; shout against peace*

	To knyt and knave, this is my kende.	*knight; nature*
	Ya, dyngne dukys on her des	*worthy; dais*
650	In byttyr balys I hem bynde.	*torment; bind them*
	Cryinge and care, chydynge and ches	*conflict and strife*
	And sad sorwe to hem I sende,	*them*
	Ya, lowde lesyngys lacchyd in les,	*falsehoods bound in a leash*
	Of talys untrewe is al my mende.	*mind*
655	Mannys bane abowtyn I bere.	*Man's ruin; carry*
	I wyl that ye wetyn, all tho that ben here,	*know; those*
	For I am knowyn fer and nere:	
	I am the Werldys messengere,	
	My name is Bacbytere.	

660	Wyth every wyth I walke and wende	*person; go*
	And every man now lovyth me wele.	
	Wyth lowde lesyngys undyr lende	*lies stored up*
	To dethys dynt I dresse and dele.	*death's blow; prepare and give*
	To speke fayre beforn and fowle behynde	*in front*
665	Amongys men at mete and mele	*banquet; feast*
	Trewly, lordys, this is my kynde,	*nature*
	Thus I renne upon a whele,	*(Fortune's) wheel*
	I am feller thanne a fox.	*craftier*
	Fleterynge and flaterynge is my lessun,	*Flitting about*
670	Wyth lesyngys I tene bothe tour and town,	*lies; harm*
	Wyth letterys of defamacyoun	
	I bere here in my box.	

	I am lyth of lopys thorwe every londe,	*light; leaps*
	Myn holy happys may not ben hyd.	*great successes*
675	To may not togedyr stonde	*Two*
	But I, Bakbyter, be the thyrde.	*Unless*
	I schape yone boyis to schame and schonde,	*yonder youths; disgrace*
	All that wyl bowyn whanne I hem bydde.	*bow; order them*
	To lawe of londe in feyth I fonde.	*offer temptation (sedition)*
680	Whanne talys untrewe arn betydde	*stories; widespread*
	Bakbytere is wyde spronge.	*widespread*
	Thorwe the werld, be downe and dalys,	*hills; valleys*
	All abowtyn I brewe balys.	*stir up trouble*
	Every man tellyth talys	*lies*
685	Aftyr my fals tunge.	*With the aid of*

	Therfore I am mad massenger	*made*
	To lepyn ovyr londys leye	*leap over untilled land*
	Thorwe all the world, fer and ner,	*Through*
	Unsayd sawys for to seye.	*Unspoken speeches; speak*
690	In this holte I hunte here	*woods*
	For to spye a prevy pley,	*hidden trick*
	For whanne Mankynde is clothyd clere,	*splendidly*
	Thanne schal I techyn hym the wey	
	To the dedly synnys sevene.	
695	Here I schal abydyn wyth my pese	*with my peace (quietly)*
	The wronge to do hym for to chese,	*make him choose*
	For I thynke that he schal lese	*lose*
	The lyth of hey Hevene.	*light of high*

[Scene vii]

VOLUPTAS	Worthy World, in welthys wonde,	*wrapped in wealth*
700	Here is Mankynde ful fayr in folde.	*handsome on earth*
	In bryth besauntys he is bownde	*bright bezants (coins); adorned*
	And bon to bowe to you so bolde.	*ready*
	He levyth in lustys every stounde;	*lives; pleasures; moment*
	Holy to you he hathe hym yolde.	*Entirely; given himself*
705	For to makyn hym gay on grounde,	*on the earth*
	Worthy World, thou art beholde.	*obliged*
	This werld is wel at ese!	
	For to God I make a vow	
	Mankynde had lever now	*would prefer*
710	Greve God wyth synys row	*To grieve; rough (grievous)*
	Thanne the World to dysplese.	

STULTICIA	Dysplese thee he wyl for no man.	
	On me, Foly, is al hys thowth.	*thought*
	Trewly Mankynde nowth nen can	*is unable to*
715	Thynke on God that hathe hym bowth.	*bought*
	Worthy World, wyth as swan,	*white*
	In thi love lely is he lawth.	*truly; caught*
	Sythyn he cowde and fyrste began	*Since; had understanding*
	Thee forsakyn wolde he nowth,	*not*
720	But geve hym to Folye.	*gave himself*
	And sythyn he hathe to thee be trewe,	*since; been*
	I rede thee forsakyn hym for no newe.	*advise; new [follower]*
	Lete us plesyn hym tyl that he rewe	*regret [it]*
	In Hell to hangyn hye.	*high*

MUNDUS	Now, Foly, fayre thee befall,	*may good luck come to you*
726	And Luste, blyssyd be thou ay!	*Pleasure; always*
	Ye han browth Mankynde to myn hall	*brought*
	Sertys in a nobyl aray.	*Certainly*

	Wyth werldys welthys wythinne these wall	*walls*
730	I schal hym feffe if that I may.	*endow*
	Welcum, Mankynde! To thee I call,	
	Clenner clothyd thanne any clay,	*More splendidly*
	Be downe, dale, and dyche.	*(i.e., everywhere)*
	Mankynde, I rede that thou reste	*advise; stay*
735	Wyth me, the World, as it is beste.	
	Loke thou holde myn hende heste	*obey my pleasant orders*
	And evere thou schalt be ryche.	

HUMANUM GENUS	Whou schul I but I thi hestys helde?	*How; unless, obey your orders*
	Thou werkyst wyth me holy my wyll.	*entirely*
740	Thou feffyst me wyth fen and felde	*endow; fen and field*
	And hye hall, be holtys and hyll.	*high; woods*
	In werldly wele my wytte I welde,	*joy; wield*
	In joye I jette wyth juelys jentyll,	*strut; elegant jewelry*
	On blysful banke my bowre is bylde,	*delightful; dwelling is built*
745	In veynglorye I stonde styll.	*pride; continually*
	I am kene as a knyt.	*brave; knight*
	Whoso ageyn the Werld wyl speke	
	Mankynde schal on hym be wreke,	*avenged*
	In stronge presun I schal hym steke,	*prison; put*
750	Be it wronge or ryth.	*right*

MUNDUS	A, Mankynde, wel thee betyde	*may good luck come to you*
	That thi love on me is sette!	
	In my bowrys thou schalt abyde	*bowers*
	And yyt fare mekyl the bette.	*much the better*
755	I feffe thee in all my wonys wyde	*endow; widespread dwellings*
	In dale of dros tyl thou be deth.	*valley of death; placed*
	I make thee lord of mekyl pryde,	*great*
	Syr, at thyn owyn mowthis mette.	*in accord with your own desire expressed by mouth*
	I fynde in thee no tresun.	
760	In all this worlde, be se and sonde,	*sea; shore*
	Parkys, placys, lawnde and londe,	*glade*
	Here I gyfe thee wyth myn honde,	
	Syr, an opyn sesun.	*clear possession*

	Go to my tresorer, Syr Covetouse.	*Greed*
765	Loke thou tell hym as I seye.	
	Bydde hym make thee maystyr in hys house	
	Wyth penys and powndys for to pleye.	*pennies*
	Loke thou geve not a lous	*louse (trifle)*
	Of the day that thou schalt deye.	
770	Messenger, do now thyne use;	*office*
	Bakbytere, teche hym the weye!	*show*
	Thou art swetter thanne mede.	*sweeter; mead*

Mankynde, take wyth thee Bakbytynge.

Lefe hym for no maner thynge.   *Leave; on no account*

775   Flepergebet wyth hys flaterynge   *Flibbertigibbet (Backbiter)*

Standyth Mankynde in stede.   *in [good] stead*

DETRACCIO   Bakbytynge and Detracion

Schal goo wyth thee fro toun to toun.

Have don, Mankynde, and cum doun.   *Finish up*

780   I am thyne owyn page.   *servant*

I schal bere thee wyttnesse wyth my myth   *might*

Whanne my lord the Werlde it behyth.   *promises it*

Lo, where Syr Coveytyse sytt   *Greed*

And bydith us in his stage.   *waits for us on his scaffold*

HUMANUM GENUS   Syr Worlde, I wende,   *intend*

786   In Covetyse to chasyn my kende.   *Greed; follow my own nature*

MUNDUS   Have hym in mende,   *mind*

And iwys thanne schalt thou be ryth thende.   *truly; very successful*

BONUS ANGELUS   Alas, Jhesu, jentyl justyce,   *judge*

790   Whedyr may mans Good Aungyl wende?   *Where; go*

Now schal careful Coveytyse   *dangerous Greed*

Mankende trewly al schende.   *destroy*

Hys sely goste may sore agryse;   *foolish spirit; be very afraid*

Bakbytynge bryngyth hym in byttyr bonde.

795   Worldly wyttys, ye are not wyse,

Your lovely lyfe amys ye spende   *wrongly*

And that schal ye sore smert.   *sorely pain*

Parkys, ponndys, and many pens   *ponds; pennies*

Thei semyn to you swetter thanne sens,   *seem; sweeter; incense*

800   But Goddys servyse nyn hys commaundementys   *nor*

Stondyth you not at hert.   *in*

MALUS ANGELUS   Ya, whanne the fox prechyth, kepe wel yore gees!   *preaches; guard*

He spekyth as it were a holy pope.   *as if he were*

Goo, felaw, and pyke off tho lys   *those lice*

805   That crepe ther upon thi cope!

Thi part is pleyed al at the dys   *dice*

That thou schalt have here, as I hope.   *think*

Tyl Mankynde fallyth to podys prys,   *a frog's worth*

Coveytyse schal hym grype and grope   *Greed; grasp; pull*

810   Tyl sum schame hym schende.   *destroy*

Tyl man be dyth in dethys dow   *put in death's pit*

He seyth nevere he hath inow.   *will say; enough*

Therfore, goode boy, cum blow

At my nether ende!

[Scene viii]

DETRACCIO   Syr Covetyse, God thee save,

816   Thi pens and thi poundys all!   *pennies*

        I, Bakbyter, thyn owyn knave,

        Have browt Mankynde unto thine hall.   *brought*

        The Werlde bad thou schuldyst hym have   *commanded*

820   And feffen hym, whatso befall.   *endow; whatever*

        In grene gres tyl he be grave   *grass; buried*

        Putte hym in thi precyous pall,   *cloak*

           Coveytyse, it were ell rewthe.   *a pity otherwise*

        Whyl he walkyth in worldly wolde   *ground*

825   I, Bakbyter, am wyth hym holde.   *bound to him*

        Lust and Folye, tho barouns bolde,   *Pleasure; those*

           To hem he hath plyth hys trewthe.   *pledged*

AVARICIA   Ow, Mankynde, blyssyd mote thou be!   *GREED; Ah; may*

        I have lovyd thee derworthly many a day,   *dearly*

830   And so I wot wel that thou dost me.   *know*

        Cum up and se my ryche aray.   *fine clothes*

        It were a gret poynte of pyté   *very unfortunate*

        But Coveytyse were to thi pay.   *Unless; liking*

        Sit up ryth here in this se.   *right; seat*

835   I schal thee lere of werldys lay   *teach; law*

           That fadyth as a flode.   *passes; river*

        Wyth good inow I schal thee store,   *enough goods*

        And yyt oure game is but lore   *lost*

        But thou coveyth mekyl more   *Unless; covet much more*

840   Thanne evere schal do thee goode.   *Than you actually need*

        Thou muste gyfe thee to symonye,   *selling church offices*

        Extorsion, and false asyse.   *measures*

        Helpe no man but thou have why.   *unless; cause*

        Pay not thi servauntys here servyse.   *their wages*

845   Thi neyborys loke thou dystroye.

        Tythe not on non wyse.   *Pay no tithes in any manner*

        Here no begger thou he crye;   *Hear; although*

        And thanne schalt thou ful sone ryse.   *soon become wealthy*

           And whanne thou usyste marchaundyse   *handle*

850   Loke that thou be sotel of sleytys,   *subtle; tricks*

        And also swere al be deseytys,   *by deceits*

        Bye and sell be fals weytys,   *Buy; weights*

           For that is kynde coveytyse.   *the nature of greed*

        Be not agaste of the grete curse.   *afraid of excommunication*

855   This lofly lyf may longe leste.   *last*

        Be the peny on thi purs,   *If there be a penny in*

        Lete hem cursyn and don here beste.   *them; their*

What, devyl of Hell, art thou the wers   *the worse off*
Thow thow brekyste Goddys heste?   *Although; commandment*
860 Do aftyr me, I am thi nors.   *nurse (teacher)*
Alwey gadyr and have non reste.   *gather [wealth]*
    In wynnynge be al thi werke.   *effort*
To pore men take none entent,   *pay no attention*
For that thou haste longe tyme hent   *that [which]; got*
865 In lytyl tyme it may be spent;
    Thus seyth Caton, the gret clerke.   *Cato*

Labitur exiguo quod partum tempore longo.[1]

HUMANUM GENUS A, Avaryce, wel thou spede!   *Greed; prosper*
Of werldly wytte thou canst iwys.   *wisdom; are truly knowledgeable*
Thou woldyst not I hadde nede
870 And schuldyst be wrothe if I ferd amys.   *angry; fared amiss*
I schal nevere begger bede   *offer*
Mete nyn drynke, be Hevene blys;
Rather, or I schulde hym clothe or fede   *before*
He schulde sterve and stynke, iwys.   *die (starve) and rot, truly*
875   Coveytyse, as thou wylt I wyl do.   *Greed; wish*
Whereso that I fare, be fenne or flod,   *Wherever; go*
I make a vow be Goddys blod   *by*
Of Mankynde getyth no man no good
    But if he synge "*Si dedero.*"[2]

AVARICIA Mankynd, that was wel songe.   *sung*
881 Sertys now thou canst sum skyll.   *Certainly; know*
Blyssyd be thi trewe tonge!
In this bowre thou schalt byde and byll.   *bower; abide and dwell*
Moo synnys I wolde thou undyrfonge: *More; wish you to undertake*
885 Wyth coveytyse thee feffe I wyll;   *greed; endow*
And thanne sum pryde I wolde spronge,   *set up*
Hyye in thi hert to holdyn and hyll   *High; hold and cherish*
    And abydyn in thi body.
Here I feffe thee in myn hevene   *endow; haven*
890 Wyth gold and sylvyr lyth as levene.   *bright; lightning*
The dedly synnys, all sevene,
    I schal do comyn in hy.   *cause to come in haste*

Pryde, Wrathe, and Envye,
Com forthe, the Develys chyldryn thre!

---

[1] *That which is acquired over a long time slips away quickly (Distichs of Cato 2:17)*

[2] *Unless he sings "If I shall give (I will expect recompense)."* See "Addresses of the Commons," line 23, in Dean, *Medieval English Political Writings*, p. 138.

895   Lecchery, Slawth, and Glotonye,
        To mans Flesch ye are fendys fre.   *noble fiends*
        Dryvyth downne ovyr dalys drye,   *Hurry*
        Beth now blythe as any be,   *bee*
        Ovyr hyll and holtys ye you hyye   *woods; hasten yourself*
900   To com to Mankynde and to me
            Fro youre dowty dennys.   *worthy dwellings*
        As dukys dowty ye you dresse.   *noble; prepare yourselves*
        Whanne ye sex be comne, I gesse,   *six have come*
        Thanne be we sevene and no lesse
905   Of the dedly synnys.

[Scene ix]

SUPERBIA Wondyr hyye howtys on hyll herd I houte;   *PRIDE; loud cries; shouted*
        Koveytyse kryeth, hys karpynge I kenne.   *Greed; speech I recognize*
        Summe lord or summe lordeyn lely schal loute   *rascal truly; agree*
        To be pyth wyth perlys of my proude penne.   *adorned; plume*
910   Bon I am to braggyn and buskyn abowt,   *Ready; brag; bustle*
        Rapely and redyly on rowte for to renne.   *Quickly; in a crowd to run*
        Be doun, dalys, nor dennys no duke I dowt,   *hills; fear*
        Also fast for to fogge, be flodys and be fenne.   *run*
           I rore whanne I ryse.   *rise up*
915   Syr Belyal, bryth of ble,   *bright of countenance*
        To you I recomaunde me.   *commend myself*
        Have good day, my fadyr fre,   *noble*
           For I goo to Coveytyse.

IRA Whanne Coveytyse cried and carpyd of care,   *WRATH; spoke*
920   Thanne must I, wod wreche, walkyn and wend   *mad creature; go*
        Hyye ovyr holtys, as hound aftyr hare.   *High; woods*
        If I lette and were the last, he schuld me sore schend.   *delay; scold*
        I buske my bold baston, be bankys ful bare.   *prepare; club*
        Sum boy schal be betyn and browth undyr bonde.   *brought into bondage*
925   Wrath schal hym wrekyn and weyin hys ware.   *avenge; measure; goods*
        Forlorn schal al be for lusti laykys in londe[1]
           As a lythyr page.   *useless servant*
        Syr Belyal, blak and blo,   *blue*
        Have good day, now I goo
930   For to fell thi foo
           Wyth wyckyd wage.   *payment [of blows]*

INVIDIA Whanne Wrath gynnyth walke in ony wyde wonys,   *ENVY; any far-ranging places*
        Envye flet as a fox and folwyth on faste.   *runs like*
        Whanne thou steryste or staryste or stumble upon stonys,   *move; stare*

---

[1] *All shall be destroyed, for merry games in the land .*

935	I lepe as a lyon; me is loth to be laste.	*I am loath*
	Ya, I breyde byttyr balys in body and in bonys,	*breed; torments*
	I frete myn herte and in kare I me kast.	*gnaw at; throw myself*
	Goo we to Coveytyse, all thre at onys,	
	Wyth oure grysly gere a grome for to gast.	*weapons; lad; terrify*
940	This day schal he deye.	*die*
	Belsabubbe, now have good day,	
	For we wyl wendyn in good aray,	*go; order*
	Al thre in fere, as I thee say,	*together*
	Pride, Wrath, and Envye.	

BELIAL Farewel now, chyldryn fayre to fynde!   *know*
946 Do now wel youre olde owse.   *custom (use)*
Whanne ye com to Mankynde
Make hym wroth and envyous.   *angry*
Levyth not lytly undyr lynde;   *Stay; carelessly; lime tree*
950 To his sowle brewyth a byttyr jous.   *For; brew; juice*
Whanne he is ded I schal hym bynde
In Hell, as catte dothe the mows.
Now buske you forthe on brede.   *hasten; abroad*
I may be blythe as any be,   *bee*
955 For Mankynde in every cuntré
Is rewlyd be my chyldyr thre,   *controlled*
Envye, Wrathe, and Pryde.

[Scene x]
GULA A grom gan gredyn gayly on grounde.   *GLUTTONY; lad; shouted; earth*
Of me, gay Glotoun, gan al hys gale.   *was all his song*
960 I stampe and I styrte and stynt upon stounde,   *leap; stop suddenly*
To a staunche deth I stakyr and stale.   *certain; stagger; stand*
What boyes wyth her belys in my bondys ben bownd,   *Whatever; their bellies*
Bothe her bak and her blod I brewe al to bale.   *their; torment*
I fese folke to fyth tyl her flesch fond.   *incite; fight; fails*
965 Whanne summe han dronkyn a drawth thei drepyn in a dale;   *draught; droop*
In me is her mynde.   *On; their*
Mans florchynge Flesch,   *flourishing*
Fayre, frele, and fresch,   *frail*
I rape to rewle in a rese   *hasten; in haste*
970 To kloye in my kynde.[1]

LUXURIA In mans kyth I cast me a castel to kepe.   *LECHERY; loins; prepare*
I, Lechery, wyth lykynge, am lovyd in iche a lond.   *pleasure; each*
Wyth my sokelys of swettnesse I sytte and I slepe.   *flowers*
Many berdys I brynge to my byttyr bonde.   *ladies*

---

[1] *To ensnare [it] according to my nature*

975	In wo and in wrake wyckyd wytys schal wepe	*torment; creatures*
	That in my wonys wylde wyl not out wende.	*dwellings; go*
	Whanne Mankynde is castyn undyr clourys to crepe,	*thrown; sod*
	Thanne tho ledrouns for her lykynge I schal al to-schende,[1]	
	Trewly to tell.	
980	Syr Flesch, now I wende,	
	Wyth lust in my lende,	*pleasure; loins*
	To cachyn Mankynde	*drive*
	To the Devyl of Hell.	

ACCIDIA	Ya, what seyst thou of Syr Slawth, wyth my soure syth?	*SLOTH; appearance (sight)*
985	Mankynde lovyth me wel, iwys, as I wene.	*truly; think*
	Men of relygyon I rewle in my ryth;	*control; right*
	I lette Goddys servyse, the sothe may be sene.	*hinder; truth; seen*
	In bedde I brede brothel wyth my berdys bryth;	*breed lechers; fair ladies*
	Lordys, ladys, and lederounnys to my lore leene.	*rascals; wisdom incline*
990	Mekyl of Mankynd in my clokys schal be knyth	*Much; held fast*
	Tyl deth dryvyth hem down in dalys bedene.	*valleys together*
	We may non lenger abyde.	
	Syr Flesch, comly kynge,	
	In thee is al oure bredynge.	*ancestry*
995	Geve us now thi blyssynge,	
	For Coveytyse hath cryde.	*called [us]*

CARO	Glotony and Slawth, farewel in fere,	*FLESH; together*
	Lovely in londe is now your lesse;	*comfort (prosperity)*
	And Lecherye, my dowtyr so dere,	
1000	Dapyrly ye dresse you so dyngne on desse.	*Splendidly; place yourself; nobly; dais*
	All thre my blessynge ye schal have here.	
	Goth now forth and gyve ye no fors.	*care*
	It is no nede you for to lere	*to teach you*
	To cachyn Mankynd to a careful clos	*drive; terrible prison*
1005	Fro the bryth blysse of Hevene.	*From; bright*
	The Werld, the Flesch, and the Devyl are knowe	*acknowledged*
	Grete lordys, as we wel owe,	*ought [to be]*
	And thorwe Mankynd we settyn and sowe	*throughout; plant*
	The dedly synnys sevene.	

Tunc ibunt Superbia, Ira, Individia, Gula, Luxuria, et Accidia ad Avariciam et dicet Superbia:[2]

---

[1] *Then those rascals for their pleasure I will destroy completely*

[2] *Then Pride, Wrath, Envy, Gluttony, Lechery, and Sloth go to Covetousness, and Pride says*

[Scene xi]

SUPERBIA   What is thi wyll, Syr Coveytyse?

1011   Why hast thou afftyr us sent?

Whanne thou creydyst we ganne agryse   *shouted; shudder*

And come to thee now par asent.   *by agreement*

Oure love is on thee lent.   *set*

1015   I, Pryde, Wrath, and Envye,

Gloton, Slawth, and Lecherye,

We arn cum all sex for thi crye

To be at thi commaundement.

AVARICIA   Welcum be ye, bretheryn all,

1020   And my systyr, swete Lecherye!

Wytte ye why I gan to call?   *Do you know; began*

For ye must me helpe and that in hy.   *quickly*

Mankynde is now com to myn hall

Wyth me to dwell, be downys dry.   *hills*

1025   Therfore ye must, whatso befall,   *whatever happens*

Feffyn hym wyth youre foly,   *Endow*

And ell ye don hym wronge.   *Or else*

For whanne Mankynd is kendly koveytous   *naturally*

He is proud, wrathful, and envyous;

1030   Glotons, slaw, and lecherous   *Gluttonous, slothful*

Thei arn othyrwhyle amonge.   *also sometimes there (see note)*

Thus every synne tyllyth in othyr   *cultivates the other*

And makyth Mankynde to ben a foole.

We sevene fallyn on a fodyr   *in a group*

1035   Mankynd to chase to pynyngys stole.   *to the seat of punishment*

Therfore, Pryde, good brothyr,

And brethyryn all, take ye your tol.   *weapons*

Late iche of us take at othyr[1]

And set Mankynd on a stomlynge stol   *stumbling stool*

1040   Whyl he is here on lyve.   *alive*

Lete us lullyn hym in oure lust   *to our pleasure*

Tyl he be drevyn to dampnynge dust.

Colde care schal ben hys crust   *breadcrust (food)*

To deth whanne he schal dryve.

SUPERBIA   In gle and game I growe glad.   *sport; play*

1046   Mankynd, take good hed

And do as Coveytyse thee bad,

Take me in thyn hert, precyous Pride.

Loke thou be not ovyrlad,   *bullied*

---

[1] This seems to mean "*Let each of us take up our own weapons*"

1050	Late no bacheler thee mysbede,
	Do thee to be dowtyd and drad,
	Bete boyes tyl they blede,
	Kast hem in careful kettys.
	Frende, fadyr and modyr dere,
1055	Bowe hem not in non manere,
	And hold no maner man thi pere,
	And use these new jettys.

young man use you badly
Make yourself feared and dreaded
Beat
Chop them into hunks of meat

Obey them
kind of; equal
styles

Loke thou blowe mekyl bost
Wyth longe crakows on thi schos.
1060 Jagge thi clothis in every cost,
And ell men schul lete thee but a goos.
It is thus, man, wel thou wost,
Therfore do as no man dos
And every man sette at a thost
1065 And of thiself make gret ros.
        Now se thiself on every syde.
Every man thou schalt schende and schelfe
And holde no man betyr thanne thiselfe.
Tyl dethys dynt thi body delfe
1070   Put holy thyn hert in Pride.

shout great boasts
pointed toes; shoes
Slash (serrate) with dags; manner
Or else; think
know

turd's value
boast
look at; opportunity
insult; push

stroke; pierce
completely

HUMANUM GENUS Pryde, be Jhesu, thou seyst wel.
Whoso suffyr is ovyrled al day.
Whyl I reste on my rennynge whel
I schal not suffre, if that I may.
1075 Myche myrthe at mete and mel
I love ryth wel, and ryche aray.
Trewly I thynke, in every sel,
On grounde to be graythyd gay
        And of myselfe to take good gard.
1080 Mykyl myrthe thou wylt me make,
Lordlyche to leve, be londe and lake.
Myn hert holy to thee I take
        Into thyne owyn award.

permits [it]; oppressed
wheel [of Fortune]
permit [it]
banquet; meal
very; clothing
time
dressed
care
Much
To live like a lord
entirely
keeping

SUPERBIA In thi bowre to abyde
1085 I com to dwelle be thi syde.

bower

[Pride ascends to Covetousness' scaffold]

HUMANUM GENUS Mankynde and Pride
Schal dwell togedyr every tyde.

forever

IRA Be also wroth as thou were wode.
Make thee be dred, be dalys derne.

angry; mad
feared; hidden valleys (i.e., everywhere)

1090   Whoso thee wrethe, be fen or flode,   *angers*
          Loke thou be avengyd yerne.   *quickly*
          Be redy to spylle mans blod.
          Loke thou hem fere, be feldys ferne.   *frighten; distant fields*
          Alway, man, be ful of mod.   *anger*
1095   My lothly lawys loke thou lerne,   *terrible*
                I rede, for any thynge.   *advise, before*
          Anon take venjaunce, man, I rede,
          And thanne schal no man thee ovyrlede,   *oppress*
          But of thee they schul have drede
1100   And bowe to thi byddynge.   *submit*

HUMANUM GENUS   Wrethe, for thi councel hende,   *Wrath; gracious*
          Have thou Goddys blyssynge and myn.
          What caytyf of al my kende   *Whatever rascal; [human] race*
          Wyl not bowe, he schal abyn.   *obey; suffer*
1105   Wyth myn venjaunce I schal hym schende   *destroy*
          And wrekyn me, be Goddys yne.   *avenge myself; eyes*
          Rathyr or I schulde bowe or bende   *before*
          I schuld be stekyd as a swyne   *stuck; pig*
                Wyth a lothly launce.
1110   Be it erly or late,
          Whoso make wyth me debate   *fights with me*
          I schal hym hyttyn on the pate   *head*
                And takyn anon venjaunce.

IRA   Wyth my rewly rothyr   *fierce guidance*
1115   I com to thee, Mankynde, my brothyr.

          [Wrath ascends to Covetousness' scaffold]

HUMANUM GENUS   Wrethe, thi fayr fothyr   *company*
          Makyth iche man to be vengyd on othyr.

INVIDIA   Envye wyth Wrathe muste dryve   *Envy; hurry*
          To haunte Mankynde also.   *accompany*
1120   Whanne any of thy neyborys wyl thryve
          Loke thou have Envye therto.   *concerning that*
          On the hey name I charge thee belyve   *In God's name; quickly*
          Bakbyte hym, whowso thou do.   *Slander; however*
          Kyll hym anon wythowtyn knyve
1125   And speke hym sum schame were thou go,   *wherever*
                Be dale or downys drye.
          Speke thi neybour mekyl schame,   *much*
          Pot on hem sum fals fame,   *Put; him*
          Loke thou undo hys nobyl name
1130   Wyth me, that am Envye.

HUMANUM GENUS   Envye, thou art bothe good and hende   *gracious*
          And schalt be of my counsel chefe.   *chief*
          Thi counsel is knowyn thorwe mankynde,   *throughout*
          For ilke man callyth othyr "hore" and "thefe."   *whore*
1135   Envye, thou art rote and rynde,   *root and rind (beginning and end)*
          Thorwe this werld, of mykyl myschefe.   *Throughout; great*
          In byttyr balys I schal hem bynde   *great torment*
          That to thee puttyth any reprefe.   *offer any reproof*
             Cum up to me above.
1140   For more envye thanne is now reynynge
          Was nevere syth Cryst was kynge.   *since*
          Cum up, Envye, my dere derlynge.
             Thou hast Mankyndys love.

INVIDIA   I clymbe fro this crofte   *from; enclosure*
1145   Wyth Mankynde to syttyn on lofte.   *aloft*

     [Envy ascends to Covetousness' scaffold]

HUMANUM GENUS   Cum, syt here softe,
          For in abbeys thou dwellyst ful ofte.

GULA   In gay Glotony a game thou begynne,   *With*
          Ordeyn thee mete and drynkys goode.   *Order*
1150   Loke that no tresour thou part atwynne   *you part with*
          But thee feffe and fede wyth al kynnys fode.   *Unless it provide; all kinds of*
          Wyth fastynge schal man nevere Hevene wynne,
          These grete fasterys I holde hem wode.   *fasters; think them mad*
          Thou thou ete and drynke, it is no synne.   *Although*
1155   Fast no day, I rede, be the Rode,   *advise; by the Cross*
           Thou chyde these fastyng cherlys.   *Although complain; churls*
          Loke thou have spycys of goode odoure
          To feffe and fede thy fleschly floure   *provide; fleshly growth*
          And thanne mayst thou bultyn in thi boure   *fornicate; chamber*
1160   And serdyn gay gerlys.   *copulate with; girls*

HUMANUM GENUS   A, Glotony, wel I thee grete!
          Soth and sad it is, thy sawe.   *True; serious; speech*
          I am no day wel, be sty nor strete,   *never; path (i.e., anywhere)*
          Tyl I have wel fyllyd my mawe.   *mouth*
1165   Fastynge is fellyd undyr fete,   *kicked*
          Thou I nevere faste, I ne rekke an hawe,   *Although; care; hawthorn berry*
          He servyth of nowth, be the Rode, I lete,   *It [fasting] is of no use, by the Cross, I think*
          But to do a mans guttys to gnawe.   *cause*
            To faste I wyl not fonde.   *attempt*
1170   I schal not spare, so have I reste,
          To have a mossel of the beste.   *morsel*

The lenger schal my lyfe mow leste   *be able to last*
    Wyth gret lykynge in londe.   *pleasure on earth*

GULA   Be bankys on brede,   *By broad banks*
1175   Othyrwhyle to spew thee spede!   *Sometimes; vomit; succeed*

    [Gluttony ascends to Covetousness' scaffold]

HUMANUM GENUS Whyl I lyf lede
    Wyth fayre fode my flesche schal I fede.   *food*

LUXURIA   Ya, whanne thi flesche is fayre fed,   *LECHERY*
    Thanne schal I, lovely Lecherye,
1180   Be bobbyd wyth thee in bed;   *bounced*
    Hereof serve mete and drynkys trye.   *For this; rich*
    In love thi lyf schal be led;
    Be a lechour tyl thou dye.
    Thi nedys schal be the better sped   *satisfied*
1185   If thou gyf thee to fleschly folye
      Tyl deth thee down drepe.   *strike*
    Lechery syn the werld began
    Hath avauncyd many a man.   *profited*
    Therfore, Mankynd, my leve lemman,   *dear lover*
1190   In my cunte thou schalt crepe.

HUMANUM GENUS   A, Lechery, wel thee be.
    Mans sed in thee is sowe.   *seed; sown*
    Fewe men wyl forsake thee
    In any cuntré that I knowe.
1195   Spousebreche is a frend ryth fre,   *Adultery; very gracious*
    Men use that mo thanne inowe.   *more than enough*
    Lechery, cum syt be me.
    Thi banys be ful wyd iknowe,   *proclamations; widely known*
      Lykynge is in thi lende.   *Pleasure; loins*
1200   On nor othyr, I se no wythte   *One; person*
    That wyl forsake thee day ner nyth.   *nor night*
    Therfore cum up, my berd bryth,   *bright lady*
      And reste thee wyth Mankynde.

LUXURIA   I may soth synge   *truly*
1205   "Mankynde is kawt in my slynge."   *noose (trap, vagina)*

    [Lechery ascends to Covetousness' scaffold]

HUMANUM GENUS For ony erthyly thynge,   *any*
    To bedde thou muste me brynge.

ACCIDIA   Ya, whanne ye be in bedde bothe,
      Wappyd wel in worthy wede,   *Wrapped; bedclothes*
1210   Thanne I, Slawthe, wyl be wrothe   *angry*
      But two brothelys I may brede.   *Unless; lechers; breed*
      Whanne the messe-belle goth   *rings*
      Lye stylle, man, and take non hede.   *pay no attention*
      Lappe thyne hed thanne in a cloth   *Wrap; then*
1215   And take a swet, I thee rede,   *sweat; advise*
         Chyrche-goynge thou forsake.
      Losengerys in londe I lyfte   *Flatterers; raise up*
      And dyth men to mekyl unthryfte.   *drive; great decadence*
      Penaunce enjoynyd men in schryfte   *given to; confession*
1220   Is undone, and that I make.   *I cause that*

HUMANUM GENUS   Owe, Slawthe, thou seyst me skylle.   *Oh; good advice*
      Men use thee mekyl, God it wot.   *much; knows*
      Men lofe wel now to lye stylle   *love*
      In bedde to take a morowe swot.   *morning sweat*
1225   To chyrcheward is not her wylle;   *their*
      Her beddys thei thynkyn goode and hot.   *Their*
      Herry, Jofferey, Jone, and Gylle
      Arn leyd and logyd in a lot   *laid; lodged in turn*
         Wyth thyne unthende charmys.   *unprofitable*
1230   Al mankynde, be the holy Rode,   *by; Cross*
      Are now slawe in werkys goode.   *slow to do*
      Com nere therfore, myn fayre foode,   *companion*
         And lulle me in thyne armys.

ACCIDIA   I make men, I trowe,   *believe*
1235   In Goddys servyse to be ryth slowe.   *very*

HUMANUM GENUS   Com up this throwe.   *at this time*
      Swyche men thou schalt fynden inowe.   *enough*

[Sloth ascends to Covetousness' scaffold]

HUMANUM GENUS   "Mankynde" I am callyd be kynde,   *nature*
      Wyth curssydnesse in costys knet.   *Joined with wickedness in my habits*
1240   In sowre swettenesse my syth I sende,   *bitter; sight; use*
      Wyth sevene synnys sadde beset.   *sorely*
      Mekyl myrthe I move in mynde,   *Much; stir*
      Wyth melody at my mowthis met.   *at my mouth's commandment*
      My prowd power schal I not pende   *limit*
1245   Tyl I be putte in peynys pyt,   *the pit of pain*
         To Helle hent fro hens.   *taken*
      In dale of dole tyl we are downe   *valley of pain; put*
      We schul be clad in a gray gowne.

I se no man but they use somme	*see*
1250 Of these sevene dedly synnys.	
For comouly it is seldom seyne,	*seen*
Whoso now be lecherows,	*Whoever*
But of othyr men he schal have dysdeyne	
And ben prowde or covetous.	
1255 In synne iche man is founde.	*each*
Ther is pore nor ryche, be londe ne lake,	
That alle these sevene wyl forsake,	
But wyth on or othyr he schal be take	*one or another; taken*
And in her byttyr bondys bownde.	

BONUS ANGELUS So mekyl the werse, weleawoo,	*much the worse, alas*
1261 That evere good aungyl was ordeynyd thee.	*for you*
Thou art rewlyd aftyr the fende that is thi foo	*ruled; fiend*
And nothynge certys aftyr me.	*clearly not at all by me*
Weleaway, wedyr may I goo?	*where*
1265 Man doth me bleykyn blody ble.	*cause [my] rosy complexion to become pale*
Hys swete sowle he wyl now slo.	*slay*
He schal wepe al hys game and gle	*for all his sport and play*
At on dayes tyme.	*one*
Ye se wel all sothly in syth	*truly; sight*
1270 I am abowte bothe day and nyth	*night*
To brynge hys sowle into blis bryth,	*bright*
And hymself wyl it brynge to pyne.	*pain*

MALUS ANGELUS No, Good Aungyl, thou art not in sesun,	*fashion*
Fewe men in thee feyth they fynde.	
1275 For thou hast schewyd a ballyd resun,	*bare (pointless)*
Goode syre, cum blowe myn hol behynde.	*arsehole*
Trewly man hath non chesun	*cause*
On thi God to grede and grynde,	*beg; gnash [his teeth]*
For, that schuld cunne Cristis lessoun,	*he who would know*
1280 In penaunce hys body he muste bynde	
And forsake the Worldys mende.	*intent*
Men arn loth on thee to crye	
Or don penaunce for her folye.	*their*
Therfore have I now maystrye	*control*
1285 Welny ovyr al mankynde.	*Almost over all*

BONUS ANGELUS Alas, Mankynde	
Is bobbyd and blent as the blynde.	*mocked; misled*
In feyth, I fynde,	
To Crist he can nowt be kynde.	
1290 Alas, Mankynne	
Is soylyd and saggyd in synne.	*sunk*

	He wyl not blynne	*cease*
	Tyl body and sowle parte atwynne.	*separate*
	Alas, he is blendyd,	*blinded*
1295	Amys mans lyf is ispendyd,	*spent*
	Wyth fendys fendyd.	*surrounded (?)*
	Mercy, God, that man were amendyd!	

CONFESCIO	What, mans Aungel, good and trewe,	*CONFESSION*
	Why syest thou and sobbyst sore?	*sigh*
1300	Sertys, sore it schal me rewe	*Certainly; grieve*
	If I se thee make mornynge more.	*see*
	May any bote thi bale brewe	*remedy ease your sorrow*
	Or any thynge thi stat astore?	*situation restore*
	For all felechepys olde and newe	*fellowships*
1305	Why makyst thou grochynge undyr gore	*complaint; gown (in your heart)*
	Wyth pynynge poyntys pale?	*By tormenting pricks [made]*
	Why was al this gretynge gunne	*weeping begun*
	Wyth sore syinge undyr sunne?	*sighing*
	Tell me and I schal, if I cunne,	*can*
1310	Brewe thee bote of bale.	*Create a remedy for your torment*

BONUS ANGELUS	Of byttyr balys thou mayste me bete,	*torment; cure*
	Swete Schryfte, if that thou wylt.	*Confession*
	For Mankynde it is that I grete;	*weep*
	He is in poynt to be spylt.	*about to be destroyed*
1315	He is set in sevene synnys sete	*seat*
	And wyl, certys, tyl he be kylt.	*surely; killed*
	Wyth me he thynkyth nevere more to mete,	
	He hath me forsake, and I have no gylt.	*guilt*
	No man wyl hym amende.	
1320	Therfore, Schryfte, so God me spede,	
	But if thou helpe at this nede	*Unless*
	Mankynde getyth nevere othyr mede	*reward*
	But peyne wythowtyn ende.	

CONFESCIO	What, Aungel, be of counfort stronge,	
1325	For thi lordys love that deyed on Tre.	*died; Cross*
	On me, Schryfte, it schal not be longe	*It will not take me, Shrift, long*
	And that thou schalt the sothe se.	*If; truth see*
	If he wyl be aknowe hys wronge	*acknowledge*
	And nothynge hele, but telle it me,	*hide*
1330	And don penaunce sone amonge,	*also*
	I schal hym stere to gamyn and gle	*sport and play*
	In joye that evere schal last.	
	Whoso schryve hym of hys synnys alle	*Whoever will absolve*
	I behete hym Hevene halle.	*promise*

1335   Therfor go we hens, whatso befalle,   *whatever happens*
          To Mankynde fast.

          Tunc ibunt ad Humanum Genus et dicet: *Then they go to Mankind and he (Confession) says*

CONFESCIO   What, Mankynde, whou goth this?   *how*
          What dost thou wyth these develys sevene?
          Alas, alas, man, al amys!
1340   Blysse in the name of God in Hevene,
          I rede, so have I rest.   *advise, as I hope for salvation*
          These lotly lordeynys awey thou lyfte   *loathsome rascals; drive*
          And cum doun and speke wyth Schryfte
          And drawe thee yerne to sum thryfte.   *quickly; [spiritual] prosperity*
1345   Trewly it is the best.

HUMANUM GENUS   A, Schryfte, thou art wel be note   *Confession; known*
          Here to Slawthe that syttyth here-inne.   *Sloth*
          He seyth thou mytyst a com to mannys cote   *might have come; dwelling*
          On Palme Sunday al betyme;   *soon enough*
1350   Thou art com al to sone.   *too soon*
          Therfore, Schryfte, be thi fay,   *faith*
          Goo forthe tyl on Good Fryday.
          Tente to thee thanne wel I may;   *Pay attention*
          I have now ellys to done.   *other things to do*

CONFESCIO   Ow, that harlot is now bold!   *Oh; villain*
1356   In bale he byndyth Mankynd belyve.   *torment; quickly*
          Sey Slawthe I preyd hym that he wold   *Say to*
          Fynd a charter of thi lyve.   *pardon for*
          Man, thou mayst ben undyr mold   *earth*
1360   Longe or that tyme, kyllyd wyth a knyve,   *before; knife*
          Wyth podys and froskys manyfold.   *many toads and frogs*
          Therfore schape thee now to schryve   *prepare yourself; confess*
          If thou wylt com to blys.
          Thou synnyste, or sorwe thee ensense.   *before; consume*
1365   Behold thynne hert, thi prevé spense,   *storeroom*
          And thynne owyn consyense,
          Or sertys thou dost amys.

HUMANUM GENUS   Ya, Petyr, so do mo!   *by St. Peter; many others*
          We have etyn garlek everychone.   *each one*
1370   Thou I schulde to Helle go,   *Although*
          I wot wel I schal not gon alone,
          Trewly I tell thee.
          I dyd nevere so evyl trewly
          That othyr han don as evyl as I.   *others*

1375   Therfore, syre, lete be thy cry   *cease*
            And go hens fro me.

PENITENCIA Wyth poynt of penaunce I schal hym prene   *PENANCE; pierce*
            Mans pride for to felle.   *bring down*
            Wyth this launce I schal hym lene,   *give*
1380   Iwys, a drope of mercy welle.   *the well (fountain) of mercy*
            Sorwe of hert is that I mene;   *that [which]*
            Trewly ther may no tunge telle   *tongue*
            What waschyth sowlys more clene
            Fro the foul fend of Helle   *fiend*
1385   Thanne swete sorwe of hert.
            God, that syttyth in Hevene on hye,   *high*
            Askyth no more or that thou dye   *before*
            But sorwe of hert wyth wepynge eye
                For all thi synnys smert.   *severe*

1390   Thei that syh in synnynge,   *sigh*
            In sadde sorwe for her synne,   *their*
            Whanne thei schal make her endynge,   *their*
            Al here joye is to begynne.   *their; about to begin*
            Thanne medelyth no mornynge   *mixes no sorrow*
1395   But joye is joynyd wyth jentyl gynne.   *skill*
            Therfore, Mankynde, in this tokenynge,   *tokening of this*
            Wyth spete of spere to thee I spynne,   *point; move rapidly*
                Goddys lawys to thee I lerne.   *teach*
            Wyth my spud of sorwe swote   *dagger; sweet*
1400   I reche to thyne hert rote.   *strike; root*
            Al thi bale schal torne thee to bote.   *torment; comfort*
                Mankynde, go schryve thee yerne.   *confess; quickly*

HUMANUS GENUS A sete of sorwe in me is set;   *seed*
            Sertys for synne I syhe sore.   *sigh*
1405   Mone of mercy in me is met;   *Moan; lamentation; come*
            For werldys myrthe I morne more.   *Because of*
            In wepynge wo my wele is wet.   *joy is wet [with tears]*
            Mercy, thou muste myn stat astore.   *condition restore*
            Fro oure Lordys lyth thou hast me let,   *light; restricted*
1410   Sory synne, thou grysly gore,   *wretched filth*
                Owte on thee, dedly synne!   *Fie*
            Synne, thou haste Mankynde schent.   *injured*
            In dedly synne my lyfe is spent.
            Mercy, God omnipotent!
1415   In youre grace I begynne.

            For, thou Mankynde have don amys,   *although*
            And he wyl falle in repentaunce,

Crist schal hym bryngyn to bowre of blys	*bower*
If sorwe of hert lache hym wyth launce.	*prick*
1420 Lordyngys, ye se wel alle thys,	
Mankynde hathe ben in gret bobaunce.	*vanity*
I now forsake my synne iwys	*truly*
And take me holy to Penaunce.	*entirely*
On Crist I crye and calle.	
1425 A, mercy, Schryfte! I wyl no more.	*Confession*
For dedly synne myn herte is sore.	
Stuffe Mankynde wyth thyne store	*Fill; store [of wisdom]*
And have hym to thyne halle.	

CONFESCIO Schryffte may no man forsake.	*Confession*
1430 Whanne Mankynde cryeth I am redy.	
Whanne sorwe of hert thee hathe take	*taken possession of*
Schryfte profytyth veryly.	
Whoso for synne wyl sorwe make	*lamentation*
Crist hym heryth whanne he wyl criye.	*hears*
1435 Now, man, lete sorwe thyn synne slake	*lessen*
And torne not ageyn to thi folye,	
For that makyth dystaunce.	*strife*
And if it happe thee turne ageyn to synne,	
For Goddys love lye not longe therinne.	
1440 He that dothe alwey evyl and wyl not blynne,	*cease*
That askyth gret venjaunce.	*asks for*

HUMANUM GENUS Nay, sertys, that schal I not do,	*truly*
Schryfte, thou schalte the sothe se;	*truth see*
For thow Mankynde be wonte therto	*although; accustomed*
1445 I wyl now al amende me.	

Tunc descendit ad Confessionem.	*Then he descends to Confession*

I com to thee, Schryfte, alholy, lo!	*entirely*
I forsake you, synnys, and fro you fle.	*from*
Ye schapyn to man a sory scho;	*make for man an ill-fitting shoe*
Whanne he is begylyd in this degré	*deceived to this extent*
1450 Ye bleykyn al hys ble.	*make pale; countenance*
Synne, thou art a sory store.	*treasure*
Thou makyst Mankynd to synke sore.	
Therfor of you wyl I no more.	
I aske schryfte, for charyté.	*absolution*

CONFESCIO If thou wylt be aknowe here	*will acknowledge*
1456 Only al thi trespas,	*Entirely*
I schal thee schelde fro Helle fere	*fire*
And putte thee fro peyne unto precyouse place.	*torment; safe*

	If thou wylt not make thynne sowle clere	*clean*
1460	But kepe hem in thyne hert cas,	*them [the sins]; your heart's box*
	Anothyr day they schul be rawe and rere	*will be unatoned and unconfessed*
	And synke thi sowle to Satanas	
	In gastful glowynge glede.	*As a ghastly glowing coal*
	Therfore, man, in mody monys,	*sorrowful laments*
1465	If thou wylt wende to worthi wonys,	*go; dwellings [Heaven]*
	Schryve thee now, al at onys,	*Confess; at once*
	Holy of thi mysdede.	*Entirely*

	HUMANUM GENUS A, yys, Schryfte, trewly I trowe,	*believe*
	I schal not spare, for odde nor even,	*for anything*
1470	That I schal rekne, al on a rowe,	*give an account, in order*
	To lache me up to lyvys levene.	*raise; the light of life*
	To my Lord God I am aknowe	*acknowledged*
	That syttyth aboven in hey Hevene	*high*
	That I have synnyd many a throwe	*times*
1475	In the dedly synnys sevene,	
	Bothe in home and halle.	
	Pride, Wrathe, and Envye,	
	Coveytyse and Lecherye,	
	Slawth and also Glotonye,	
1480	I have hem usyd alle.	*them*

	The ten comaundementys brokyn I have	
	And my fyve wyttys spent hem amys.	
	I was thanne wood and gan to rave.	*mad; began*
	Mercy, God, forgeve me thys!	
1485	Whanne any pore man gan to me crave	*to beg of me*
	I gafe hym nowt, and that forthynkyth me, iwys.	*I truly regret*
	Now, Seynt Saveour, ye me save	
	And brynge me to your boure of blys!	*bower*
	I can not alle say,	*any more*
1490	But to the erthe I knele adown,	
	Bothe wyth bede and orison,	*beads; prayer*
	And aske myn absolucion,	
	Syr Schryfte, I you pray.	

	CONFESCIO Now Jhesu Cryste, God holy,	
1495	And all the seyntys of Hevene hende,	*gracious*
	Petyr and Powle, apostoly,	*apostles*
	To whom God gafe powere to lese and bynde,	*loose*
	He forgeve thee thi foly	*[May] he forgive*
	That thou hast synnyd wyth hert and mynde.	
1500	And I, up my powere, thee asoly	*through; pardon*
	That thou hast ben to God unkynde	
	Quantum peccasti.	*However much you have sinned*

	In Pride, Ire, and Envye,	
	Slawthe, Glotony, and Lecherye,	
1505	And Coveytyse continuandelye	*Covetousness continually*
	Vitam male continuasti.	*You have led your life evilly*

	I thee asoyle wyth goode entent	*pardon*
	Of alle the synnys that thou hast wrowth	*done*
	In brekynge of Goddys commaundement	
1510	In worde, werke, wyl, and thowth.	*thought*
	I restore to thee the sacrament	
	Of penauns weche thou nevere rowt;	*which; heeded*
	Thi fyve wyttys mysdyspent	*misspent*
	In synne the weche thou schuldyst nowt,	*which; not*
1515	*Quicquid gesisti,*	*Whatsoever you have committed*
	Wyth eyne sen, herys herynge,	*Seen with eyes, heard [with] ears*
	Nose smellyd, mowthe spekynge,	
	And al thi bodys bad werkynge,	
	Vicium quodcumque fecisti.	*Whatsoever sins you have committed*

	I thee asoyle wyth mylde mod	*pardon*
1520	Of al that thou hast ben ful madde	
	In forsakynge of thyn aungyl good,	
	And thi fowle Flesche that thou hast fadde,	*fed*
	The Werld, the Devyl that is so woode,	*mad*
1525	And folwyd thyne aungyl that is so badde.	
	To Jhesu Crist that deyed on Rode	*died; Cross*
	I restore thee ageyn ful sadde.	*solemnly*
	Noli peccare!	*Do not sin*
	And all the goode dedys that thou haste don	*deeds*
1530	And all thi tribulacyon	
	Stonde thee in remyssion.	
	Posius noli viciare.	*Sin no more*

HUMANUM GENUS	Now, Syr Schryfte, where may I dwelle	
	To kepe me fro synne and woo?	
1535	A comly counseyl ye me spelle	*suitable; tell*
	To fende me now fro my foo.	*defend; from; foes*
	If these sevene synnys here telle	*hear*
	That I am thus fro hem goo,	*from them gone*
	The Werld, the Flesche, and the Devyl of Hell	
1540	Schul sekyn my soule for to sloo	*seek; slay*
	Into balys bowre.	*place of torment*
	Therfore I pray you putte me	
	Into sum place of sureté	*safety*
	That thei may not harmyn me	*So that*
1545	Wyth no synnys sowre.	*bitter*

CONFESCIO   To swyche a place I schal thee kenne   *such; direct*
       Ther thou mayst dwelle wythoutyn dystaunsce   *strife*
       And alwey kepe thee fro synne,
       Into the Castel of Perseveraunce.
1550   If thou wylt to Hevene wynne
       And kepe thee fro werldly dystaunce,   *from; strife*
       Goo to yone castel and kepe thee therinne,
       For it is strenger thanne any in Fraunce.   *stronger*
          To yone castel I thee seende.
1555   That castel is a precyous place,
       Ful of vertu and of grace;
       Whoso levyth there hys lyvys space   *lives; his lifetime*
          No synne schal hym schende.   *injure*

HUMANUM GENUS   A, Schryfte, blyssyd mote thou be!   *may*
1560   This castel is here but at honde.   *close by*
       Thedyr rapely wyl I tee,   *Thither quickly; go*
       Sekyr ovyr this sad sonde.   *Safely; solid land*
       Good perseveraunce God sende me
       Whyle I leve here in this londe.   *live*
1565   Fro fowle fylthe now I fle,
       Forthe to faryn now I fonde   *go; undertake*
       To yone precyous port.
       Lord, what man is in mery lyve   *a blissful life*
       Whanne he is of hys synnys schreve!   *pardoned*
1570   Al my dol adoun is dreve.   *sorrow is overthrown*
          Criste is myn counfort.

MALUS ANGELUS   Ey, what devyl, man, wedyr schat?   *where are you going*
       Woldyst drawe now to holynesse?   *turn*
       Goo, felaw, thi goode gate,   *your way*
1575   Thou art forty wyntyr olde, as I gesse.
       Goo ageyn, the develys mat,   *mate*
       And pleye thee a whyle wyth Sare and Sysse.   *Sarah and Cecily*
       Sche wolde not ellys, yone olde trat,   *hag*
       But putte thee to penaunce and to stresse,   *Except*
1580   Yone foule feterel fyle.   *deceitful wretch*
       Late men that arn on the pyttys brynke   *brink of the grave*
       Forberyn bothe mete and drynke   *Avoid*
       And do penaunce as hem good thynke,   *seems good to them*
          And cum and pley thee a whyle.

BONUS ANGELUS   Ya, Mankynde, wende forthe thi way
1586   And do nothynge aftyr hys red.   *according to his advice*
       He wolde thee lede ovyr londys lay   *fallow land*
       In dale of dros tyl thou were ded.   *valley of dust*
       Of cursydnesse he kepyth the key

1590	To bakyn thee a byttyr bred.	*bread*
	In dale of dol tyl thou schuldyst dey	*valley of sorrow; die*
	He wolde drawe thee to cursydhed,	*wickedness*
	In synne to have myschaunce.	*ill fortune*
	Therfor spede now thy pace	*hurry*
1595	Pertly to yone precyouse place	*Quickly*
	That is al growyn ful of grace,	
	The Castel of Perseveraunce.	

HUMANUM GENUS Goode Aungyl, I wyl do as thou wylt,

	In londe whyl my lyfe may leste,	*last*
1600	For I fynde wel in holy wryt	*scripture*
	Thou counseylyste evere for the beste.	

- - - - - - - - - - - - - - - -   *(see note)*

[Scene xii]

CARITAS To Charyté, man, have an eye   *CHARITY*

	In al thynge, man, I rede.	*advise*
	Al thi doynge as dros is drye	*dust*
1605	But in Charyté thou dyth thi dede.	*Unless; perform; deeds*
	I dystroye alwey Envye;	
	So dyd thi God whanne he gan blede;	*began to bleed*
	For synne he was hangyn hye	*high*
	And yyt synnyd he nevere in dede,	
1610	That mylde mercy welle.	*well of mercy*
	Poule in hys pystyl puttyth the prefe,	*St. Paul; epistle gives the proof*
	"But charyté be wyth thee chefe."[1]	*Unless; foremost*
	Therfore, Mankynde, be now lefe	*glad*
	In Charyté for to dwelle.	

ABSTINENCIA In abstinens lede thi lyf,

1616	Take but skylful refeccyon;	*moderate food*
	For Gloton kyllyth wythoutyn knyf	*Gluttony*
	And dystroyeth thi complexion.	
	Whoso ete or drynke ovyrblyve	*excessively*
1620	It gaderyth to corrupcion.	*leads to*
	This synne browt us alle in stryve	*strife*
	Whanne Adam fel in synne down	
	Fro precyous Paradys.	*From*
	Mankynd, lere now of oure lore.	*learn; wisdom*
1625	Whoso ete or drynke more	
	Thanne skylfully hys state astore,	*his estate can reasonably maintain*
	I holde hym nothynge wys.	*not at all wise*

---

[1] See 1 Corinthians 13:13

CASTITAS   Mankynd, take kepe of Chastyté   *CHASTITY; heed*
        And move thee to maydyn Marye.   *address; virgin Mary*
1630   Fleschly foly loke thou fle,
        At the reverense of Oure Ladye.   *Out of respect for*

        Quia qui in carne vivunt Domino placere non possunt.[1]

        That curteys qwene, what dyd sche?   *courteous queen*
        Kepte hyre clene and stedfastly,   *herself chaste*
        And in her was trussyd the Trinité;   *enclosed*
1635   Thorwe gostly grace sche was worthy,   *Through spiritual*
            And al for sche was chaste.   *because*
        Whoso kepyt hym chast and wyl not synne,
        Whanne he is beryed in bankys brymme   *buried; brim (edge)*
        Al hys joye is to begynne.
1640   Therfore to me take taste.   *take heed of me*

SOLICITUDO   In Besynesse, man loke thou be,   *INDUSTRY*
        Wyth worthi werkys goode and thykke.   *frequent*
        To Slawthe if thou cast thee
        It schal thee drawe to thowtys wyckke.   *wicked thoughts*

        Otiositas parit omne malum.   *Idleness begets all evil*

1645   It puttyth a man to poverté
        And pullyth hym to peynyns prycke.   *the torment of pain*
        Do sumwhat alwey for love of me,   *something*
        Thou thou schuldyst but thwyte a stycke.   *Although; whittle*
            Wyth bedys sumtyme thee blys   *beads; bless yourself*
1650   Sumtyme rede and sumtyme wryte   *read*
        And sumtyme pleye at thi delyte.
        The devyl thee waytyth wyth dyspyte   *waits for; malice*
            Whanne thou art in idylnesse.

LARGITAS   In Largyté, man, ley thi love.   *GENEROSITY; place*
1655   Spende thi good, as God it sent.
        In worchep of hym that syt above
        Loke thi goodys be dyspent.   *spent*
        In dale of dros whanne thou schalt drove   *dust; be forced*
        Lytyl love is on thee lent;   *placed*
1660   The sekatourys schul seyn it is her behove   *executors; their duty*
        To make us mery, "For he is went   *gone*
            That al this good gan owle."   *wealth accumulated*
        Ley thi tresour and thy trust

---

[1] *Since those who live in the flesh cannot be pleasing to God* (see Romans 8:8)

	In place where no ruggynge rust	*destroying*
1665	May it dystroy to dros ne dust¹	*dirt*
	But al to helpe of sowle.	

HUMANUM GENUS   Ladys in londe, lovely and lyt,   *bright*
Lykynge lelys, ye be my leche.   *Kindly lilies; physician*
I wyl bowe to your byddynge bryth;   *beautiful advice*
1670   Trewe tokenynge ye me teche.   *meaning*
Dame Meknes, in your myth   *Meekness; power*
I wyl me wryen fro wyckyd wreche.   *turn away; wretchedness*
Al my purpos I have pyt,   *set*
Paciens to don, as ye me preche;   *do*
1675   Fro Wrathe ye schal me kepe.
Charyté, ye wyl to me entende.   *pay attention*
Fro fowle Envye ye me defende.
Manns mende ye may amende,   *mind; change*
        Whethyr he wake or slepe.

1680   Abstynens, to you I tryst;   *trust*
Fro Glotony ye schal me drawe.   *From*
In Chastyté to levyn me lyst,   *I wish to live*
That is Oure Ladys lawe.
Besynes, we schul be cyste;   *Industry; kiss each other*
1685   Slawthe, I forsake thi sleper sawe.   *slippery speech*
Largyté, to you I tryst,   *trust*
Coveytyse to don of dawe.   *Greed; put to death*
    This is a curteys cumpany.   *courteous*
What schuld I more monys make?   *moans*
1690   The sevene synnys I forsake
And to these sevene vertuis I me take.   *virtues*
        Maydyn Meknes, now mercy!   *Meekness*

HUMILITAS   Mercy may mende al thi mone.   *MEEKNESS; change; lamentation*
Cum in here at thynne owyn wylle.
1695   We schul thee fende fro thi fon   *defend from; foes*
If thou kepe thee in this castel stylle.   *continually*

Cum sancto sanctus eris, et cetera.
Tunc intrabit.²

Stonde hereinne as stylle as ston;
Thanne schal no dedly synne thee spylle.   *harm*
Whethyr that synnys cumme or gon,

---

¹ See Matthew 6:19.

² Lines 1696a–b: *You will be holy with the holy ones, etcetera* (see Psalm 17:26). / *Then he goes in*

1700	Thou schalt wyth us thi bowrys bylle,	*make your home*
	Wyth vertuse we schul thee vaunce.	*virtues; lift up*
	This castel is of so qweynt a gynne	*such ingenious construction*
	That whoso evere holde hym therinne	*keep*
	He schal nevere fallyn in dedly synne;	
1705	It is the Castel of Perseveranse.	

Qui perseveraverit usque in finem, hic salvus erit.
Tunc cantabunt "Eterne Rex altissime," et dicet:[1]

HUMILITAS	Now blyssyd be Oure Lady, of Hevene Emperes!	*Empress*
	Now is Mankynde fro foly falle	*fallen away from folly*
	And is in the Castel of Goodnesse.	
	He hauntyth now Hevene halle	*occupies; halls of Heaven*
1710	That schal bryngyn hym to Hevene.	
	Crist that dyed wyth dyen dos	*with a deadly potion*
	Kepe Mankynd in this castel clos	
	And put alwey in hys purpos	*keep; mind*
	To fle the synnys sevene!	

MALUS ANGELUS	Nay, be Belyals bryth bonys,	*bright bones*
1716	Ther schal he no whyle dwelle.	
	He schal be wonne fro these wonys	*won from; dwellings*
	Wyth the Werld, the Flesch, and the Devyl of Hell!	*By*
	Thei schul my wyl awreke.	*carry out*
1720	The synnys sevene, tho kyngys thre,	*those*
	To Mankynd have enmyté.	
	Scharpely thei schul helpyn me	*Fiercely*
	This castel for to breke.	
	Howe, Flypyrgebet, Bakbytere!	*Ho, Flibbertigibbet, Backbiter*
1725	Yerne oure message loke thou make.	*Quickly; proclaim*
	Blythe about loke thou bere.	*Quickly; go*
	Sey Mankynde hys synnys hath forsake.	
	Wyth yene wenchys he wyl hym were,	*yon; take refuge*
	Al to holynesse he hath hym take.	
1730	In myn hert it doth me dere,	*harm*
	The bost that tho moderys crake;	*those bitches brag*
	My galle gynnyth to grynde.	*guts begin*
	Flepyrgebet, ronne upon a rasche.	*quickly*
	Byd the Werld, the Fend, and the Flesche	*Devil*
1735	That they com to fytyn fresche	*fight vigorously*
	To wynne ageyn Mankynde.	

[1] Lines 1705a–b: *He who perseveres to the end will be saved* (see Matthew 10:22). / *Then they will sing "Eternal King most high," and [Meekness] says*

DETRACCIO   I go, I go, on grounde glad,   *BACKBITER*
            Swyftyr thanne schyp wyth rodyr.   *rudder*
            I make men masyd and mad   *confused*
1740   And every man to kyllyn odyr   *others*
                Wyth a sory chere.   *evil attitude*
            I am glad, be Seynt Jamys of Galys,
            Of schrewdnes to tellyn talys   *To spread tales of malice*
            Bothyn in Ingelond and in Walys,   *England; Wales*
1745   And feyth I have many a fere.   *truly; companion*

            Tunc ibit ad Belial.   *Then he goes to Belial (the Devil)*

[Scene xiii]
            Heyl, set in thyn selle!   *on; seat*
            Heyl, dynge Devyl in thi delle!   *worthy; pit*
            Heyl, lowe in Helle!   *deep*
            I cum to thee talys to telle

BELYAL   Bakbyter, boy,
1751   Alwey be holtys and hothe,   *woods; cleared land (everywhere)*
            Sey now, I sey,   *Tell me now*
            What tydyngys? Telle me the sothe!   *truth*

DETRACCIO   Teneful talys I may thee sey,   *Distressing; tell*
1755   To thee no good, as I gesse:
            Mankynd is gon now awey
            Into the Castel of Goodnesse.
            Ther he wyl bothe lyvyn and deye
            In dale of dros tyl deth hym dresse;   *dust; place*
1760   Hathe thee forsakyn, forsothe I sey,
            And all thi werkys more and lesse;
                To yone castel he gan to crepe.   *Into*
            Yone modyr Meknes, sothe to sayn,   *bitch Meekness, truth*
            And all yene maydnys on yone playn   *those*
1765   For to fytyn thei be ful fayn   *fight; glad*
                Mankynd for to kepe.

            Tunc vocabit Superbiam, Indiviam, et Iram.   *Then he will call Pride, Envy, and Wrath*

SUPERBIA   Syr kynge, what wytte?   *what is on your mind*
            We be redy throtys to kytte.   *throats to cut*

BELYAL   Sey, gadelyngys — have ye harde grace   *rascals; bad luck*
1770   And evyl deth mote ye deye! —   *may*
            Why lete ye Mankynd fro you pase   *from; escape*
            Into yene castel fro us aweye?   *yon; from*
                Wyth tene I schal you tey.   *pain; bind*

	Harlotys, at onys	*Rascals, [go] at once*
1775	Fro this wonys!	*place*
	Be Belyals bonys,	*By*
	Ye schul abeye.	*pay [for it]*

Et verberabit eos super terram.   *And he will beat them on the ground*

DETRACCIO   Ya, for God, this was wel goo,   *by; done*
          Thus to werke wyth bakbytynge.
1780   I werke bothe wrake and woo   *vengeance; injury*
          And make iche man othyr to dynge.   *to strike others*
          I schal goo abowte and makyn moo   *more*
          Rappys for to route and rynge.   *Blows; roar and yell*
          Ye bakbyterys, loke that ye do so.
1785   Make debate abowtyn to sprynge   *strife*
            Betwene systyr and brothyr.
          If any bakbyter here be lafte,
          He may lere of me hys crafte.   *learn*
          Of Goddys grace he schal be rafte   *bereft*
1790   And every man to kyllyn othyr.   *others*

Ad Carnem.   *[He goes] to [the scaffold of] Flesh*

[Scene xiv]
          Heyl, kynge, I calle!
          Heyl, prinse, proude prekyd in palle!   *proudly dressed in rich robes*
          Heyl, hende in halle!   *gracious*
          Heyl, syr kynge, fayre thee befalle!   *good luck*

CARO   Boy Bakbytynge,   *FLESH*
1796   Ful redy in robys to rynge,   *shout*
          Ful glad tydynge,
          Be Belyalys bonys, I trow thow brynge.   *By; bones; believe*

DETRACCIO   Ya, for God, "owt" I crye   *shame*
1800   On thi too sonys and thi dowtyr yynge: *two; young*
          Glotoun, Slawthe, and Lechery
          Hath put me in gret mornynge.   *lamentation*
          They let Mankynd gon up hye   *high*
          Into yene castel at hys lykynge,   *yon; pleasure*
1805   Therin for to leve and dye,
          Wyth tho ladys to make endynge,   *those*
            Tho flourys fayre and fresche.
          He is in the Castel of Perseverauns
          And put hys body to penauns.
1810   Of hard happe is now thi chauns,   *bad luck; fortune*
            Syre kynge, Mankyndys Flesche.

Tunc Caro clamabit ad Gulam, Accidiam, et Luxuriam.[1]

LUXURIA Sey now thi wylle,		*Say*
Syr Flesch, why cryest thou so schylle?		*shrilly*

CARO A, Lechery, thou skallyd mare!		*scurvy mare*
1815 And thou Gloton, God geve thee wo!		
And vyle Slawth, evyl mote thou fare!		*may*
Why lete ye Mankynd fro you go		*from*
In yone castel so hye?		*high*
Evele grace com on thi snowte!		*Bad luck; nose*
1820 Now I am dressyd in gret dowte.		*put*
Why ne had ye lokyd betyr abowte?		*kept closer watch*
Be Belyalys bonys, ye schul abye.		*By; pay [for it]*

Tunc verberabit eos in placeam.   *Then he will beat them in the place*

DETRACCIO Now, be God, this is good game!		
I, Bakbyter, now bere me wel.		*enjoy myself*
1825 If I had lost my name,		
I vow to God it were gret del.		*pity*
I schape these schrewys to mekyl schame;		*direct; rascals; great*
Iche rappyth on othyr wyth rowtynge rele.		*Each beats [the] other in riotous tumult*
I, Bakbyter, wyth fals fame		*report*
1830 Do brekyn and brestyn hodys of stele.		*break; burst helmets*
Thorwe this cuntré I am knowe.		*known*
Now wyl I gynne forth to goo		*begin*
And make Coveytyse have a knoke or too,		*Greed; blow or two*
And thanne iwys I have doo		*truly; done*
1835 My dever, as I trowe.		*duty; believe*

Ad Mundum.   *[He goes] to [the scaffold of] the World*

[Scene xv]

Heyl, styf in stounde!		*steadfast in a fight*
Heyl, gayly gyrt upon grounde!		*dressed*
Heyl, fayre flowr ifounde!		
Heyl, Syr Werld, worthi in wedys wonde!		*splendid clothes*

MUNDUS Bakbyter in rowte,		*with [your] retinue*
1841 Thou tellyst talys of dowte,		*deception*
So styf and so stowte.		*steadfast; strong*
What tydyngys bryngyst thou abowte?		

---

[1] *Then Flesh will shout to Gluttony, Sloth, and Lechery*

DETRACCIO Nothynge goode, that schalt thou wete.   *know*

1845   Mankynd, Syr Werld, hath thee forsake.

       Wyth Schryfte and Penauns he is smete   *struck*

       And to yene castel he hath hym take   *yon*

           Amonge yene ladys whyt as lake.   *linen*

       Lo, Syr Werld, ye moun agryse   *should be upset*

1850   That ye be servyd on this wyse.   - *dealt with in this manner*

       Go pley you wyth Syr Coveytyse   *Greed*

           Tyl hys crowne crake.   *head crack*

Tunc buccinabit cornu ad Avariciam.[1]

AVARICIA Syr bolnynge bowde,   *swollen dung beetle*

           Tell me why blowe ye so lowde?

MUNDUS Lewde losel, the Devel thee brenne!   *Base rascal; burn*

1856   I prey God geve thee a fowl hap!   *bad luck*

       Sey, why letyst thou Mankynd

       Into yene castel for to skape?   *yon; escape*

           I trowe thou gynnyst to rave.   *think; begin to go mad*

1860   Now, for Mankynd is went,   *gone*

       Al oure game is schent.   *sport is ruined*

       Therfore a sore dryvynge dent,   *strong blow*

           Harlot, thou schalt have.   *Rascal*

Tunc verberabit eum.   *Then he will beat him*

AVARICIA Mercy, mercy! I wyl no more.

1865   Thou hast me rappyd wyth rewly rowtys.   *struck; severe blows*

       I snowre, I sobbe, I sye sore.   *scowl; sigh*

       Myn hed is clateryd al to clowtys.   *shattered; pieces*

       In al youre state I schal you store   *To; rank; restore*

       If ye abate youre dyntys dowtys.   *stop; terrible blows*

1870   Mankynd, that ye have forlore,   *whom; completely lost*

       I schal do com owt fro yone skowtys   *make come out; sluts*

           To youre hende hall.   *gracious*

       If ye wyl no more betyn me,   *beat*

       I schal do Mankynd com out fre.   *make; voluntarily*

1875   He schal forsake, as thou schalt se,

           The fayre vertus all.   *virtues*

MUNDUS Have do thanne, the Devyl thee tere!   *Do it then; tear [apart]*

           Thou schalt ben hangyn in Hell herne.   *a corner of Hell*

           Bylyve my baner up thou bere   *Quickly*

---

[1] *Then he (Mundus) will blow a horn towards [the scaffold of] Covetousness*

1880 And besege we the castel yerne	*besiege; quickly*
Mankynd for to stele.	
Whanne Mankynd growyth good,	*becomes*
I, the Werld, am wyld and wod.	*crazy; mad*
Tho bycchys schul bleryn in her blood	*bitches; wail (stream at the eyes) in their*
1885 Wyth flappys felle and fele.	*many cruel blows*
Yerne lete flapyr up my fane	*Quickly; flutter; banner*
And schape we schame and schonde.	*let us create; disgrace*
I schal brynge wyth me tho bycchys bane;	*those bitches' ruin*
Ther schal no vertus dwellyn in my londe.	*virtues*
1890 Mekenes is that modyr that I mene,	*Meekness; bitch*
To hyre I brewe a byttyr bonde.	*For; bondage*
Sche schal dey upon this grene	*die*
If that sche com al in myn honde,	*into my power*
Yene rappokys wyth her rumpys.	*Yon rascals; their rumps*
1895 I am the Werld! It is my wyll	
The Castel of Vertu for to spyll.	*destroy*
Howtyth hye upon yene hyll,	*Shout loudly; yon*
Ye traytours, in youre trumpys.	*with your trumpets*

Tunc Mundus, Cupiditas, et Stulticia ibunt ad castellum cum vexillo et dicet Demon:[1]

[Scene xvi]

BELYAL I here trumpys trebelen al of tene.	*hear trumpets proclaim; wrath*
1900 The worthi Werld walkyth to werre	*goes; war*
For to clyvyn yone castel clene,	*split; entirely*
Tho maydnys meyndys for to merre.	*Those; intentions; destroy*
Sprede my penon upon a prene	*banner; spike*
And stryke we forthe now undyr sterre.	*stars*
1905 Schapyth now youre scheldys schene	*Prepare; shining shields*
Yene skallyd skoutys for to skerre	*Yon scurvy sluts to scare*
Upon yone grene grese.	*grass*
Buske you now, boyes, belyve.	*Prepare yourselves; quickly*
For evere I stonde in mekyl stryve;	*great anxiety*
1910 Whyl Mankynd is in clene lyve	*a virtuous life*
I am nevere wel at ese.	
Make you redy, all three,	
Bolde batayl for to bede.	*offer*
To yone feld let us fle	
1915 And bere my baner forth on brede.	*far and wide*
To yone castel wyl I te;	*go*

---

[1] *Then the World, Covetousness, and Folly shall go to the castle with a banner and the Devil will say [from his scaffold]*

Tho mamerynge modrys schul have her mede. *chattering women; reward*
But thei yeld up to me, *Unless*
Wyth byttyr balys thei schul blede, *torments; bleed*
1920   Of her reste I schal hem reve. *their; despoil*
In woful watyrs I schal hem wasche.
Have don, felaws, and take youre trasche *Go to it; course*
And wende we thedyr on a rasche *go; quickly*
    That castel for to cleve. *split*

SUPERBIA   Now, now, now, go now!
1926 On hye hyllus lete us howte *high; shout*
For in pride is al my prow *profit*
Thi bold baner to bere abowte.
To Golyas I make a vow *Goliath*
1930 For to schetyn yone iche skowte. *shoot each of yon sluts*
On hyr ars, raggyd and row, *In her; rough*
I schal bothe clatyr and clowte *clatter; strike*
    And geve Meknesse myschanse. *Meekness bad luck*
Belyal bryth, it is thyn hest *bright; command*
1935 That I, Pride, goo thee nest *next to you*
And bere thi baner beforn my brest
    Wyth a comly contenaunce. *gracious*

[Scene xvii]
CARO   I here an hydowse whwtynge on hyt. *hear a hideous hooting of loud voices*
Belyve, byd my baner forth for to blase. *Quickly, shine*
1940 Whanne I syt in my sadyl it is a selkowth syt; *splendid sight*
I gape as a gogmagog whanne I gynne to gase. *giant; begin to stare*
This worthy wylde werld I wagge wyth a wyt; *move; weight*
Yone rappokys I ruble and al to-rase *rascals; crush; demolish*
Bothe wyth schot and wyth slynge I caste wyth a sleyt *skillfully*
1945 Wyth care to yone castel to crachen and to crase *sorrow; crack; shatter*
    In flode. *Into the river*
I am mans Flesch; where I go
I am mans most fo; *greatest foe*
Iwys, I am evere wo *Truly; woeful*
1950   Whane he drawyth to goode. *turns*

Therfore, ye bolde boyes, buske you abowte. *get ready*
Scharply on scheldys your schaftys ye schevere. *shields; spears; break*
And Lechery ledron, schete thou a skoute. *rogue, shoot; slut*
Help we Mankynd fro yone castel to kevere. *escape*
1955   Helpe we moun hym wynne. *must regain him*
Schete we all at a schote *Shoot we together*
Wyth gere that we cunne best note *equipment; can best use*
To cache Mankynd fro yene cote *chase; yon dwelling*
    Into dedly synne.

GULA	Lo, Syr Flesch, whow I fare to the felde,	*how; go*
1961	Wyth a faget on myn hond for to settyn on a fyre.	*faggot*
	Wyth a wrethe of the wode wel I can me welde;	*twist; acquit myself well*
	Wyth a longe launce tho loselys I schal lere.	*rascals I shall teach [a lesson]*
	Go we wyth oure gere.	*equipment*
1965	Tho bycchys schul bleykyn and blodyr;	*bitches; turn pale; blubber*
	I schal makyn swyche a powdyr,	*dust*
	Bothe wyth smoke and wyth smodyr,	*fumes*
	Thei schul schytyn for fere.	*shit out of fear*

Tunc descendent in placeam.	*Then they descend into the place*

[Scene xviii]

MALUS ANGELUS	*Dicet ad Belyal*:	*Says to the Devil*
	As armys! As an herawd hey now I howte!	*To; Like a herald loudly; shout*
1970	Devyl, dyth thee as a duke to do tho damyselys dote.[1]	
	Belyal, as a bolde boy thi brodde I bere abowte;	*banner*
	Helpe to cache Mankynd fro caytyfys cote.	*chase; the villains' dwelling*
	Pryd, put out thi penon of raggys and of rowte.	*banner; rags; riot*
	Do this modyr Mekenes meltyn to mote.	*Make; bitch Meekness melt to a speck*
1975	Wrethe, prefe Paciens, the skallyd skowte.	*take on; scurvy slut*
	Envye, to Charyté schape thou a schote	*on; prepare an attack*
	Ful yare.	*Quickly*
	Wyth Pryde, Wrethe, and Envye,	
	These develys, be downys drye,	*barren hills*
1980	As comly kynge I dyscrye	*noble; see*
	Mankynd to kachyn to care.	*[we will] drive*

Ad Carnem:	*[He speaks] to Flesh*

	Flesche, frele and fresche, frely fed,	*frail; lavishly*
	Wyth Gloton, Slawthe, and Lechery mans sowle thou slo.	*slay*
	As a duke dowty do thee to be dred.	*brave make yourself feared*
1985	Gere thee wyth gerys fro toppe to the too.	*Equip yourself; toe*
	Kyth this day thou art a kynge frely fedde.	*Show; lavishly*
	Gloton, sle thou Abstynensce wyth wyckyd woo.	
	Wyth Chastyté, thou Lechour, be not ovyrledde.	*By; oppressed*
	Slawthe, bete thou Besynes on buttokys bloo.	*Industry; blue*
1990	Do now thi crafte, in coste to be knowe.	*skill, its value known*

Ad Mundum:	*[He speaks] to the World*

	Worthy, wytty, and wys, wondyn in wede,	*dressed in garments*
	Lete Coveytyse karpyn, cryen, and grede.	*Greed shout, yell; call*

---

[1] *Devil, prepare yourself nobly to make those maidens look silly*

| | Here ben bolde bacheleris batyl to bede, | *are; soldiers; offer* |
| | Mankynd to tene, as I trowe. | *injure; believe* |

HUMANUM GENUS	That dynge duke that deyed on Rode	*worthy man; Cross*
1996	This day my sowle kepe and safe!	*save*
	Whanne Mankynd drawyth to goode	*turns*
	Beholde what enmys he schal have!	*enemies*
	The Werld, the Devyl, the Flesche arn wode;	*angry*
2000	To men thei casten a careful kave;	*prepare; terrible cavern*
	Byttyr balys thei brewyn on brode	*torments; brew far and wide*
	Mankynd in wo to weltyr and wave,	*to roll and toss*
	Lordyngys, sothe to sey.	*truth*
	Therfore iche man be war of this,	*each; wary*
2005	For whyl Mankynd clene is	*virtuous*
	Hys enmys schul temptyn hym to don amys	*enemies; amiss*
	If thei mown be any wey.	*are able; means*

Omne gaudium existimate cum variis temptacionibus insideritis.[1]

	Therfore, lordys, beth now glad	*be*
	Wyth elmesdede and orysoun	*almsdeeds; prayer*
2010	For to don as Oure Lord bad,	*do; bade*
	Styfly wythstonde youre temptacyoun.	*Steadfastly*
	Wyth this foul fende I am ner mad.	*almost*
	To batayle thei buskyn hem bown.	*make themselves ready*
	Certys I schuld ben ovyrlad,	*Certainly; defeated*
2015	But that I am in this castel town,	*Were I not*
	Wyth synnys sore and smerte.	*painful*
	Whoso wyl levyn oute of dystresse	*live*
	And ledyn hys lyf in clennesse	*virtue*
	In this Castel of Vertu and of Goodnesse	
2020	Hym muste have holé hys hert.	*entirely*

Delectare in Domino et dabit tibi peticiones cordis tui.[2]

BONUS ANGELUS	A, Mekenesse, Charyté, and Pacyens,	*Meekness*
	Prymrose pleyeth parlasent.	*(see note)*
	Chastyté, Besynes, and Abstynens,	*Industry*
	Myn hope, ladys, in you is lent.	*placed*
2025	Socoure, paramourys, swetter thanne sens,	*Help, ladies; incense*
	Rode as rose on rys irent.	*Red; torn from a branch*
	This day ye dyth a good defens.	*prepare*
	Whyl Mankynd is in good entent	*Although; has good intentions*

---

[1] *Consider it all joy, when you fall into many temptations* (see James 1:2)

[2] *Take pleasure in the Lord, and He will give you the desires of your heart* (see Psalm 36:4)

	His thoutys arn unhende.	*thoughts; unstable*
2030	Mankynd is browt into this walle	
	In freelté to fadyn and falle.	*frailty; decline*
	Therfore, ladys, I pray you alle,	
	Helpe this day Mankynde.	

HUMILITAS	God, that syttyth in Hevene on hy,	*MEEKNESS; high*
2035	Save al Mankynd be se and sonde!	*sea; shore (i.e., everywhere)*
	Lete hym dwellyn here and ben us by	*be with us*
	And we schul puttyn to hym helpynge honde.	*give him*
	Yyt forsothe nevere I sy	*have seen*
	That any fawte in us he fonde	*defect; found*
2040	But that we savyd hym fro synne sly	*crafty*
	If he wolde be us styfly stonde	*by us steadfastly*
	In this castel of ston.	
	Therfore drede thee not, mans aungel dere.	
	If he wyl dwellyn wyth us here	
2045	Fro sevene synnys we schul hym were	*defend*
	And his enmys ichon.	*each of his enemies*

	Now my sevene systerys swete,	
	This day fallyth on us the lot	*destiny*
	Mankynd for to schylde and schete	*shield; guard*
2050	Fro dedly synne and schamely schot.	*shameful attack*
	Hys enmys strayen in the strete	*enemies wander*
	To spylle man wyth spetows spot.	*destroy; cruel disgrace*
	Therfor oure flourys lete now flete	*flowers; float down*
	And kepe we hym, as we have het,	*promised*
2055	Among us in this halle.	
	Therfor, sevene systerys swote,	*sweet*
	Lete oure vertus reyne on rote.	*rain down; roots*
	This day we wyl be mans bote	*man's remedy*
	Ageyns these develys alle.	

BELYAL	This day the vaward wyl I holde.	*vanguard*
2061	Avaunt my baner, precyous Pride,	*Forward*
	Mankynd to cache to karys colde.	*drive; cares*
	Bold batayl now wyl I byde.	*offer*
	Buske you, boyes, on brede.	*Prepare; widely*
2065	Alle men that be wyth me wytholde,	*that follow me*
	Bothe the yonge and the olde,	
	Envye, Wrathe, ye boyes bolde,	
	To rounde rappys ye rape, I rede.	*strong blows; rush; advise*

SUPERBIA	As armys, Mekenes! I brynge thi bane,	*PRIDE; To; ruin*
2070	Al wyth pride peyntyd and pyth.	*decorated*
	What seyst thou, faytour? Be myn fayr fane,	*deceiver; banner*

Wyth robys rounde rayed ful ryth,   *on all sides arrayed lavishly*
Grete gounse, I schal thee gane.   *gowns; overcome*
To marre thee, Mekenes, wyth my myth,   *destroy; might*
2075   No werldly wyttys here ar wane.   *missing*
Lo, thi castel is al beset!   *surrounded*
    Moderys, whow schul ye do?   *Bitches; how*
Mekenes, yelde thee to me, I rede.   *yield yourself; advise*
Myn name in londe is precyous Prede.
2080   Myn bolde baner to thee I bede.   *present*
    Modyr, what seyste therto?   *Bitch*

HUMILITAS Ageyns thi baner of pride and bost   *MEEKNESS; boasting*
A baner of meknes and mercy
I putte ageyns pride, wel thou wost,   *know*
2085   That schal schende thi careful cry.   *destroy; grievous*
This meke kynge is knowyn in every cost   *meek; everywhere*
That was croysyd on Calvary.   *crucified*
Whanne he cam doun fro Hevene ost   *host*
And lytyd wyth mekenes in Mary,   *alighted*
2090   This lord thus lytyd lowe.   *settled humbly*
Whanne he cam fro the Trynyté
Into a mayden lyted he,   *alighted*
And al was for to dystroye thee,
    Pride, this schalt thou knowe.

Deposuit potentes de sede, et cetera.[1]

2095   For whanne Lucyfer to Helle fyl,   *fell*
Pride, therof thou were chesun,   *cause*
And thou, Devyl, wyth wyckyd wyl
In Paradys trappyd us wyth tresun.
So thou us bond in balys ille,   *bound; terrible torments*
2100   This may I preve be ryth resun,   *prove; proper reason*
Tyl this duke that dyed on hylle   *nobleman (i.e., Jesus); hill (Golgatha)*
In Hevene man myth nevere han sesun;   *might; have a place*
    The gospel thus declaryt.
For whoso lowe hym schal ben hy,   *humbles himself; high*
2105   Therfore thou schalt not comen us ny,   *near*
And thou thou be nevere so sly,   *although; crafty*
    I schal felle al thi fare.   *destroy; attempts*

Qui se exaltat humiliabitur, et cetera.[2]

---

[1] *He has put down the mighty from their seats, etc.* (see Luke 1:52)

[2] *Whoever exalts himself will be abased, etc.* (see Luke 14:11 and 18:14)

IRA   Dame Pacyens, what seyst thou to Wrathe and Ire?
          Putte Mankynd fro thi castel clere,   *out of; virtuous*
2110   Or I schal tappyn at thi tyre   *strike; attire*
          Wyth styffe stonys that I have here.   *heavy*
          I schal slynge at thee many a vyre   *crossbow bolt*
          And ben avengyd hastely here.
          Thus Belsabub, oure gret syre,
2115   Bad me brenne thee wyth wyld fere,   *burn; wild fire*
              Thou bycche, blak as kole.   *bitch*
          Therfor fast, fowle skowte,   *slut*
          Putte Mankynd to us owte,
          Or of me thou schalt have dowte,   *fear*
2120   Thou modyr, thou motyhole!   *bitch; filthy cunt*

PACIENCIA   Fro thi dowte Crist me schelde   *fear of you; protect*
          This iche day, and al mankynde!   *Today*
          Thou wrecchyd Wrethe, wood and wylde,   *mad*
          Pacyens schal thee schende.   *destroy*

          Quia ira viri justiciam Dei non operatur.[1]

2125   For Marys sone, meke and mylde,   *son*
          Rent thee up, rote and rynde,   *Ripped; root; bark*
          Whanne he stod meker thanne a chylde   *meeker*
          And lete boyes hym betyn and bynde,
              Therfor, wrecche, be stylle.
2130   For tho pelourys that gan hym pose,   *despoilers; push*
          He myth a drevyn hem to dros,   *might have forced; dust*
          And yyt, to casten hym on the Cros,   *crucify*
              He sufferyd al her wylle.   *their*

          Thowsentys of aungellys he myth han had   *might have*
2135   To a wrokyn hym ther ful yerne,   *To have avenged; quickly*
          And yyt to deyen he was glad   *die*
          Us pacyens to techyn and lerne.   *patience*
          Therfor, boy, wyth thi boystous blad,   *fierce blade*
          Fare awey be feldys ferne.   *into distant fields*
2140   For I wyl do as Jhesu bad,
          Wrecchys fro my wonys werne   *turn from my dwellings*
              Wyth a dyngne defens.   *worthy*
          If thou fonde to comyn alofte   *attempt*
          I schal thee cacche fro this crofte   *chase from*
2145   Wyth these rosys swete and softe,
              Peyntyd wyth pacyens.

---

[1] *For the wrath of man does not produce the justice of God* (see James 1:20)

INVIDIA Out, myn herte gynnyth to breke, — *begins*
For Charyté that stondyth so stowte. — *steadfast*
Alas, myn herte gynnyth to wreke. — *begins to seek vengeance*
2150 Yelde up this castel, thou hore clowte, — *gray rag*
It is myn offyce fowle to speke, — *function foully*
Fals sklaundrys to bere abowte. — *slanders*
Charyté, the Devyl mote thee cheke — *may the Devil choke you*
But I thee rappe wyth rewly rowte, — *Unless; strike; terrible blow*
2155 Thi targe for to tere. — *shield; break*
Let Mankynde cum to us doun
Or I schal schetyn to this castel town — *shoot at*
A ful fowle defamacyoun.
Therfore this bowe I bere.

CARITAS Thou thou speke wycke and fals fame, — *CHARITY; Although; wickedness*
2161 The wers schal I nevere do my dede. — *worse*
Whoso peyryth falsly anothyr mans name, — *damages*
Crystys curs he schal have to mede. — *as a reward*

Vae homini illi per quem scandalum venit.[1]

Whoso wyl not hys tunge tame, — *control*
2165 Take it sothe as mes-crede, — *true; the Creed*
Wo, wo to hym and mekyl schame! — *much*
In holy wrytte this I rede. — *scripture; read*
For evere thou art a schrewe. — *villain*
Thou thou speke evyl, I ne geve a gres; — *Although; blade of grass*
2170 I schal do nevere the wers. — *worse*
At the last the sothe vers — *true teaching*
Certys Hymself schal schewe. — *demonstrate*

Oure lovely Lord wythowtyn lak — *flaw*
Gaf example to charyté, — *of*
2175 Whanne he was betyn blo and blak — *blue*
For trespas that nevere dyd he.
In sory synne had he no tak — *spot*
And yyt for synne he bled blody ble. — *a bloody countenance*
He toke hys Cros upon hys bak,
2180 Synful man, and al for thee.
Thus he mad defens.
Envye, wyth thi slaundrys thycke, — *prolific*
I am putte at my Lordys prycke; — *placed in; torment*
I wyl do good ageyns the wycke — *wicked*
2185 And kepe in sylens — *remain*

---

[1] *Woe to the man through whom offense comes* (see Matthew 18:7)

BELYAL   What, for Belyalys bonys,   *bones*
                  Whereabowtyn chyde ye?   *What are you jabbering about*
                  Have don, ye boyes, al at onys.   *all together*
                  Lasche don these moderys, all three.   *Strike down; bitches*
2190   Werke wrake to this wonys.   *Make destruction; dwelling*
                  The vaunward is grauntyd me.   *vanguard*
                  Do these moderys to makyn monys.   *Cause; bitches; moans*
                  Youre dowty dedys now lete se.   *brave deeds*
                       Dasche hem al to daggys.   *pieces*
2195   Have do, boyes, blo and blake   *Go to it; blue*
                  Wirke these wenchys wo and wrake.   *vengeance*
                  Claryouns, cryeth up at a krake,   *Trumpets; loudly*
                       And blowe your brode baggys!   *bagpipes*

         Tunc pugnabunt diu.   *Then they will fight for a long time*

SUPERBIA   Out, my proude bak is bent!
2200   Mekenes hath me al forbete.   *severely beaten*
                  Pride wyth Mekenes is forschent.   *by; destroyed*
                  I weyle and wepe wyth wondys wete;   *wail; bloody wounds*
                       I am betyn in the hed.
                  My prowde pride adoun is drevyn;
2205   So scharpely Mekenes hath me schrevyn   *humbled*
                  That I may no lengyr levyn,   *live*
                       My lyf is me berevyd.   *taken away*

INVIDIA   Al myn enmyté is not worth a fart;   *hatred*
                  I schyte and schake al in my schete.   *underwear*
2210   Charyté, that sowre swart,   *swarthy person*
                  Wyth fayre rosys myn hed gan breke.
                       I brede the malaundyr.   *I'm covered with scabs*
                  Wyth worthi wordys and flourys swete   *noble*
                  Charyté makyth me so meke
2215   I dare neythyr crye nore crepe,   *creep*
                       Not a schote of sklaundyr.   *shot*

IRA   I, Wrethe, may syngyn "Weleawo."
                  Pacyens me gaf a sory dynt.   *terrible blow*
                  I am al betyn blak and blo   *blue*
2220   Wyth a rose that on Rode was rent.   *was torn from the Cross*
                       My speche is almost spent.
                  Hyr rosys fel on me so scharpe
                  That myn hed hangyth as an harpe.   *hangs [in strings]*
                  I dar neythyr crye nor carpe,   *complain*
2225   Sche is so pacyent.

MALUS ANGELUS   Go hens, ye do not worthe a tord.   *are not; turd*

Foule falle you, alle foure!   *Bad luck to you*

Yerne, yerne, let fall on bord,   *Quickly; attack again*

Syr Flesch, wyth thyn eyn soure.   *eyes*

2230   For care I cukke and koure.   *sorrow; shit and cower*

Syr Flesch, wyth thyn company,

Yerne, yerne, make a cry.   *Quickly*

Helpe! we have no velony   *disgrace*

That this day may be oure.   *By which*

CARO   War, war, late mans Flesche go to!   *let; go to [work]*

2236   I com wyth a company.

Have do, my chyldryn, now have do,   *Let's go*

Glotoun, Slawth, and Lechery.

Iche of you wynnyth a scho.   *Each; gain fame*

2240   Lete not Mankynde wynne maystry.   *mastery*

Lete slynge hem in a fowl slo   *Let them be thrown; ditch*

And fonde to feffe hym wyth foly.   *try to endow*

Dothe now wel youre dede.   *Do*

Yerne lete se whow ye schul gynne   *Quickly; how; begin*

2244   Mankynde to temptyn to dedly synne.

If ye muste this castelle wynne   *are able to*

Hell schal be your mede.   *reward*

GULA   War, Syr Gloton schal makyn a smeke   *Beware; smoke*

Ageyns this castel, I vowe.

2250   Abstynens, thou thou bleyke,   *although you turn pale*

I loke on thee wyth byttyr browe.

I have a faget in myn necke   *torch on my shoulder*

To settyn Mankynd on a lowe.   *on fire*

My foul leye schalt thou not let,   *flame; hinder*

2255   I vow to God, as I trowe.   *believe*

Therfor putte hym out here.

In meselynge Glotonye,   *disease-ridden*

Wyth goode metys and drynkys trye,   *rich*

I norche my systyr Lecherye   *nourish*

2260   Tyl man rennyth on fere.   *on fire*

ABSTINENCIA   Thi metys and drynkys arn unthende   *ABSTINENCE; unhealthy*

Whanne thei are out of mesure take.

Thei makyn men mad and out of mende   *mind*

And werkyn hem bothe wo and wrake.   *cause them; injury*

2265   That for thi fere thou thou here kyndyl,   *fire although*

Certys I schal thi wele aslake   *diminish your prosperity*

Wyth bred that browth us out of Hell   *bread; brought*

And on the Croys sufferyd wrake: *Cross; injury*

I mene the sacrament.   *mean*

2270	That iche blysful bred	*same blessed*

That iche blysful bred — *same blessed*
That hounge on hyl tyl he was ded
Schal tempere so myn maydynhed — *assist*
    That thi purpos schal be spent. — *wasted*

In abstynens this bred was browth, — *bread; brought*
2275 Certys, Mankynde, and al for thee.
Of fourty dayes ete he nowth — *nothing*
And thanne was naylyd to a tre.

Cum jejunasset quadraginta diebus, et cetera.[1]

Example us was betawth, — *taught*
In sobyrnesse he bad us be.
2280 Therfor Mankynd schal not be cawth, — *caught*
Glotony, wyth thy degré — *condition*
    The sothe thou schalt se. — *truth*
To norysch fayre thou thou be fawe, — *nourish pleasantly although; eager*
Abstynens it schal wythdrawe
2285 Tyl thou be schet undyr schawe — *shut up; earth*
    And fayn for to fle. — *eager*

LUXURIA Lo, Chastyté, thou fowle skowte! — *LECHERY; slut*
This ilke day here thou schalt deye. — *same*
I make a fer in mans towte — *fire; genitals*
2290 That launcyth up as any leye. — *leaps; flame*
These cursyd colys I bere abowte — *coals*
Mankynde in tene for to teye. — *pain; tie up*
Men and wommen hathe no dowte — *fear*
Wyth pyssynge pokys for to pleye. — *private parts*
2295   I bynde hem in my bondys.
I have no reste, so I rowe, — *hope for repose*
Wyth men and wommen, as I trowe, — *believe*
Tyl I, Lechery, be set on a lowe — *on fire*
    In al Mankyndys londys. — *loins*

CASTITAS I, Chastyté, have power in this place
2301 Thee, Lechery, to bynd and bete.
Maydyn Marye, well of grace,
Schal quenche that fowle hete. — *heat*

Mater et Virgo, extingue carnales concupiscentias! *Mother and Virgin, quench carnal lusts!*

---

[1] *When he had fasted forty days, etc.* (see Matthew 4:2)

	Oure Lord God mad thee no space	*made no room for you*
2305	Whanne his blod strayed in the strete.	*flowed*
	Fro this castel he dyd thee chase	
	Whanne he was crounyd wyth thornys grete	*crowned*
	And grene.	
	To drery deth whanne he was dyth	*put*
2310	And boyes dyd hym gret dyspyth,	*ruffians; harm*
	In lechery had he no delyth,	
	And that was ryth wel sene.	*very*

	At Oure Lady I lere my lessun	*From; have learned; lesson*
	To have chaste lyf tyl I be ded.	
2315	Sche is qwene and beryth the croun,	*wears*
	And al was for hyr maydynhed.	
	Therfor go fro this castel toun,	
	Lechery, now I thee rede,	*advise*
	For Mankynd getyst thou nowth doun	*not*
2320	To soloyen hym wyth synful sede.	*sully; seed (semen)*
	In care thou woldys hym cast.	*would*
	And if thou com up to me,	
	Trewly thou schalt betyn be	*beaten*
	Wyth the yerde of Chastyté	*rod*
	Whyl my lyf may last.	

	ACCIDIA Ware, war, I delve wyth a spade.	*SLOTH; Beware; dig*
	Men calle me the lord Syr Slowe.	
	Gostly grace I spylle and schade;	*Spiritual; pour out; shed*
	Fro the watyr of grace this dyche I fowe.	*ditch; empty*
2330	Ye schulyn com ryth inowe	*meet soon enough*
	Be this dyche drye, be bankys brede.	*With; ditch; broad*
	Thyrti thousende that I wel knowe	
	In my lyf lovely I lede	*I'm well acquainted with*
	That hed levere syttyn at the ale	*would prefer; alehouse*
2335	Thre mens songys to syngyn lowde	
	Thanne toward the chyrche for to crowde.	*Than*
	Thou, Besynesse, thou bolnyd bowde,	*Industry; swollen dung beetle*
	I brewe to thee thyne bale.	*for you; ruin*

	SOLICITUDO A, good men, be war now all	*INDUSTRY*
2340	Of Slugge and Slawthe, this fowl thefe!	*Sluggishness*
	To the sowle he is byttyrer thanne gall;	
	Rote he is of mekyl myschefe.	*Root*
	Goddys servyse, that ledyth us to Hevene hall,	
	This lordeyn for to lettyn us is lefe.	*rascal; hinder; glad*
2345	Whoso wyl schryvyn hym of hys synnys all,	*confess*
	He puttyth this brethel to mykyl myschefe,	*rascal; great distress*
	Mankynde he that myskaryed.	*led astray*

Men moun don no penauns for hym this,	*should do; this fellow*
Nere schryve hem whanne they don amys,	*Nor absolve them*
2350 But evyr he wold in synne, iwys,	*truly*
That Mankynd were taryed.	*remained*
Therfor he makyth this dyke drye	*ditch*
To puttyn Mankynde to dystresse.	
He makyth dedly synne a redy weye	*for deadly sin an easy path*
2355 Into the Castel of Goodnesse.	
But wyth tene I schal hym teye,	*torment; bind*
Thorwe the helpe of Hevene emperesse.	
Wyth my bedys he schal abeye,	*beads; pay [for it]*
And othyr ocupacyons more and lesse	*great and small*
2360 I schal schape hym to schonde,	*plan to shame him*
For whoso wyle Slawth putte doun	*Sloth*
Wyth bedys and wyth orysoun	*beads; prayer*
Or sum oneste ocupacyoun,	*honest*
As, boke to have in honde.	*Such as a Bible; hand*

Nunc lege, nunc ora, nunc disce, nuncque labora.[1]

CARO Ey, for Belyalys bonys, the kynge,	*bones*
2366 Whereabowte stonde ye al-day?	*Why*
Caytyvys, lete be your kakelynge	*Rascals; jabbering*
And rappe at rowtys of aray.	*strike at crowds in [military] array*
Glotony, thou fowle gadlynge,	*rascal*
2370 Sle Abstynens, if thou may.	*Slay; if you can*
Lechery, wyth thi werkynge,	*deeds*
To Chastyté make a wyckyd aray	*display*
A lytyl throwe.	*For a little while*
And whyl we fyth	*fight*
2375 For owre ryth,	*right*
In bemys bryth	*With bright trumpets*
Late blastys blowe.	*Let*

Tunc pugnabunt diu.   *Then they will fight for a long time*

GULA Out, Glotoun, adown I dryve.	*fall*
Abstynens hathe lost my myrth.	*destroyed*
2380 Syr Flesch, I schal nevere thryve;	
I do not worthe the develys dyrt;	*am not; turd*
I may not levyn longe.	*live*
I am al betyn, toppe and tayl;	*beaten, head*
Wyth Abstynens wyl I no more dayl;	*deal*

---

[1] *Now read, now pray, now learn, and now work*

2385	I wyl gon cowche qwayl	*go crouch like a quail*
	At hom in your gonge.	*privy*

LUXURIA Out on Chastyté, be the Rode! *Cross*
Sche hathe me dayschyd and so drenchyd. *beaten; drowned*
Yyt have sche the curs of God *let her have*
2390 For al my fere the qwene hath qwenchyd. *fire*
For ferd I fall and feynt. *fear*
In harde ropys mote sche ryde! *be hanged*
Here dare I not longe abyde.
Sumwhere myn hed I wolde hyde
2395 As an irchoun that were schent. *urchin (child); disgraced*

ACCIDIA Out, I deye! Ley on watyr! *die; Pour*
I swone, I swete, I feynt, I drulle! *swoon; stagger(?)*
Yene qwene wyth hyr pytyr-patyr *Yon; jabbering*
Hath al to-dayschyd my skallyd skulle. *smashed; scabbed*
2400 It is as softe as wulle. *wool*
Or I have here more skathe, *Before; injury*
I schal lepe awey, be lurkynge lathe, *by a secret path*
There I may my ballokys bathe *testicles*
And leykyn at the fulle. *rest (play; lick?) entirely*

MALUS ANGELUS Ya, the Devyl spede you, al the packe! *help*
2406 For sorwe I morne on the mowle, *ground*
I carpe, I crye, I coure, I kacke, *complain; cower; shit*
I frete, I fart, I fesyl fowle. *fizzle (break wind) foully*
I loke lyke an howle. *glare; owl*

Ad Mundum: *[He goes] to the World*

2410 Now, Syr World, whatso it cost, *whatever*
Helpe now, or this we have lost; *this [battle]*
Al oure fare is not worth a thost; *turd*
That makyth me to mowle. *whimper*

MUNDUS How, Coveytyse! Banyour avaunt! *Greed; Banner forward*
2415 Here comyth a batayl nobyl and newe;
For syth thou were a lytyl faunt, *since; infant*
Coveytyse, thou hast ben trewe.
Have do that damysel, do hyr dawnt. *Finish off; tame her*
Byttyr balys thou hyr brewe. *torments; for her*
2420 The medys, boy, I thee graunt, *rewards*
The galows of Canwyke to hangyn on newe, *Canwick; again*
That wolde thee wel befalle. *be appropriate*
Have don, Syr Coveytyse.
Wyrke on the best wyse. *manner*

2425   Do Mankynde com and aryse   *Make*
             Fro yone vertuse all.   *virtues*

AVARICIA   How, Mankynde! I am atenyde   *GREED; troubled*
             For thou art there so in that holde.   *Since; stronghold*
             Cum and speke wyth thi best frende,
2430   Syr Coveytyse, thou knowyst me of olde.
             What devyl schalt thou ther lenger lende   *stay*
             Wyth grete penaunce in that castel colde?
             Into the werld if thou wylt wende,   *go*
             Amonge men to bere thee bolde,   *carry yourself boldly*
2435   I rede, be Seynt Gyle.   *advise*
             How, Mankynde! I thee sey.
             Com to Coveytyse, I thee prey.
             We to schul togedyr pley,   *two*
                 If thou wylt, a whyle.

LARGITAS   A, God helpe! I am dysmayed,   *GENEROSITY*
2441   I curse thee, Coveytyse, as I can;
             For certys, treytour, thou hast betrayed
             Nerhand now iche erthely man.   *Almost; each mortal*
             So myche were men nevere afrayed   *much; tormented*
2445   Wyth Coveytyse, syn the werld began.   *By*
             God almythy is not payed.   *almighty; pleased*
             Syn thou, fende, bare the Werldys bane,   *Since; gave birth to; ruin*
                 Ful wyde thou gynnyst wende.   *widely; begin to spread*
             Now arn men waxyn ner woode;   *become almost mad*
2450   They wolde gon to Helle for werldys goode.   *because of; wealth*
             That Lord that restyd on the Rode   *Cross*
                 Is maker of an ende.   *Will make*

             Maledicti sunt avariciosi hujus temporis.   *Cursed are the avaricious from this time forth*

             Ther is no dysese nor debate   *trouble; strife*
             Thorwe this wyde werld so rounde,
2455   Tyde nor tyme, erly nor late,   *At any time*
             But that Coveytyse is the grounde.   *Except; cause*
             Thou norchyst pride, envye, and hate,   *nourish*
             Thou Coveytyse, thou cursyd hounde.
             Criste thee schelde fro oure gate   *keep from*
2460   And kepe us fro thee saf and sounde   *from*
                 That thou no good here wynne!   *gain*
             Swete Jhesu, jentyl justyce,
             Kepe Mankynde fro Coveytyse,   *from*
             For iwys he is, in al wyse,   *truly; in every way*
2465   Rote of sorwe and synne.   *Root*

AVARICIA   What eylyth thee, Lady Largyté,   *ails; Generosity*
                Damysel dyngne upon thi des?   *worthy; dais (platform)*
                And I spak ryth not to thee,   *not at all*
                Therfore I prey thee holde thi pes.
2470   How, Mankynde! cum speke wyth me,
                Cum ley thi love here in my les.   *place; control*
                Coveytyse is a frend ryth fre,   *very generous*
                Thi sorwe, man, to slake and ses.   *abate; put an end to*
                    Coveytyse hathe many a gyfte.
2475   Mankynd, thyne hande hedyr thou reche.   *stretch out*
                Coveytyse schal be thi leche.   *physician*
                The ryth wey I schal thee teche   *proper*
                    To thedom and to thryfte.   *prosperity; wealth*

HUMANUM GENUS   Coveytyse, whedyr schuld I wende?   *go*
2480   What wey woldyst that I sulde holde?   *take*
                To what place woldyst thou me sende?
                I gynne to waxyn hory and olde.   *become*
                My bake gynnyth to bowe and bende,
                I crulle and crepe and wax al colde.   *crawl; become*
2485   Age makyth man ful unthende,   *feeble*
                Body and bonys and al unwolde;   *weak*
                    My bonys are febyl and sore.
                I am arayed in a sloppe,   *loose gown*
                As a yonge man I may not hoppe,
2490   My nose is colde and gynnyth to droppe,   *drip*
                    Myn her waxit al hore.   *hair becomes; gray*

AVARICIA   Petyr! thou hast the more nede   *[By St.] Peter*
                To have sum good in thyn age;
                Markys, poundys, londys and lede,   *servants*
2495   Howsys and homys, castell and cage.   *prisons*
                Therfor do as I thee rede;   *advise*
                To Coveytyse cast thi parage.   *give your allegiance*
                Cum, and I schal thyne erdyn bede;   *present your petition*
                The worthi Werld schal geve thee wage,
2500   Certys not a lyth.   *little*
                Com on, olde man, it is no reprefe   *disgrace*
                That Coveytyse be thee lefe.   *dear*
                If thou deye at any myschefe   *because of*
                    It is thiselfe to wyth.   *your own fault*

HUMANUM GENUS   Nay, nay, these ladys of goodnesse
2506   Wyl not lete me fare amys,   *do ill*
                And thou I be a whyle in dystresse,   *although*
                Whanne I deye I schal to blysse.   *go to*
                It is but foly, as I gesse,

2510 Al this werldys wele iwys.   *wealth truly*
    These lovely ladys, more and lesse,
    In wyse wordys thei telle me thys.
      Thus seyth the Bok of Kendys.   *Book of Nature*
    I wyl not do these ladys dyspyt   *insult*
2515 To forsakyn hem for so lyt.   *little*
    To dwellyn here is my delyt;   *delight*
      Here arn my best frendys.

AVARICIA Ya, up and don thou take the wey   *down*
    Thorwe this werld to walkyn and wende   *wander*
2520 And thou schalt fynde, soth to sey,   *truth*
    Thi purs schal be thi best frende.
    Thou thou syt al-day and prey,   *Although; pray*
    No man schal com to thee nor sende,
    But if thou have a peny to pey,   *Unless*
2525 Men schul to thee thanne lystyn and lende   *pay attention*
      And kelyn al thi care.   *cool*
    Therfore to me thou hange and helde   *cling; hold tight*
    And be coveytous whylys thou may thee welde.   *manage yourself*
    If thou be pore and nedy in elde   *needy; age*
2530   Thou schalt oftyn evyl fare.

HUMANUM GENUS Coveytyse, thou seyst a good skyl.   *advice*
    So grete God me avaunce,   *help*
    Al thi byddynge don I wyl.
    I forsake the Castel of Perseveraunce.
2535 In Coveytyse I wyl me hyle   *shelter myself*
    For to gete sum sustynaunce.
    Aforn mele men mete schul tyle;   *Before a meal; get*
    It is good for al chaunce   *contingencies*
      Sum good owhere to hyde.   *wealth somewhere*
2540 Certys this ye wel knowe,
    It is good, whouso the wynde blowe,   *however*
    A man to have sumwhat of hys owe,   *something; own*
      What happe so-evere betyde.   *occasion; happen*

BONUS ANGELUS A, ladyse, I prey you of grace,
2545 Helpyth to kepe here Mankynne.
    He wyl forsake this precyous place
    And drawe ageyn to dedly synne.   *turn*
    Helpe, ladys, lovely in lace.   *fine clothes*
    He goth fro this worthi wonnynge.   *dwelling*
2550 Covetyse awey ye chace
    And schyttyth Mankynd sumwhere here-inne,   *shut up*
      In youre worthi wyse.   *appropriate manner*
    Ow, wrechyd man, thou schalt be wroth,

	That synne schal be thee ful loth.	*loathsome*
2555	A, swete ladys, helpe, he goth	
	Awey wyth Coveytyse.	

Tunc descendit ad Avariciam.   *Then he (Mankind) goes down to Covetousness*

HUMILITAS	Good Aungyl, what may I do therto?	*MEEKNESS; about that*
	Hymselfe may hys sowle spylle.	*destroy*
	Mankynd to don what he wyl do,	*whatever*
2560	God hath govyn hym a fre wylle.	*given*
	Thou he drenche and hys sowle slo,	*Although; drown; slay*
	Certys we may not do theretylle.	*do [anything] about that*
	Syn he cam this castel to,	
	We dyd to hym that us befelle	*what was appropriate to us*
2565	And now he hath us refusyd.	
	As longe as he was wythinne this castel walle,	
	We kepte hym fro synne, ye sawe wel alle;	
	And now he wyl ageyn to synne falle,	
	I preye you holde us excusyd.	*consider us*

PACIENCIA	Resun wyl excusyn us alle.	*Reason*
2571	He helde the ex be the helve.	*axe; haft*
	Thou he wyl to foly falle,	
	It is to wytyn but hymselve.	*There is no one to blame*
	Whyl he held hym in this halle,	*kept himself*
2575	Fro dedly synne we dyd hym schelve.	*protect*
	He brewyth hymselfe a byttyr galle;	
	In dethys dynt whanne he schal delve	*By death's blow; be buried*
	This game he schal begrete.	*regret*
	He is endewyd wyth wyttys fyve	*endowed*
2580	For to rewlyn hym in hys lyve.	*control*
	We vertuse wyl not wyth hym stryve:	*virtues; fight*
	Avyse hym and hys dede.	*Let him think of himself; deed (choice)*

CARITAS	Of hys dede have we nowt to done;	*nothing to do*
	He wyl no lenger wyth us be lad.	*led*
2585	Whanne he askyd out, we herd hys bone,	*asked for anything; request*
	And of hys presens we were ryth glad.	*very*
	But, as thou seste, he hath forsakyn us sone;	*see; quickly*
	He wyl not don as Crist hym bad.	
	Mary, thi Sone abovyn the mone	*moon*
2590	As make Mankynd trewe and sad,	*Make; steadfast*
	In grace for to gon.	
	For if he wyl to foly flyt,	*fly*
	We may hym not wythsyt.	*prevent*
	He is of age and can hys wyt,	*knows his mind*
2595	Ye knowe wel everychon.	*each one*

ABSTINENCIA	Ichon ye knowyn he is a fole,	*Each of you*
	In Coveytyse to dyth hys dede.	*perform; deeds*
	Werldys wele is lyke a thre-fotyd stole,	*stool*
	It faylyt a man at hys most nede.	*fails*

Mundus transit et concupiscencia ejus.[1]

2600	Whanne he is dyth in dedys dole,	*placed; death's torment*
	The ryth regystre I schal hym rede;	*true account; read*
	He schal be tore wyth teneful tole;	*torn; painful tools*
	Whanne he schal brenne on glemys glede	*burn; bright coals*
	He schal lere a new lawe.	*learn*
2605	Be he nevere so ryche of werldys wone,	*wealth*
	Hys seketouris schul makyn her mone:	*executors; complaint*
	"Make us mery and lete hym gone!	*go*
	He was a good felawe."	

CASTITAS	Whanne he is ded her sorwe is lest.	*their; very little*
2610	The ton sekatour seyth to the tothyr:	*one executor; other*
	"Make we mery and a ryche fest	
	And lete hym lyn in dedys fodyr."	*lie; death's company*

Et sic relinquent alienis divicias suas.[2]

	So hys part schal be the lest;	*least*
	The systyr servyt thus the brothyr.	*deals with*
2615	I lete a man no betyr thanne a best,	*consider; beast*
	For no man can be war be othyr	*be prudent about another*
	Tyl he hathe al ful spunne.	*experienced everything himself*
	Thou schalt se that day, man, that a bede	*bead [prayer]*
	Schal stonde thee more in stede	*avail more for you*
2620	Thanne al the good that thou mytyst gete,	*wealth; are able to*
	Certys, undyr sunne.	*on the earth*

SOLICITUDO	Mankynde, of on thynge have I wondyr:	*INDUSTRY; one*
	That thou takyst not into thyn mende,	*mind*
	Whanne body and sowle schul partyn on sundyr	*separate*
2625	No werldys good schal wyth thee wende.	*go*

Non descendet cum illo gloria ejus.[3]

---

[1] *The world passes away, and the desire thereof* (see I John 2:17)

[2] *And thus they [the foolish] leave their wealth to others* (see Psalm 48:11)

[3] *His glory (wealth) shall not descend with him* (see Psalm 48:18)

Whanne thou art ded and in the erthe leyd undyr

Mysgotyn good thee schal schende;   *Ill-gotten wealth; destroy*

It schal thee weyen as peys in pundyr   *weigh down; weight; scales*

Thi sely sowle to bryngyn in bende   *foolish; bondage*

2630   And make it ful unthende.   *feeble*

And yyt Mankynd, as it is sene,

Wyth Coveytyse goth on this grene.

The treytor doth us al this tene   *injury*

      Aftyr hys lyvys ende.   *life's*

LARGITAS Out, I crye, and nothynge lowe,   *GENEROSITY; not softly*

2636 On Coveytyse, as I wel may.

Mankynd seyth he hath nevere inowe   *enough*

Tyl hys mowthe be ful of clay.

Avarus numquam replebitur pecunia.[1]

Whanne he is closyd in dethis dow   *enclosed in the grave*

2640 What helpyt ryches or gret aray?   *fine clothes*

It flyet awey as any snow   *flies*

Anon aftyr thye endynge day,

      To wylde werldys wyse.   *As is the fashion of the fickle world*

Now good men alle that here be,

2645 Have my systerys excusyd and me,

Thou Mankynde fro this castel fle.   *Although*

      Wyte it Coveytyse.   *Blame it on Greed*

MALUS ANGELUS Ya, go forthe and lete the qwenys cakle!   *whores*

Ther wymmen arn, are many wordys.   *Wherever*

2650 Lete hem gon hoppyn wyth her hakle!   *their feathers*

Ther ges syttyn are many tordys.   *Wherever geese; turds*

Wyth Coveytyse thou renne on rakle   *run quickly*

And hange thyne hert upon hys hordys.   *hoards [of money]*

Thou schalt be schakyn in myn schakle;   *placed; shackles*

2655 Unbynde thi baggys on hys bordys,   *Untie; moneybags; tables*

      On hys benchys above.

Pardé, thou gost owt of Mankynde   *Certainly, you are no part of*

But Coveytyse be in thi mende.   *Unless; mind*

If evere thou thynke to be thende,   *prosperous*

2660   On hym thou ley thi love.   *place*

HUMANUM GENUS Nedys my love muste on hym lende,   *Necessarily; be placed*

Wyth Coveytyse to waltyr and wave.   *float; toss*

I knowe non of al my kynde   *kind (species)*

---

[1] *The miser will never be satisfied with money* (see Ecclesiastes 5:9–10)

	That he ne coveytyth for to have.	
2665	Penyman is mekyl in mynde;	*Money [personified]; much*
	My love in hym I leye and lave.	*on; place; put*
	Where that evere I walke or wende	*Wherever; go*
	In wele and woo he wyl me have;	*good and bad times; maintain*
	He is gret of grace.	*lavish*
2670	Whereso I walke in londe or lede	*Wherever; in crowds*
	Penyman best may spede;	*prosper*
	He is a duke to don a dede	*good man to get something done*
	Now in every place.	

BONUS ANGELUS   Alas, that evere Mankynde was born!

2675	On Coveytyse is al hys lust.	*pleasure*
	Nyth and day, mydnyth and morn,	*Night; midnight*
	In Penyman is al hys trust.	
	Coveytyse schal makyn hym lorn	*lost*
	Whanne he is dolven al to dust;	*buried*
2680	To mekyl schame he schal be schorn,	*much shame; reduced*
	Wyth foule fendys to roten and rust.	*rot and deteriorate*
	Alas, what schal I do?	
	Alas, alas, so may I say.	
	Man goth wyth Coveytyse away.	
2685	Have me excusyd, for I ne may	*Consider*
	Trewly not do therto.	*do [anything] about it*

MUNDUS   A, a, this game goth as I wolde.

	A, a, this game goth as I wolde.	*goes*
	Mankynde wyl nevere the Werld forsake.	
	Tyl he be ded and undyr molde	*earth*
2690	Holy to me he wyl hym take.	*Entirely*
	To Coveytyse he hath hym yolde;	*given himself*
	Wyth my wele he wyl awake;	*wealth; be excited*
	For a thousende pounde I nolde	*would wish nothing*
	But Coveytyse were Mans make,	*Except; companion*
2695	Certys on every wyse.	*Certainly*
	All these gamys he schal bewayle,	*regret*
	For I, the Werld, am of this entayle,	*disposition*
	In hys moste nede I schal hym fayle,	
	And al for Coveytyse.	*because of Greed*

[Scene xix]

AVARICIA   Now, Mankynd, be war of this:

2701	Thou art a-party wele in age.	*somewhat advanced*
	I wolde not thou ferdyst amys;	*fared ill*
	Go we now knowe my castel cage.	*to become acquainted with*
	In this bowre I schal thee blys;	*bower; make happy*
2705	Worldly wele schal be thi wage;	*wealth*
	More mucke thanne is thyne, iwys,	*wealth; truly*

Take thou in this trost terage   *of this full possession*
    And loke that thou do wronge.
Coveytyse, it is no sore,   *sorrow*
2710   He wyl thee feffen ful of store,   *endow; goods*
And alwey, alwey sey "More and more,"
    And that schal be thi songe.

HUMANUM GENUS   A, Coveytyse, have thou good grace!
    Certys thou beryst a trewe tonge.
2715   "More and more," in many a place,
Certys that songe is oftyn songe.   *Truly; sung*
I wyste nevere man, be bankys bace,   *knew; low banks (i.e., everywhere)*
So seyn, in cley tyl he were clonge: *Say that; clay until; buried*
"Inow, inow" hadde nevere space,   *Enough; opportunity*
2720   That ful songe was nevere songe,   *sung*
    Nor I wyl not begynne.
Goode Coveytyse, I thee prey
That I myth wyth thee pley.   *am able; to play*
Geve me good inow, or that I dey,   *enough, before; die*
2725   To wonne in werldys wynne.   *live; joy (comfort)*

AVARICIA   Have here, Mankynd, a thousend marke.
    I, Coveytyse, have thee this gote.   *got this for you*
Thou mayst purchase therwyth bothe ponde and parke
And do therwyth mekyl note.   *many great things*
2730   Lene no man hereof, for no karke,   *Lend; injury*
Thou he schulde hange be the throte,
Monke nor frere, prest nor clerke,
Ne helpe therwyth chyrche nor cote,   *cottage*
    Tyl deth thi body delve.   *bury*
2735   Thou he schuld sterve in a cave,   *Although; starve*
Lete no pore man therof have.
In grene gres tyl thou be grave   *grass; buried*
    Kepe sumwhat fore thiselve.

HUMANUM GENUS   I vow to God, it is gret husbondry.   *thrift*
2740   Of thee I take these noblys rownde.
I schal me rapyn, and that in hye,   *hurry; in haste*
To hyde this gold undyr the grownde.
Ther schal it ly tyl that I dye,
It may be kepte ther save and sownde.
2745   Thou my neybore schuld be hangyn hye,   *Although*
Therof getyth he neythyr peny nor pownde.
    Yyt am I not wel at ese.   *comfortable*
Now wolde I have castel wallys,
Stronge stedys and styf in stallys.   *horses; powerful*

2750	Wyth hey holtys and hey hallys,	*tall woods*
	Coveytyse, thou muste me sese.	*endow*

AVARICIA Al schalt thou have al redy, lo,
At thyn owyn dysposycyoun.
Al this good take thee to,   *these goods*
2755   Clyffe and cost, toure and toun.
Thus hast thou gotyn in synful slo   *by evil means*
Of thyne neyborys be extorcyoun.   *by*
"More and more" sey yyt, have do,   *go ahead*
Tyl thou be ded and drepyn dounn;   *struck down*
2760   Werke on wyth werldys wrenchys.   *Proceed; deceits*
"More and more" sey yyt, I rede,   *advise*
To more thanne inow thou hast nede.   *enough*
Al this werld, bothe lenthe and brede,   *length; breadth*
        Thi coveytyse may not qwenche.   *satisfy*

HUMANUM GENUS Qwenche nevere no man may;   *Satisfy*
2766   Me thynkyth nevere I have inow.   *enough*
Ther ne is werldys wele, nyth nor day,   *wealth, night*
But that me thynkyth it is too slow.   *it seems to me*
"More and more" yit I say
2770   And schal evere whyl I may blow;   *breathe*
On Coveytyse is al my lay   *About; song*
And schal tyl deth me ovyrthrow.
        "More and more," this is my stevene.   *petition (vow)*
If I myth alwey dwellyn in prosperyté,   *may*
2775   Lord God, thane wel were me.   *I would be happy*
I wolde, the medys, forsake thee   *as a reward*
        And nevere to comyn in Hevene.

[Scene xx]
MORS Ow, now it is tyme hye   *DEATH; high time*
        To castyn Mankynd to Dethys dynt.   *stroke*
2780   In all hys werkys he is unslye;   *foolish*
Mekyl of hys lyf he hath myspent.   *Much*
To Mankynd I ney ny,   *come close*
Wyth rewly rappys he schal be rent.   *terrible blows; torn*
Whanne I com iche man drede forthi,   *each; is fearful of it*
2785   But yyt is ther no geyn-went,   *no road back*
        Hey hyl, holte, nyn hethe.   *High; nor heath*
Ye schul me drede everychone;   *everyone*
Whanne I come ye schul grone;   *lament*
My name in londe is lefte alone: *remains alone on earth*
2790   I hatte drery Dethe.   *am called dreadful*

Drery is my deth-drawth;   *Dreadful; death-potion*
Ageyns me may no man stonde.
I durke and downbrynge to nowth   *lurk; nought*
Lordys and ladys in every londe.
2795   Whomso I have a lessun tawth,   *To whom; taught*
Onethys sythen schal he mowe stonde;   *Scarcely afterwards; be able to stand*
In my carful clothys he schal be cawth,   *clothes of care; caught*
Ryche, pore, fre and bonde;   *bondsman*
        Whanne I come thei goo no more.
2800   Whereso I wende in any lede,   *go; crowd*
Every man of me hat drede.   *has*
Lette I wyl for no mede   *Stop; reward*
        To smyte sadde and sore.   *forcibly; sorely*

Dyngne dukys arn adred   *Worthy; afraid*
2805   Whanne my blastys arn on hem blowe.   *blown at them*
Lordys in londe arn ovyrled;   *overcome*
Wyth this launce I leye hem lowe.
Kyngys kene and knytys kyd,   *bold; famous knights*
I do hem delvyn in a throwe,   *bury in a moment*
2810   In banke I buske hem a bed,   *On a hill I prepare for them*
Sad sorwe to hem I sowe,
        I tene hem, as I trowe.   *injure; believe*
As kene koltys thow they kynse,   *spirited colts although; shy away*
Ageyns me is no defens.
2815   In the grete pestelens
        Thanne was I wel knowe.   *known*

But now almost I am forgete;   *forgotten*
Men of Deth holde no tale   *pay no attention*
In coveytyse her good they gete;   *their goods*
2820   The grete fyschys ete the smale.   *fish*
But whanne I dele my derne dette   *give; stealthy blow*
Tho prowde men I schal avale.   *Those; bring down*
Hem schal helpyn nothyr mel or mete   *Shall help them; banquet nor feast*
Tyl they be drewyn to dethys dale;   *driven to death's valley*
2825   My lawe thei schul lerne.
Ther ne is peny nor pownde   *There is neither*
That any of you schal save sownde.
Tyl ye be gravyn undyr grownde   *buried*
        Ther may no man me werne.   *avoid me*

2830   To Mankynde now wyl I reche;   *proceed*
He hathe holé hys hert on Coveytyse.   *entirely [set]*
A newe lessun I wyl hym teche
That he schal bothe grwcchyn and gryse.   *complain; tremble*
No lyf in londe schal ben hys leche;   *No person; physician*

2835	I schal hym prove of myn empryse;	*show him my power*
	Wyth this poynt I schal hym broche	*pierce*
	And wappyn hym in a woful wyse.	*strike; manner*
	Nobody schal ben hys bote.	*help*
	I schal thee schapyn a schenful schappe.	*make for you; shameful appearance*
2840	Now I kylle thee wyth myn knappe!	*blow*
	I reche to thee, Mankynd, a rappe	*give; blow*
	To thyne herte rote.	*root*

HUMANUM GENUS A, Deth, Deth! Drye is thi dryfte.		*Hard; power*
	Ded is my desteny.	*Death*
2845	Myn hed is clevyn al in a clyfte;	*split; gash*
	For clappe of care now I crye;	*blow; sorrow*
	Myn eyeledys may I not lyfte;	
	Myn braynys waxyn al emptye;	*become*
	I may not onys myn hod up schyfte;	*once; head; lift*
2850	Wyth Dethys dynt now I dey!	*Death's stroke; die*
	Syr Werld, I am hent.	*taken (seized)*
	Werld, Werld, have me in mende!	*mind*
	Goode Syr Werld, helpe now Mankend!	
	But thou me helpe, Deth schal me schende.	*Unless; destroy*
2855	He hath dyth to me a dynt.	*dealt me a [mortal] blow*

	Werld, my wyt waxyt wronge;	*becomes twisted*
	I chaunge bothe hyde and hewe;	*complexion; color*
	Myn eyeledys waxyn al outewronge;	*wrung out [with tears]*
	But thou me helpe, sore it schal me rewe.	*Unless; regret*
2860	Now holde that thou haste behete me longe,	*keep that [which]; promised; for a long time*
	For all felachepys olde and newe,	
	Lesse me of my peynys stronge.	*Release; pains*
	Sum bote of bale thou me brewe	*remedy for torment*
	That I may of thee yelpe.	*praise you*
2865	Werld, for olde aqweyntawns,	
	Helpe me fro this sory chawns.	*miserable fortune*
	Dethe hathe lacchyd me wyth hys launce.	*struck*
	I deye but thou me helpe.	*unless*

MUNDUS Owe, Mankynd, hathe Dethe wyth thee spoke?		*Oh*
2870	Ageyns hym helpyth no wage.	*payment*
	I wolde thou were in the erthe beloke	*locked up*
	And anothyr hadde thyne erytage.	*heritage*
	Oure bonde of love schal sone be broke;	*broken*
	In colde clay schal be thy cage;	*prison*
2875	Now schal the Werld on thee be wroke	*avenged*
	For thou hast don so gret outrage.	*Because; crimes*
	Thi good thou schalt forgoo.	*goods; lose*
	Werldys good thou hast forgon	*goods; lost*

	And wyth tottys thou schalt be torn.	*by devils*
2880	Thus have I servyd here-beforn	*previously*
	A hundryd thousend moo.	*more*

HUMANUM GENUS   Ow, Werld, Werld, evere worthe wo!   *woe to you forever*
　　　　　And thou, synful Coveytyse!
　　　　　Whanne that a man schal fro you go   *from*
2885　　Ye werke wyth hym on a wondyr wyse.   *deal; in a strange manner*
　　　　　The wytte of this werld is sorwe and wo.   *wisdom*
　　　　　Be ware, good men, of this gyse!   *trick*
　　　　　Thus hathe he servyd many on mo.   *many others*
　　　　　In sorwe slakyth al hys asyse;   *ends; fashion*
2890　　　　He beryth a tenynge tungge.   *harmful tongue*
　　　　　Whyl I leyd wyth hym my lott   *placed; destiny*
　　　　　Ye seyn whow fayre he me behott;   *how fairly; made promises*
　　　　　And now he wolde I were a clott   *clod*
　　　　　　　In colde cley for to clynge.   *waste away*

MUNDUS   How, boy, aryse! now thou muste wende   *go*
2896　　On myn erdyn, be steppe and stalle.   *errand; stable*
　　　　　Go brewe Mankynd a byttyr bende   *bondage*
　　　　　And putte hym oute of hys halle.
　　　　　Lete hym therinne no lenger lende.   *remain*
2900　　Forbrostyn, I trowe, be hys galle   *Shattered; let be; gall bladder*
　　　　　For thou art not of hys kende.   *Because; kinship*
　　　　　All hys erytage wyl thee wele befalle.   *heritage; fall properly to you*
　　　　　　　Thus faryth myn fayre feres.   *dear companions*
　　　　　Oftyn tyme I have you told,
2905　　Tho men that ye arn to lest behold   *Those; to whom you owe the least*
　　　　　Comynly schal youre wonnynge wold   *Often; rule your dwelling*
　　　　　　　And ben youre next eyrys.   *heirs*

GARCIO   Werld worthy, in wedys wounde,   *BOY; dressed in [fine] clothes*
　　　　　I thanke thee for thi grete gyfte.
2910　　I go glad upon this grounde
　　　　　To put Mankynde out of hys thryfte.   *estate*
　　　　　I trowe he stynkyth this ilke stounde.   *believe; very moment*
　　　　　Into a lake I schal hym lyfte.   *pit; throw*
　　　　　Hys parkys, placys, and penys rounde,   *pennies*
2915　　Wyth me schul dryven in this dryfte   *be taken by force*
　　　　　　　In baggys as thei ben bownde.
　　　　　For I thynke for to dele,   *share*
　　　　　I vow to God, neythyr corn nore mele.   *grain*
　　　　　If he have a schete he beryth hym wele   *sheet (shroud); does well*
2920　　　　Whereinne he may be wounde.

Tunc iet ad Humanum Genus.   *Then he goes to Mankind*

Whou faryst, Mankynde? Art thou ded?	*How are you*
Be Goddys body, so I wene.	*think*
He is hevyer thanne any led.	
I wold he were gravyn undyr grene.	*buried; grass*

HUMANUM GENUS   Abyde, I breyd uppe wyth myn hed. *lift*
2926   What art thou? What woldyst thou mene? *do you intend*
    Wheydyr comyst thou for good or qwed? *Do you come; evil*
    Wyth peynys prycke thou dost me tene, *torment of pain; hurt*
        The sothe for to sey. *truth*
2930   Telle me now, so God thee save,
    Fro whom comyst thou, good knave? *From*
    What dost thou here? what woldyst thou have?
        Telle me or I deye. *before; die*

GARCIO   I am com to have al that thou hast,
2935   Ponndys, parkys, and every place.
    Al that thou hast gotyn fyrst and last,
    The Werld hathe grauntyd it me of hys grace
        For I have ben hys page. *servant*
    He wot wel thou schalt be ded, *knows*
2940   Nevermore to ete bred;
    Therfore he hath for thee red *decided*
        Who schal have thyne erytage. *estate*

HUMANUM GENUS   What devyl! Thou art not of my kyn!
    Thou dedyst me nevere no maner good. *kind of*
2945   I hadde lever sum nyfte or sum cosyn *would prefer; nephew*
    Or sum man hadde it of my blod. *of my family*
        In sum stede I wold it stod. *I wish it were of some use*
    Now schal I in a dale be delve *buried in a valley*
    And have no good therof myselve. *benefit from it*
2950   Be God and be hys apostelys twelve, *By*
        I trowe the Weerld be wod. *think; mad*

GARCIO   Ya, ya, thi parte schal be the leste. *You don't have anything to say about this*
    Deye on, for I am maystyr here. *Go ahead and die*
    I schal thee makyn a nobyl feste
2955   And thanne have I do myn devere. *done my duty*
    The Werld bad me this gold areste, *seize*
    Holt and hallys and castell clere. *Woods*
    The Werldys joye and hys jentyl jeste *game*
    Is now thyne, now myn, bothe fere and nere. *far and near*
2960   Go hens, for this is myne.
    Syn thou art ded and browth of dawe, *brought to death*
    Of thi deth, syr, I am ryth fawe. *very pleased*

        Thou thou knowe not the Werldys lawe,   *Although*
             He hath gove me al that was thyne.   *given*

HUMANUM GENUS I preye thee now, syn thou this good schalt gete,   *wealth*
2966   Telle thi name or that I goo.

GARCIO Loke that thou it not forgete:
        My name is I-Wot-Nevere-Whoo.   *I-Don't-Know-Who*

HUMANUM GENUS I-Wot-Nevere-Who! so welaway!
2970   Now am I sory of my lyf.
        I have purchasyd many a day
        Londys and rentys wyth mekyl stryf.   *much*
        I have purchasyd holt and hay,   *woods; fields*
        Parkys and ponndys and bowrys blyfe,   *pleasant bowers*
2975   Goode gardeynys wyth gryffys gay,   *groves*
        To myne chyldyr and to myn wyfe   *For; children*
             In dethe whanne I were dyth.   *should be put*
        Of my purchas I may be wo,   *woeful*
        For, as I thout, it is not so,   *thought*
2980   But a gedelynge I-Wot-Nevere-Who   *rascal*
             Hath al that the Werld me behyth.   *promised*

        Now, alas, my lyf is lak.   *poor*
        Bittyr balys I gynne to brewe.   *torment*
        Certis, a vers that David spak   *Certainly*
2985   In the sawter I fynde it trewe: *In the Psalms*

        Thesaurizat, et ignorat cui congregabit ea.[1]

        Tresor, tresor, it hathe no tak;   *endurance*
        It is othyr mens, olde and newe.
        Ow, ow, my good gothe al to wrak!   *Oh; wealth; ruin*
        Sore may Mankynd rewe.   *regret*
2990   God kepe me fro dyspayr!
        Al my good, wythout fayle,   *goods*
        I have gadryd wyth gret travayle,   *gathered; effort*
        The Werld hathe ordeynyd of hys entayle *determined testamentary disposition*
             I-Wot-Nevere-Who to be myn eyr.   *heir*

2995   Now, good men, takythe example at me.   *by*
        Do for youreself whyl ye han spase.   *Provide; time*
        For many men thus servyd be
        Thorwe the werld in dyverse place.   *Throughout*

---

[1] *Man heaps up treasure and does not know to whom it will accumulate* (see Psalm 38:7)

	I bolne and bleyke in blody ble	*swell; grow pale; countenance*
3000	And as a flour fadyth my face.	*flower*
	To Helle I schal bothe fare and fle	*go*
	But God me graunte of hys grace.	*Unless*
	I deye certeynly.	
	Now my lyfe I have lore.	*lost*
3005	Myn hert brekyth, I syhe sore.	*sigh*
	A word may I speke, no more.	
	I putte me in Goddys mercy.	

[Scene xxi]

ANIMA	"Mercy," this was my last tale	*SOUL; word*
	That evere my body was abowth.	*concerned with*
3010	But Mercy helpe me in this vale,	*Unless; valley (see Psalm 23:6)*
	Of dampnynge drynke sore I me doute.	*damning; sorely; fear*
	Body, thou dedyst brew a byttyr bale	*sorrow*
	To thi lustys whanne gannyst loute.	*pleasures when you yielded*
	Thi sely sowle schal ben akale;	*wretched; cold*
3015	I beye thi dedys wyth rewly rowte,	*pay for; terrible blows*
	And al it is for gyle.	*deceit*
	Evere thou hast be coveytows	*greedy*
	Falsly to getyn londe and hows.	
	To me thou hast browyn a byttyr jows.	*brewed; potion*
3020	So welaway the whyle!	

	Now, swet aungel, what is thi red?	*advice*
	The ryth red thou me reche.	*right way; direct*
	Now my body is dressyd to ded	*for death*
	Helpe now me and be my leche.	*physician*
3025	Dyth thou me fro develys drede.	*Put me; from*
	Thy worthy weye thou me teche.	*proper*
	I hope that God wyl helpyn and be myn hed	*guide*
	For "mercy" was my laste speche;	
	Thus made my body hys ende.	

- - - - - - - - - - - - - - - -

[**MALUS ANGELUS**]	Wyttnesse of all that ben abowte,	
3031	Syr Coveytyse he had hym owte.	
	Therfor he schal, wythoutyn dowte,	
	Wyth me to Helle pytt.	*the pit of Hell*

BONUS ANGELUS	Ye, alas, and welawo!	
3035	Ageyns Coveytyse can I not telle.	*argue*
	Resun wyl I fro thee goo,	*Reason determines; from*
	For, wrechyd Sowle, thou muste to Helle.	
	Coveytyse, he was thi fo;	*foe*

He hathe thee schapyn a schameful schelle; — *prepared; dwelling*
3040 Thus hathe he servyd many on mo — *many others*
Tyl thei be dyth to dethys delle, — *put in death's pit*
　　To byttyr balys bowre. — *bower of sorrow*
Thou muste to peyne, be ryth resun, — *by just reason*
Wyth Coveytyse, for he is chesun. — *[the] cause*
3045 Thou art trappyd ful of tresun
　　But Mercy be thi socowre. — *Unless*

For ryth wel this founde I have
Ageyns Rythwysnesse may I not holde. — *Justice; argue*
Thou muste wyth hym to careful cave — *cave of sorrow*
3050 For grete skyllys that he hathe tolde. — *good reasons; explained*
Fro thee awey I wandyr and wave; — *turn and toss*
For thee I clynge in carys colde. — *waste*
Alone now I thee lave — *leave*
Whylyst thou fallyst in fendys folde, — *[the] devil's enclosure*
3055 　　In Helle to hyde and hylle. — *take shelter*
Rytwysnesse wyl that thou wende — *Justice determines; go*
Forthe awey wyth the fende.
But Mercy wyl to thee sende, — *Unless*
　　Of thee I can no skylle. — *I have no power to help you*

ANIMA Alas, Mercy, thou art too longe! — *too long [coming]*
3061 Of sadde sorwe now may I synge.
Holy wryt it is ful wronge — *Scripture*
But Mercy pase alle thynge. — *Unless; surpass*
I am ordeynyd to peynys stronge, — *condemned to terrible pains*
3065 In wo is dressyd myn wonnynge, — *prepared; dwelling*
In Helle on hokys I schal honge, — *hooks*
But mercy fro a welle sprynge. — *Unless; fountain*
　　This devyl wyl have me away.
Weleaway! I was ful wod — *mad*
3070 That I forsoke myn Aungyl Good
And wyth Coveytyse stod
　　Tyl that day that I schuld dey.

MALUS ANGELUS Ya, why woldyst thou be coveytous — *greedy*
And drawe thee agayn to synne? — *turn*
3075 I schal thee brewe a byttyr jous; — *potion*
In bolnynnge bondys thou schalt brenne. — *swelling; burn*
In hye Helle schal be thyn hous, — *In the depths of Hell*
In pycke and ter to grone and grenne; — *pitch; tar; gnash your teeth*
Thou schalt lye drenkelyd as a mous; — *drowned*
3080 Ther may no man therfro thee werne — *defend*
　　For that ilke wyll. — *Because of; same desire*
That day the ladys thou forsoke

And to my counsel thou thee toke,
Thou were betyr anhangyn on hoke   *hanged on a hook*
3085   Upon a jebet hyll.   *gallows*

Farter fowle, thou schalt be frayed   *foul; bruised*
Tyl thou be frettyd and al forbled.   *gnawed; bloody*
Foule mote thou be dysmayed   *Foully may*
That thou schalt thus ben ovyrled.   *overpowered*
3090   For Coveytyse thou hast asayed   *tried*
In byttyr balys thou schalt be bred.   *torments; roasted*
Al mankynd may be wel payed   *satisfied*
Whou Coveytyse makyth thee adred.   *How; afraid*
      Wyth rappys I thee rynge.   *blows; surround*
3095   We schul to Hell, bothe to,   *two*
And bey in Inferno.   *suffer; Hell*
Nulla est redempcio.   *There is no redemption*
      For no kynnys thynge.   *manner of*

Now dagge we hens a dogge trot.   *jog; hence*
3100   In my dongion I schal thee dere.   *dungeon; injure*
On thee is many a synful spot;
Therfore this schame I schal thee schere   *cut off*
      Whanne thou comyst to my neste.
Why woldyst thou, schrewe schalt nevere thé,   *rascal [who] will never prosper*
3105   But in thi lyve don aftyr me?   *Only; follow after*
And thi Good Aungyl tawth thee   *taught*
      Alwey to the beste,

Ya, but thou woldyst hym not leve.   *believe*
To Coveytyse alwey thou drow.   *turned*
3110   Therfore schalt thou evyl preve;   *thrive in anguish*
That foul synne thi soule slow.   *killed*
I schal fonde thee to greve   *make you grieve*
And putte thee in peynys plow.   *harness you to pain's plow*
Have this, and evyl mote thou scheve,   *Take this [blow]; may you thrive evilly*
3115   For thou seydyst nevere "inow, inow."   *enough*
      Thus lacche I thee thus lowe.   *strike; down*
Thow thou kewe as a kat,   *Although; mew*
For thi coveytyse have thou that!   *(i.e., he strikes another blow)*
I schal thee bunche wyth my bat   *strike*
3120   And rouge thee on a rowe.   *rough you up in order*

Lo, synful tydynge,   *story*
Boy, on thi bak I brynge.
Spedely thou sprynge.   *jump*
Thi "*Placebo*" I schal synge.   *"I will please"*
3125   To devylys delle   *In; pit*

I schal thee bere to Helle.

I wyl not dwelle.

Have good day! I goo to Helle.   *delay*

[Scene xxii]

MISERICORDIA   A mone I herd of mercy meve   *MERCY; moan; spoken*

3130   And to me, Mercy, gan crye and call;

But if it have mercy, sore it schal me greve,   *Unless; grieve*

For ell it schal to Hell fall.   *otherwise*

Rythwysnes, my systyr cheve,   *Justice; chief*

Thys ye herde; so dyde we all.

3135   For we were mad frendys leve   *made; dear*

Whanne the Jewys proferyd Criste eysyl and gall   *vinegar*

On the Good Fryday.

God grauntyd that remission,

Mercy, and absolicion,

3140   Thorwe vertu of hys passion,   *Through virtue*

To no man schuld be seyd nay.

Therfore, my systyr Rytwysnes,   *Justice*

Pes, and Trewth, to you I tell,

Whanne man crieth mercy, and wyl not ses,   *cease*

3145   Mercy schal be hys waschynge-well: *fountain of purification*

Wytnesse of Holy Kyrke.   *As Holy Church testifies*

For the leste drope of blode   *least*

That God bledde on the Rode   *Cross*

It hadde ben satysfaccion goode   *would be*

3150   For al Mankyndys werke.   *deeds*

JUSTICIA   Systyr, ye sey me a good skyl,   *good argument*

That mercy pasyt mannys mysdede.   *is greater than*

But take mercy whoso wyl   *receive; whoever*

He muste it aske wyth love and drede;   *fear*

3155   And everyman that wyl fulfyll

The dedly synnys and folw mysdede,   *practice sin*

To graunte hem mercy me thynkyth it no skyl;   *no good reason*

And therfore, systyr, you I rede   *advise*

Lete hym abye hys mysdede.   *pay for*

3160   For thou he lye in Hell and stynke,   *although*

It schal me nevere ovyrthynke.   *bother*

As he hath browyn, lete hym drynke;   *brewed*

The Devyl schal quyte hym hys mede.   *pay; reward*

Unusquisque suum honus portabit.   *Everyone shall bear his own burden (Galatians 6:5)*

Trowe ye that whanne a man schal deye,   *Do you believe*

3165   Thanne thow that he mercy crave,   *Then although; beg*

That anon he schal have mercye?
Nay, nay, so Crist me save!

Non omne qui dicit "Domine, Domine" intrabit regnum celorum.[1]

For schuld no man do no good
All the dayes of hys lyve
3170 But hope of mercy be the Rode   *by; Cross*
Schulde make bothe werre and stryve   *war; strife*
  And torne to gret grewaunse.   *turn; injury*
Whoso in hope dothe any dedly synne
To hys lyvys ende, and wyl not blynne,   *cease*
3175 Rytfully thanne schal he wynne   *gain*
  Crystis gret vengaunse.

VERITAS Rytwysnes, my systyr fre,   *TRUTH; Justice; noble*
  Your jugement is good and trewe.
In good feyth so thynkyth me;   *it seems to me*
3180 Late hym hys owyn dedys rewe.   *Let; deeds regret*
I am Veritas and trew wyl be
In word and werke to olde and newe.   *deed*
Was nevere man in fawte of me   *default*
Dampnyd nor savyd, but it were dew.   *deserved*
3185   I am evere at mans ende.   *death*
Whanne body and sowle partyn atwynne,   *separate*
Thanne wey I hys goode dedys and hys synne,   *weigh*
And weydyr of hem be more or mynne   *which of them; less*
  He schal it ryth sone fynde.   *very quickly*

3190 For I am Trewthe and trewthe wyl bere,   *bear [witness]*
As grete God hymself us byd.   *commanded*
Ther schal nothynge the sowle dere   *injure*
But synne that the body dyd.
Syth that he deyed in that coveytous synne,
3195 I, Trewthe, wyl that he goo to pyne.   *torment*
Of that synne cowde he not blynne;   *could; cease*
Therfore he schal hys sowle tyne   *lose*
  To the pytte of Hell.
Ellys schuld we, bothe Trewthe and Rytwysnes,   *Otherwise; Justice*
3200 Be put to ovyrmekyl dystresse   *too much*
And every man schul be the wers   *worse*
  That therof myth here tell.   *might hear tell [of it]*

---

[1] *Not everyone who says, "Lord, Lord" will enter the kingdom of Heaven* (see Matthew 7:21)

PAX	Pes, my systyr Verité!	PEACE; Peace; Truth
	I preye you, Rytwysnes, be stylle!	
3205	Lete no man be you dampnyd be	by
	Nor deme ye no man to Helle.	condemn
	He is on kyn tyl us thre,	related to
	Thow he have now not al hys wylle.	Although
	For hys love that deyed on Tre,	died on the Cross
3210	Late save Mankynd fro al peryle	Let Mankind be saved; peril
	And schelde hym fro myschaunsse	defend; disaster
	If ye tweyne putte hym to dystresse	two
	It schuld make gret hevynesse	
	Betwene us tweyne, Mercy and Pes,	
3215	And that were gret grevaunce.	injury

	Rytwysnes and Trewthe, do be my red,	advice
	And Mercy, go we to yone hey place.	high
	We schal enforme the hey Godhed	explain to; high
	And pray hym to deme this case.	judge
3220	Ye schal tell hym youre entent	argument
	Of Trewthe and of Rytwysnesse,	
	And we schal pray that hys jugement	
	May pase be us, Mercy and Pes.	be rendered by
	All foure, now go we hens	
3225	Wytly to the Trinité	Quickly
	And ther schal we sone se	
	What that hys jugement schal be,	
	Wythoutyn any deffens.	appeal

Tunc ascendent ad Patrem omnes pariter et dicet Veritas:[1]

[Scene xxiii]

VERITAS	Heyl, God almyth!	
3230	We cum, thi dowterys in syth,	sight (presence)
	Trewth, Mercy, and Ryth,	Justice
	And Pes, pesyble in fyth.	peaceably in discussion

MISERICORDIA	We cum to preve	decide
	If Man, that was thee ful leve,	very dear to you
3235	If he schal cheve	attain
	To Hell or Hevene, be thi leve.	permission

| JUSTICIA | I, Rytwysnes, | |
| | Thi dowtyr as I ges, | believe |

---

[1] *Then they go to the Father all together and Truth says*

| | Late me, neverthelesse, | *Let* |
| 3240 | At thi dom putte me in pres. | *judgment exert myself* |

PAX	Pesyble kynge,	*Peaceful*
	I, Pes, thi dowtyr yynge,	*young*
	Here my preyinge	*Hear*
	Whanne I pray thee, Lord, of a thynge.	*concerning something*

DEUS	Welcum in fere,	*GOD; together*
3246	Bryther thanne blossum on brere!	*Brighter; briar*
	My dowterys dere,	
	Cum forth and stand ye me nere.	

VERITAS	Lord, as thou art Kyng of kyngys, crownyd wyth crowne,	
3250	As thou lovyste me, Trewthe, thi dowtyr dere,	
	Lete nevere me, Trewthe, to fall adowne,	
	My feythful Fadyr, *saunz pere*!	*without equal*

Quoniam veritatem dilexisti.   *For you have loved truth*

	For in all trewthe standyth thi renowne,	
	Thi feyth, thi hope, and thi powere,	
3255	Lete it be sene, Lord, now at thi dome,	*Let; judgment*
	That I may have my trewe prayere	
	To do trewthe to Mankynd.	
	For if Mankynd be dempte be ryth	*damned justly*
	And not be mercy, most of myth,	*might*
3260	Her my trewthe, Lord, I thee plyth,	*promise*
	In presun man schal be pynyd.	*prison; tormented*

	Lord, whow schuld Mankynd be savyd,	*how*
	Syn he dyed in dedly synne	
	And all thi comaundementys he depravyd	*broke*
3265	And of fals covetyse he wolde nevere blynne?	*greed; cease*

Aurum sitisti, aurum bibisti.   *You thirsted for gold, you have drunk gold*

	The more he hadde, the more he cravyd,	
	Whyl the lyf lefte hym wythinne.	*remained*
	But he be dampnyd I am abavyd	*Unless; amazed*
	That Trewthe schuld com of Rytwys kynne,	*Justice's*
3270	And I am thi dowtyr Trewthe.	
	Thou he cried mercy, *moriendo*,	
	Nimis tarde penitendo,	

Talem mortem reprehendo.[1]
    Lete hym drynke as he brewyth!

3275	Late repentaunce if man save scholde,	*If late repentance*
	Wheythyr he wrouth wel or wyckydnesse,	*did*
	Thanne every man wold be bolde	
	To trespas in trost of forgevenesse.	*sin; expectation*
	For synne in hope is dampnyd, I holde;	*committed in hope of redemption; argue*
3280	Forgevyn is nevere hys trespase.	
	He synnyth in the Holy Gost manyfolde.	*many time*s
	That synne, Lord, thou wylt not reles	*remit*
	In this werld nor in the tothyr.	*other [world]*
	Quia veritas manet in eternum,	
3285	*Tendit homo ad infernum,*	
	Nunquam venit ad supernum,[2]	
	Thou he were my brothyr.	*Although*
	For man on molde halt welthe and wele,	*earth holds; goods*
	Lust-and-lykynge in al hys lyfe,	*Pleasure*
3290	Techynge, prechynge, in every sele,	*season*
	But he forgetyth the Lord belyve.	*quickly*
	Hye of hert, happe and hele,	*Proud; happy; healthy*
	Gold and sylvyr, chyld and wyf,	
	Denteth drynke at mete and mele,	*Dainty*
3295	Unnethe thee to thanke he can not kyth	*Scarcely; show*
	In any maner thynge.	
	Whanne mans welthe gynnyth awake	*begins to grow*
	Ful sone, Lord, thou art forsake.	
	As he hathe browne and bake,	*brewed; baked*
3300	Trewthe wyl that he drynke.	*wishes*
	For if Man have mercy and grace	
	Thanne I, thi dowtyr Sothfastnesse,	*Truth*
	At thi dom schal have no place	*judgment*
	But be putte abak be wronge dures.	*set aside; force*
3305	Lord, lete me nevere fle thi fayr face	*flee from*
	To make my power any lesse!	
	I pray thee, Lord, as I have space,	*opportunity*
	Late Mankynd have dew dystresse	*appropriate punishment*
	In Helle fere to be brent.	*fire; burnt*
3310	In peyne loke he be stylle,	*See to it that he be in perpetual pain*
	Lord, if it be thi wylle,	

---

[1] Lines 3271–73: *in dying, / Repenting far too late, / I condemn such a death*

[2] Lines 3284–86: *Because truth endures for all time, / Man goes to Hell / By no means he comes to Heaven*

Or ell I have no skylle   *else; ability*
    Be thi trew jugement.   *By*

MISERICORDIA   *O Pater misericordiarum et Deus tocius consolacionis, qui consolatur nos in omni*
    tribulacione nostra![1]

    O thou Fadyr, of mytys moste,   *mights*
3315   Mercyful God in Trinité!
    I am thi dowtyr, wel thou woste,   *know*
    And mercy fro Hevene thou browtyst fre.   *from; brought willingly*
    Schew me thi grace in every coste!   *way*
    In this cas my conforte be!
3320   Lete me, Lord, nevere be loste
    At thi jugement, whowso it be,   *however it be [settled]*
       Of Mankynd.
    Ne had mans synne nevere cum in cas   *into question*
    I, Mercy, schuld nevere in erthe had plas.   *have been needed*
3325   Therfore graunte me, Lord, thi grace,
       That Mankynd may me fynd.

    And mercy, Lord, have on this man
    Aftyr thi mercy, that mekyl is,   *great*
    Unto thi grace that he be tan,   *taken*
3330   Of thi mercy that he not mys!   *be deprived*
    As thou descendyst fro thi trone
    And lyth in a maydyns wombe iwys,   *alighted; truly*
    Incarnat was in blod and bone,
    Lat Mankynd cum to thi blys,
3335   As thou art Kynge of Hevene!
    For werldly veynglory   *pride*
    He hathe ben ful sory,
    Punchyd in purgatory   *Punished*
       For all the synnys sevene.

    Si pro peccato vetus Adam non cecidisset,
    Mater pro nato numquam gravidata fuisset.[2]

3340   Ne had Adam synnyd here-before
    And thi hestys in Paradys had offent,   *commandments; broken*
    Nevere of thi modyr thou schuldyst a be bore,   *have been born*

---

[1] *Oh Father of Mercies and God of all comfort, who comforts us all in our tribulation* (see 2 Corinthians
1:3–4). [Since an English version of this line does not appear in the text, it is not clear whether it
should be considered part of the playtext or not.]

[2] Lines 3339a–b: *If through sin old Adam had not fallen, / Your mother would never have become heavy
with child*

	Fro Hevene to erthe to have be sent.	*been*
	But thyrti wyntyr here and more,	*years*
3345	Bowndyn and betyn and al to-schent,	*Bound; seriously injured*
	Scornyd and scourgyd sadde and sore,	*severely*
	And on the Rode rewly rent,	*Cross grievously torn*
	Passus sub Pilato Poncio.	*He suffered under Pontius Pilate*
	As thou henge on the Croys	*hung; Cross*
3350	On hye thou madyste a voys,	*Aloud*
	Mans helthe, the gospel seys,	*[For] man's salvation*
	Whanne thou seydyst "*Scitio.*"	*I thirst*

Scilicet, salutem animarum.   *That is, for the salvation of souls*

	Thane the Jewes that were unquert	*wicked*
	Dressyd thee drynke, eysyl and galle.	*Prepared for you; vinegar*
3355	It to taste thou myth nowth styrt	*could not avoid*
	But seyd "*Consummatum est*" was alle.	*It is finished*
	A knyt wyth a spere so smert,	*soldier; sharp*
	Whanne thou forgafe thi fomen thrall	*foe's servants*
	He stonge thee, Lord, unto the hert.	*pierced*
3360	Thanne watyr and blod gan oute wall,	*pour*
	Aqua baptismatis et sanguis redempcionis *The water of baptism and the blood of redemption*	
	The watyr of Baptomm,	*Baptism*
	The blod of redempcioun	
	That fro thin herte ran doun	
3365	*Est causa salvacionis.*	*It is the cause of salvation*

	Lord, thou that man hathe don more mysse thanne good	*although; ill*
	If he dey in very contricioun,	*die; true*
	Lord, the lest drope of thi blod	*least*
	For hys synne makyth satysfaccioun.	
3370	As thou deydyst, Lord, on the Rode,	*died; Cross*
	Graunt me my peticioun!	
	Lete me, Mercy, be hys fode,	*sustenance*
	And graunte hym thi salvacion,	
	Quia dixisti "Misericordia servabo."[1]	
3375	"Mercy" schal I synge and say	
	And "*Miserere*" schal I pray	*have mercy*
	For Mankynd evere and ay.	*for ever and ever*
	Misericordias Domini in eternum cantabo.[2]	

| JUSTICIA | Rythwys Kynge, Lorde God almyth, | *Righteous; almighty* |
| 3380 | I am thi dowtyr Rythwysnesse. | *Justice* |

---

[1] *Since you have said, "I will keep my mercy"* (see Psalm 88:29)

[2] *I shall sing of the mercies of the Lord forever* (see Psalm 88:1)

Thou hast lovyd me evere, day and nyth,   *night*
As wel as othyr, as I gesse.   *the others; believe*

Justicias Dominus justicia dilexit.   *The just Lord had loved justice*

If thou mans kynde fro peyne aquite,   *nature; release*
Thou dost ageyns thyne owyn processe,   *judicial procedure*
3385   Lete hym in preson to be pyth   *prison; placed*
For hys synne and wyckydnesse,
       Of a bone I thee pray.   *request*
Ful oftyn he hath thee, Lord, forsake
And to the Devyl he hathe hym take.   *taken*
3390   Lete hym lyn in Hell lake,   *lie; Hell's pit*
       Dampnyd for evere and ay.   *for ever and ever*

Quia Deum, quia se genuit, dereliquit.   *For he has forsaken God, who created him*

For whanne Man to the werld was bornn
He was browth to Holy Kyrke,   *brought*
Feythly followd in the funte-ston   *Devoutly christened; font*
3395   And wesch fro orygynal synne so dyrke.   *washed of; dark*
Satanas he forsok as hys fone,   *Satan; foe*
All hys pompe and al hys werke,   *display*
And hyth to serve thee alone;   *promised*
To kepe thi commandementys he schuld not irke,   *grow weary*
3400   *Sicut justi tui.*   *According to your laws*
But whanne he was com to mans astate   *estate*
All hys behestys he thanne forgate.   *promises; forgot*
He is worthi be dampnyd for that,
       Qui oblitus est Domini creatoris sui.   *For he has forgotten God his creator*

3405   For he hathe forgetyn thee that hym wrout   *made*
And formydiste hym lyke thyne owyn face   *made himself*
And wyth thi precyous blod hym bowth   *bought*
And in this world thou geve hym space.   *a place*
All thi benefetys he set at nowth   *nought*
3410   But toke hym to the Develys trase,   *path*
The Flesch, the World, was most in his thowth   *thought*
And purpose to plese hem in every plase,   *intended; place*
       So grymly on grounde.   *cruelly on the earth*
I pray thee, Lord lovely,
3415   Of man have no mercy,
But, dere Lord, lete hym ly,   *lie*
       In Hell lete hym be bounde!

Man hathe forsake the Kynge of Hevene
And hys Good Aungels governaunce

3420	And solwyd hys soule wyth synnys sevene	*sullied*
	Be hys Badde Aungels comberaunce.	*temptation*
	Vertuis he putte ful evyn away	*Virtues; entirely*
	Whanne Coveytyse gan hym avaunce.	*assist*
	He wende that he schulde a levyd ay,	*thought; have lived forever*
3425	Tyl Deth trypte hym on hys daunce,	*tripped; in*
	He loste hys wyttys fyve.	
	Ovyrlate he callyd Confescion;	*Too late*
	Ovyrlyt was hys contricioun;	*Too little*
	He made nevere satisfaccioun.	
3430	Dampne hym to Helle belyve!	*quickly*
	For if thou take Mans sowle to thee	
	Ageyns thi Rythwysnesse,	
	Thou dost wronge, Lorde, to Trewth and me	
	And puttys us fro oure dewnesse.	*rights*
3435	Lord, lete us nevere fro thee fle,	
	Ner streyne us nevere in stresse,	*restrain; by force*
	But late thi dom be by us thre	*judgment*
	Mankynde in Hell to presse,	*thrust*
	Lord, I thee beseche!	
3440	For Rytwysnes dwellys evere sure	
	To deme Man aftyr hys deserviture,	*judge; deserving*
	For to be dampnyd it is hys ure,	*destiny*
	On Man I crie wreche.	*vengeance*

Letabitur justus cum viderit vindictam.[1]

MISERICORDIA   Mercy, my systyr Rythwysnes!

3445	Thou schape Mankynde no schonde.	*make for; shame*
	Leve systyr, lete be thi dresse.	*Dear; severity*
	To save Man lete us fonde.	*attempt*
	For if Man be dampnyd to Hell dyrknes,	
	Thanne myth I wryngyn myn honde	*must*
3450	That evere my state schulde be les,	*condition; inferior [to yours]*
	My fredam to make bonde.	*put in restraint*
	Mankynd is of oure kyn.	
	For I, Mercy, pase al thynge	*surpass*
	That God made at the begynnynge	
3455	And I am hys dowtyr yynge,	*young*
	Dere systyr, lete be thi dyn!	*shouting*

Et misericordia ejus super omnia opera ejus.[2]

---

[1] *The righteous man will rejoice when he sees vengeance* (see Psalm 57:11)

[2] *And his mercy is over all his works* (see Psalm 144:9)

Of Mankynde aske thou nevere wreche   *vengeance*
Be day ner be nyth,   *nor; night*
For God hymself hath ben hys leche,   *physician*
3460 Of hys mercyful myth.   *power*
To me he gan hym beteche,   *entrusted him*
Besyde al hys ryth.   *Against; laws*
For hym wyl I prey and preche
To gete hym fre respyth,   *respite*
3465   And my systyr Pese.   *Peace*
For hys mercy is wythout begynnynge
And schal be wythoutyn endynge,
As David seyth, that worthy kynge;
     In scriptur is no les.   *there are no lies*

Et misericordia ejus a progenie in progenies, et cetera.[1]

Veritas Mercy is Mankynde non worthy,   *not worthy of*
3471 David thou thou recorde and rede,   *although; recite; read*
For he wolde nevere the hungry
Neythyr clothe nor fede,   *feed*
Ner drynke gyf to the thrysty,   *Nor; give*
3475 Nyn pore men helpe at nede.   *Nor*
For if he dyd non of these, forthy   *therefore*
In Hevene he getyth no mede.   *reward*
     So seyth the gospel.
For he hathe ben unkynde   *Because*
3480 To lame and to blynde
In Helle he schal be pynde.   *tormented*
     So is resun and skyl.   *reason*

Pax Pesible Kyng in majeste,   *PEACE; Peaceful*
I, Pes thi dowtyr, aske thee a boun   *favor*
3485 Of Man, whouso it be.   *however*
Lord, graunte me myn askynge soun,   *soon*
That I may evermore dwelle wyth thee
As I have evere yyt doun,
And lat me nevere fro thee fle,
3490   Specialy at thi dome   *because of your judgment*
     Of Man, thi creature.
Thou my systyr Ryth and Trewthe   *sisters Justice*
Of Mankynd have non rewthe,   *pity*
Mercy and I ful sore us mewythe   *strongly exert ourselves*
3495   To cacche hym to our cure.   *take; care*

---

[1] *And his mercy is from generation to generation, etc.* (see Luke 1:50)

	For whanne thou madyst erthe and Hevyn,	
	Ten orderys of aungelys to ben in blys,	*be*
	Lucyfer, lyter thanne the levyn	*brighter; lightning*
	Tyl whanne he synnyd, he fel iwys.	*Until; truly*
3500	To restore that place ful evyn	*completely*
	Thou madyst Mankynd wyth thys	*for this reason*
	To fylle that place that I dyd nevene.	*name*
	If thy wyl be resun it is,	*by*
	In pes and rest,	*peace*
3505	Amonge thyne aungels bryth	*bright*
	To worchep thee in syth,	*sight*
	Graunt, Lord God almyth!	*almighty*
	And so I holde it best.	

	For thou Truthe, that is my systyr dere,	
3510	Arguyth that Man schuld dwell in wo	
	And Rytwysnes wyth hyr powere	
	Wolde fayn and fast that it were so,	*eagerly; resolutely*
	But Mercy and I, Pes, bothe in fere,	*together*
	Schal nevere in feyth acorde therto.	*argument agree*
3515	Thanne schuld we evere dyscorde here	*argue*
	And stande at bate for frend or foo	*in conflict*
	And evere at dystaunce.	*in opposition*
	Therfore my counseyl is	
	Lete us foure systerys kys	
3520	And restore Man to blys,	
	As was Godys ordenaunce.	

Misericordia et Veritas obviauerunt sibi, Justicia et Pax osculate sunt.[1]

	For if ye, Ryth and Truthe, schuld have your wylle,	*Justice*
	I, Pes, and Mercy schuld evere have travest.	*opposition*
	Thanne us betwene had bene a gret perylle	*danger*
3525	That oure joyes in Hevene schuld a ben lest.	*have been lost*
	Therfore, gentyl systerys, consentyth me tyll,	*to my proposal*
	Ellys betwene oureself schuld nevere be rest.	
	Where schuld be luf and charité, late ther cum non ille.	*love*
	Loke oure joyes be perfyth, and that I holde the best,	*perfect*
3530	In Heveneryche blys.	*Heaven's bliss*
	For ther is pes wythowtyn were,	*war*
	There is rest wythowtyn fere,	*fear*
	Ther is charité wythowtyn dere.	*injury*
	Our Fadyris wyll so is.	

---

[1] *Mercy and Truth have met together, Righteousness and Peace have kissed each other* (see Psalm 84:11–12)

Hic pax, hic bonitas, hic laus, hic semper honestas.[1]

3535	Therfore, jentyl systerys, at on word,	*with one word*
	Truth, Ryth, and Mercy hende,	*gracious*
	Lete us stonde at on acord,	*in agreement*
	At pes wythowtyn ende.	
	Late love and charyté be at oure bord,	*Let; table*
3540	Alle venjauns awey wende,	*go*
	To Hevene that Man may be restoryd,	
	Lete us all be hys frende	
	Before oure Fadyrs face.	
	We schal devoutly pray	
3545	At dredful Domysday	*fearful Judgment Day*
	And I schal for us say	
	That Mankynd schal have grace.	

Et tuam, Deus, deposcimus pietatem ut ei tribuere digneris lucidas et quietas mansiones.[2]

	Lord, for thi pyté and that pes	*peace*
	Thou sufferyst in thi pascioun,	*passion*
3550	Boundyn and betyn, wythout les,	*beaten; lying*
	Fro the fote to the croun,	
	Tanquam ovis ductus es	*Like a sheep you were led*
	Whanne gutte sanguis ran adoun,	*drops of blood*
	Yyt the Jwes wolde not ses	*Jews; cease*
3555	But on thyn hed thei thryst a croun	*thrust*
	And on the Cros thee naylyd.	
	As petously as thou were pynyd,	*piteously; tormented*
	Have mercy of Mankynd,	
	So that he may fynde	
3560	Oure preyer may hym avayle.	*aid*

PATER	[*Sedens in trono:*	*Sitting on a throne*
	Ego cogito cogitaciones pacis, non affliccionis.[3]	
	Fayre falle thee, Pes, my dowtyr dere!	*May good fortune come to you*
	On thee I thynke and on Mercy.	
	Syn ye acordyd beth all in fere,	*are in agreement together*
	My jugement I wyl geve you by	*according to your proposal*
3565	Not aftyr deservynge to do reddere,	*according to punishment*
	To dampne Mankynde to turmentry,	*torments*

---

[1] *Here is peace, here is goodness, here is glory, here eternally is virtue*

[2] *And we earnestly entreat your pity, O Lord, so that you may deign to grant him a shining and peaceful dwelling*

[3] *I think thoughts of peace, not of affliction* (see Jeremias 29:11)

But brynge hym to my blysse ful clere   *perfect*
In Hevene to dwelle endelesly,
    At your prayere forthi.   *According to*
3570 To make my blysse perfyth   *perfect*
I menge wyth my most myth   *mingle; might*
Alle pes, sum treuthe, and sum ryth,   *peace; justice*
    And most of my mercy.
Misericordia Domini plena est terra.[1] Amen!

Dicet filiabus: *He says to his daughters:*

My dowters hende,   *gracious*
3575 Lufly and lusti to lende,   *joyful to consent*
Goo to yone fende   *devil*
And fro hym take Mankynd.
Brynge hym to me
And set hym here be my kne,   *by*
3580 In Hevene to be,
In blysse wyth gamyn and gle.   *joy and mirth*

VERITAS We schal fulfylle
Thin hestys, as resun and skylle,   *commands; as is reasonable*
Fro yone gost grylle   *fierce spirit*
3585 Mankynde to bryng thee tylle.   *to you*

Tunc ascendent ad Malum Angelum omnes pariter et dicet:[2]

PAX A, thou foule wyth,   *creature*
Lete go that soule so tyth!   *immediately*
In Hevene lyth   *the light of Heaven*
Mankynde sone schal be pyth.   *placed*

JUSTICIA Go thou to Helle,
3591 Thou devyl bold as a belle,
Therin to dwelle,
In bras and brimston to welle!   *brass (fetters?); boil*

Tunc ascendent ad tronum.   *Then they go up to the throne*

MISERICORDIA Lo here Mankynd,
3595 Lyter thanne lef is on lynde,   *Brighter; leaf; linden tree*

---

[1] *The earth is full of the mercy of the Lord* (see Psalm 32:5). [This line might well be part of the playtext.]

[2] *Then they all ascend to the Bad Angel together and say*

That hath ben pynyd.   *tormented*
Thi mercy, Lord, lete hym fynde!

PATER [*Sedens in judicio:*   THE FATHER; *Sitting in judgment*
          Sicut scintilla in medio maris.[1]

          My mercy, Mankynd, geve I thee.
          Cum syt at my ryth honde.   *right*
3600   Ful wel have I lovyd thee,
          Unkynd thow I thee fonde.   *though; found*
          As a sparke of fyre in the se   *sea*
          My mercy is synne-quenchand.   *sin-quenching*
          Thou hast cause to love me
3605   Abovyn al thynge in land,   *estates; under my control*
              And kepe my comaundment.
          If thou me love and drede
          Hevene schal be thi mede;   *reward*
          My face thee schal fede: *feed*
3610   This is myn jugement.

Ego occidam et vivificabo, percuciam et sanabo, et nemo est qui de manu mea possit eruere.[2]

          Kyng, kayser, knyt, and kampyoun,   *knight; champion*
          Pope, patriark, prest, and prelat in pes,
          Duke dowtyest in dede, be dale and be doun,   *bravest; valley; hill*
          Lytyl and mekyl, the more and the les,
3615   All the statys of the world is at myn renoun;   *estates; under my control*
          To me schal thei geve acompt at my dygne des.   *account; worthy throne*
          Whanne Myhel hys horn blowyth at my dred dom   *Michael; terrible judgment*
          The count of here conscience schal putten hem in pres   *account; difficulties*
              And yeld a reknynge   *yield*
3620   Of her space whou they han spent,   *time [on earth] how; have*
          And of her trew talent,   *their real good deeds*
          At my gret jugement
              An answere schal me brynge.   *to me*

Ecce, requiram gregem meum de manu pastoris.[3]

          And I schal inquire of my flok and of her pasture   *their pastors*
3625   Whou they have levyd and led her peple sojet.   *How; the people in their care*
          The goode on the ryth syd schul stond ful sure;   *right*

---

[1] *Like a spark in the midst of the sea* (see note). [This line might be part of the playtext.]

[2] *I will kill and make alive, I will wound and heal; and there is no one who can deliver out of my hand* (see Deuteronomy 32:39)

[3] *Lo, I will inquire of my flock at the hand of the shepherd* (see Ezechiel 34:10)

The badde on the lyfte syd ther schal I set.

The sevene dedys of mercy whoso hadde ure   *use*

To fylle, the hungry for to geve mete,   *food*

3630 Or drynke to thrysty, the nakyd, vesture,   *clothing*

The pore or the pylgrym hom for to fette,   *bring*

Thi neybour that hath nede;

Whoso doth mercy to hys myth   *according to his ability*

To the seke, or in presun pyth,   *sick; [those] put in prison*

3635 He doth to me; I schal hym quyth;   *requite*

Hevene blys schal be hys mede.   *reward*

Et qui bona egerunt ibunt in vitam eternam; qui vero mala, in ignem eternum.[1]

And thei that wel do in this werld, her welthe schal awake;   *grow*

In Hevene thei schal be heynyd in bounté and blys;   *exalted*

And thei that evyl do, thei schul to Helle lake   *the pit of Hell*

3640 In byttyr balys to be brent: my jugement it is.   *torment; burnt*

My vertus in Hevene thanne schal thei qwake.   *virtues; tremble*

Ther is no wyth in this werld that may skape this.   *creature; escape*

All men example here-at may take

To mayntein the goode and mendyn her mys.   *amend their sins*

3645 Thus endyth oure gamys.

To save you fro synnynge

Evyr at the begynnynge

Thynke on youre last endynge!

Te Deum laudamus!   *We praise you, O God*

---

[1] *And those who do good, they will go to eternal life; those who do evil, assuredly to eternal fire* (see note)

EXPLANATORY NOTES

ABBREVIATIONS: **B**: Bevington, *Medieval Drama; CT*: Chaucer, *Canterbury Tales*; **E**: Eccles, *The Macro Plays*; **MED**: *Middle English Dictionary*; **OED**: *Oxford English Dictionary*; **Tilley**: Tilley, *A Dictionary of the Proverbs in England in the Sixteenth and Seventeenth Centuries*; **Whiting**: Whiting, *Proverbs, Sentences, and Proverbial Phrases*.

STAGE PLAN

The *OED* connects "stytelerys" with the verb "stightle" (to arrange, set in order), perhaps related (as Eccles points out) to "stickler" (umpire, moderator), recorded first in 1538. This would suggest that the "stytelerys" were crowd-control officers; it is not clear whether the direction that there should not be too many of them indicates a common failing with large plays or an assumption that they will not be needed in this particular case.

The "copbord" of Greed at the foot of the bed from which Mankind is born and in which he dies is not necessarily a stationary piece of furniture. Tydeman questions the stage plan's placement of it within the castle, and suggests that this is an error for a position near Greed's scaffold (*English Medieval Theatre 1400–1500*, pp. 97–98). But that is unnecessary. Mankind likely stores his riches in the "copbord," especially the thousand marks which Greed gives him to entice him out of the castle (line 2726). The "copbord" might also be carried away by Garcio at line 2960, "Go hens, for this is myne." This hint of portability might well imply a chest or similar container. Although no reference is made to it in the play, the prominent description of its location on the stage plan suggests that it was intended to be used in such a manner. Although it stands by Mankind's bed, it is Greed's cupboard and thus likely holds those things which Greed gives to Mankind. Natalie Crohn Schmitt suggests a useful analogue, citing Hieronymus Bosch's "Death of the Miser," in which the Miser's goods are kept in just such a chest at the foot of the bed ("Was There a Medieval Theatre in the Round?" p. 130, n. 4, and p. 142. A reproduction of the painting can also be found at <http://www.ibiblio.org/wm/paint/auth/bosch/death-miser/death-miser.jpg>).

Gunpowder (*gunnepowdyr*) was known in England at least from the mid-thirteenth century, when Roger Bacon described it in his treatise *De nullitate magiæ*. By the middle of the fourteenth century, gunpowder was being made in the royal armories of the Tower of London. The provision of gunpowder/fireworks for Belial would strongly suggest that the actor wore an elaborate protective costume, gloved to protect his hands, and with a substantial mask to protect his ears (see Butterworth, *Theatre of Fire*, pp. 25–26).

The Four Daughters of God wear costumes in traditionally symbolic colors: white is a standard symbol for Mercy, Peace's black is the color of mourning, Justice wears the red of a judge, and Truth's green symbolizes eternity.

CAST LIST

The list of the players actually appears at the end of the play on fol. 191. The scribe has miscounted by one; including the "vexillatores" (standard-bearers) who announce the play a week before the performance, there are only thirty-five characters, not thirty-six.

18   Although the idea of a pair of forces, one malign, one benign, fighting for control of each human being is found in a wide range of popular theology and sermon literature, only here and in Marlowe's *Doctor Faustus* are they given a place on stage. There is no evidence that Marlowe knew *Castle*, though it is not outside the bounds of possibility.

29   The traditional Three Enemies of Mankind, the World, the Flesh, and the Devil, appear in several other plays as well, notably in the Digby play of Mary Magdalene. Though the idea — a sort of evil parallel to the Trinity — was widespread, it may derive ultimately from the *Meditations* attributed to St. Bernard of Clairvaux, Chapter 12, *De tribus inimicis hominis, carne, mundo et diabolo* ("On the Three Enemies of Man, the Flesh, the World, and the Devil"). See also Wenzel, "Three Enemies of Man."

44   When banns do survive for a play, discrepancies between the banns and the playtext are not uncommon, suggesting perhaps that the play has been revised without the revision having been transferred to the summary of the banns. Here, according to the summary, the Good Angel enlists the help of Conscience, Confession, and Penitence to take Mankind out of the clutches of Greed, the Three Enemies, and the Seven Deadly Sins. In the play, however, Conscience does not appear.

91   The relationship between old age and covetousness is proverbial. See, for example, Chaucer, *Troilus and Criseyde* (IV.1369), where Criseyde notes, "elde is ful of coveytise." See also Whiting C490.

99   *lake*. The "lake" is probably an alliterative reference to the pit of Hell.

124   Further evidence that the play may have been revised without reference to the banns can be seen in the absence of any description of the colloquy of the Four Daughters of God which ends the playtext as we have it. This line may suggest that an earlier version of the play concluded with the intercession of Mary, similar, perhaps, to her support for the King in *The Pride of Life*.

138   This line is ambiguous in two ways. The term "underne" could mean midmorning, midday, or midafternoon, and it is not certain whether "we shul be onward" means "our play must be underway" or "we must be finished and moving on to our next destination."

154   Eccles proposed reading the infinitive "lende" for the manuscript reading "lendys," though that is problematic since the rhyme of the passage is "-ys" (E, p. 7, n. 154).

161–63   The World is speaking to the audience, and their division into "bolde bachelerys" who will need to be prepared to fight and "syrys" who "syttyth on syde" seems to echo Mercy's division of his audience in *Mankind* into "ye soverens that sitt, and ye brothern that stonde right uppe" (line 29).

170–78   The World boasts of the extent of his reputation, and the place-names are selected largely for their alliteration. The Dry Tree is located at the site of the Garden of Eden; it dried up and withered at the moment of Adam's fall. It appears on the well-known Hereford Cathedral map of the world (ca. 1300) next to the Gates of Paradise; see Westrem, *Hereford Map*, pp. 38–39, #76.

182   Greed does not merely *give* the lands to the World but places him in legal possession (*seisin*) of them.

201   Carlisle, just south of the Scottish border in the far northwest, to Kent, in the southeast, defines the whole of England.

202   Belial's claim that he bursts into flame "Bothe the bak and the buttoke" would seem to echo the provision for gunpowder in his costume on the stage plan.

226   *grym.* "Strife." Eccles glosses: "cruelty" (E, p. 246), presumably to get at the force of Belial's boast. *MED grim* n1.c suggests "agitation," which goes well with the fiends' usual practice of working the field as agitators, trying to create disturbances that will give them clues to people's weak spots. Lucifer is an agitator when he first approaches Eve; Titivillus agitates Mankind until he breaks faith with Mercy in *Mankind*. When Belial comes upon "Fele folke on a flokke to flappyn and to flene" (line 225), his alliterative boasting implies more of an effort to create a "flap" than to actually beat and flay people — not even Belial could get away with that until he actually has someone in Hell. His intention at the moment is to impress the "folke" with his capacity for frightful violence, in which case his boasting is more an effort to stir his "boyis on this grene" (line 227) into action when he blasts his bugle than an act of cruelty.

235, 239   Flesh's scaffold would have been decorated with towers.

271   The reference here (and elsewhere, lines 906, 1897, 1926) to a "hyll" has caused some difficulties for scholars who would take it literally and equate it with a pile of earth created by digging a ditch. It is far more likely that it refers simply to the appropriate scaffold, and that the word is used for its alliterative value or its rhyme (as here). See Schmitt, "Was There a Medieval Theatre in the Round?" p. 138.

294   It is not clear whether Mankind's reference is to "chrisom," a piece of linen cloth placed over a child's head at christening, or to "chrism," the consecrated oil used in several sacraments, including christening. The difference is not important; Mankind explains that his only possession is that which he received at his first sacrament.

324   See previous note; the phrase "a crysyme" would suggest the first meaning.

345   *stylle as ston.* Mankind does not move as he tries to decide between the two angels.

361a   On this and subsequent extra-metrical Latin lines in the text, see Introduction, "Extra-metrical Latin Lines," pp. 6–7. The Good Angel has been arguing that

Mankind should avoid the World altogether, so although the Latin line seems like an expansion of the previous statement, it does not really "bere wytnesse" to the Good Angel's argument advocating, as it does, a middle way between riches and poverty. On this and other situations where the Latin quotation does not exactly fit the playtext, see Parry, "Margin of Error," p. 43.

407–10a   The point which the Good Angel makes here foreshadows the end of the play, where the actor playing God steps out of character and concludes that pondering one's ending is the proper way to avoid sin and lead a good life.

455, s.d.   "Pipe" in this context could indicate any wind instrument or combination of wind instruments. The playwright tends to be specific about trumpets ("trumpe up," lines 156, 574 s.d., etc., or "bemys," lines 617, 2376), so the reference here would more likely be to a ceremonial shawm band as illustrated in many fifteenth-century pictures of feasts and celebratory occasions.

479   The hawthorn berry is proverbial as an indication of something trivial, small, and worthless. See Whiting H190.

516   If Folly is referring here to a specific book, it would likely be either Thomas à Kempis' *Imitatio Christi*, which circulated in several different versions dating between 1418 and 1441, or Nicholas of Cusa's *De docta ignorantia*, which first appeared in 1441. Folly could not be thinking of Erasmus' *Praise of Folly* (*Morae Encomium*), which was written in 1509, well after the date of the *Castle* manuscript. See Kaiser, *Praisers of Folly*, pp. 8–10.

516a   This is a particularly good example of an extra-metrical Latin line that cannot be part of the playtext, since it would be highly inappropriate for either Folly or Pleasure to say "Wisdom is with the Lord." The line does, however, make excellent sense as an extra-dramatic gloss on the passage. See Parry, "Margin of Error," p. 44.

519   I have hyphenated Lust-and-Lykynge since it is clear in the text that the phrase refers to one person who is called "Voluptas" (Pleasure) in the speech headings.

656   Backbiter addresses the audience directly.

659   Backbiter has several names. He also calls himself Detraction (line 777), and the World calls him Flibbertigibet (lines 775, 1724, 1733). He represents the self-absorption that leads men to flatter those who can do them good and to speak ill of their neighbors. One of the two lowlifes who accuse Mary of adultery in the N-Town "Trial of Mary and Joseph" is named Bakbytere (*N-Town Plays*, ed. Spector, 1:140, line 41, or Sugano, p. 124, line 41). On Edgar's references (as Poor Tom) to Flibbertigibbet in *King Lear*, see also Cauthen, "Foule Flibbertigibbet."

672   Backbiter is carrying a letter box or dispatch box containing the lies he spreads about other people.

691   Several scholars have proposed emending "pley" to "prey" on the grounds that Backbiter's hunting in the woods would be more likely to be for prey than for play. However, if the object of his hunting is the "game" he is playing with Mankind, the

reading "pley" would also make sense. See Withington, "*Castle of Perseverance*, line 695," and Umphrey, "*Castle of Perseverance*, line 695."

716   Although the World is probably costumed as a prince, in purple or red, this line suggests that his costume is edged with white fur (or its costume equivalent).

730   *feffe*. As with "sesyd" (line 182), the World does not merely give wealth to Mankind, but formally puts him in legal possession (enfeoffs him).

750   Mankind has already cast ethical action to the winds; in the service of the World he will happily imprison anyone who speaks against the World, whether guilty or innocent of any real crime.

763   *opyn sesun*. As in line 182, "seisin" indicates the legal possession of land.

775   See note to line 659.

802   *whanne the fox prechyth*. Proverbial; compare Cain's assessment of Abel's prayer in the Towneley *Mactacio Abel*: "How! let furth youre geyse; the fox will preche" (*Towneley Plays*, ed. Stevens and Cawley, 1:14, line 86). G. R. Owst illustrates the proverb with a wood carving of a fox preaching (*Preaching in Medieval England*, p. 86).

805   The cope which the Good Angel wears indicates that he is costumed as a priest in liturgical vestments.

841   Simony, the buying or selling of church offices for profit, was a substantial problem in the Middle Ages, when many churchmen held temporal administrative positions in addition to their spiritual positions within the church. Dante's *Inferno* condemned the simoniacs to the eighth circle of Hell. A fourteenth-century poem, "The Simonie," linking simony and covetousness or greed, is found in Dean, *Medieval English Political Writings*, pp. 193–212.

866   The *Disticha* of Dionysius Cato (who is otherwise unknown) are moral statements in Latin hexameter couplets, written in the third or fourth century. They were virtually ubiquitous in the Middle Ages as a school text for the learning of Latin. Their usefulness persisted well into the early modern period; Benjamin Franklin printed an English version of them in 1735. See Chase, *Distichs of Cato*.

879   *Si dedero*. A satirical Latin song which begins with these words seems to have been very popular, though it is not certain that the reference here is to that poem. The phrase out of context seems to have been a byword for bribery, with which meaning it appears frequently, including in the Macro play of *Mankind*, line 456. In most of its appearances, the phrase "If I give [you something]" implies the continuation "I'll expect something better in return." John Lydgate's version of the Aesopian fable of the Wolf and the Lamb concludes with the statement:

> *Si dedero* ys now so mery a song,
> Hath founde a practyk by lawe to make a preef   *method; prove a case*
> To hang a trew man & save an errant theef.   *obvious*

(*Minor Poems of John Lydgate*, ed. MacCracken, 2:577, lines 327–29). A similar usage appears in the poem "The Simonie" in the Auchinleck manuscript (National

Library of Scotland, Edinburgh, Advocates Manuscript 19.2.1) which describes a clerk presenting a case at the court of Rome: "Or he shal singe *si dedero* or al geineþ him noht" ("Either he will offer a bribe or he'll get nothing at all," line 24). Both Mankind and Greed speak of "singing" the phrase, and it does appear to have existed as well as a popular tune. A setting of it in three parts by Alexander Agricola (ca. 1445–1506) was printed by Ottaviano Petrucci in *Harmonice Musices Odhecaton A* (1501), and Jacob Obrecht (ca. 1457–1505) used the tune as the *cantus firmus* of a setting of the Mass.

906   The "hyll" to which Pride refers is presumably the scaffold of Greed (see note to line 271).

941   *Belsabubbe*. The Devil's many guises are indicated by the several names he is called: Belial, Beelsabub, Satanas.

1031   The syntax is a bit messy here. "Thei" refers to the three sins, Gluttony, Sloth, and Lechery, in line 1030, but the playwright (or scribe) seems to have forgotten that the reference there is to the adjectival forms (gluttonous, slothful, lecherous) following on from "He is . . ." in line 1029, rather than to the sins themselves. The sense of the line is "They are sometimes there as well."

1035   A "pynyngys stole," like the stocks and the pillory, was a method of punishment, especially for selling food and drink at false measures. Greed's intent of making Mankind "to ben a foole" would be fulfilled by putting him to a punishment intended for alewives, butchers, and bakers.

1059   The "crakows" which Pride recommends to Mankind as the latest fashion are useful in dating the original composition of the play. These shoes with excessively long pointed toes (often so long as to require attaching to the knees) are referred to only in texts dating from about 1382 to about 1425. E (pp. 190–91) gives a full list of these references. The style seems to have come from Eastern Europe, and the name likely derives from Krakow, Poland. In the *Historia Vitae et Regni Ricardi II* it is claimed that the style was introduced by Anne of Bohemia, who married Richard in 1382 (see E, p. 191).

1060   The technique of "jagging" clothes involved the cutting of long (predominately vertical) slashes to allow a lining of contrasting color and texture to be seen through the cut.

1073   The image of the wheel of Fortune is ubiquitous in medieval literature. It is described in detail in Boethius' *Consolation of Philosophy* (Book II); see Patch, *Goddess Fortuna in Medieval Literature*.

1085a   I have followed B's practice of adding appropriate stage directions for the vices' joining of Covetousness, here and at 1145a, 1175a, 1205a, and 1237a.

1109   This line could be seen as a foreshadowing of Mankind's eventual death (line 2807).

1122   Unlike Mankind (lines 1102 and 1106), Envy is wary of taking the Lord's name in vain.

1139   *Cum up to me above.* Humanum Genus, basking proudly on Sir Covetyse's scaffold, invites Envy to join him "on lofte" (line 1145).

1152–55   The laity was required to fast (usually defined as the removal of meat from the diet) during the seasons of Advent (the four weeks leading up to Christmas) and Lent (the period from Ash Wednesday to Easter).

1215   *take a swet.* E (p. 269), B (p. 833), and *MED* gloss *swet* in this line as "sweat," the idea being, perhaps, that rather than go to Mass the lover should wrap his head in a cloth (i.e., a sweat band, line 1214) and relax in a steam bath.

1237a   *[Sloth ascends to Covetousness' scaffold]* is Bevington's stage direction (B, p. 834). It is especially necessary here to clarify the distinction between Humanum Genus' two contiguous speeches.

1350   *al to sone.* It is necessary for Mankind to go to confession before taking communion on Easter Sunday. Mankind tells Schrift that, according to Sloth, Palm Sunday (a week before Easter) is much too early for confession, and that he should return on Good Friday, five days later.

1369   *We have etyn garlek everychone.* Mankind, thinking back to his pleasures of food on Gluttony's scaffold, resists the Confessor's invitation to temper his diet. The *Castle*-playwright is drawing on a well-established tradition of the evil of rich foods mentioned by the hungry Israelites in the desert who, dissatisfied with the blandness of manna, yearn for the tasty delicacies of Egypt (Numbers 11:5). That passage gets picked up in various commentaries and also by Gower in *Vox clamantis* (3.85–90; Macaulay, ed., *Works*, 4:109), where the protagonist warns against the corruptive effects of such foods on worldly prelates; and in Chaucer's Prologue to the *Canterbury Tales*, where the Summoner, physically disfigured as a sign of his debauched love of women or men and rich food, is said to be fond of garlic, onions, and leeks (*CT* I[A]634). See Kaske, "Summoner's Garleek, Oynons, and Eek Lekes," on these foods as symbolic of moral corruption; and Biggins, who discusses such foods as stimulants of sexual desire, in "Chaucer's Summoner: 'Wel Loved He Garleek, Onyons, and eek Lekes.'" See also Wood, "Sources of Chaucer's Summoner's 'Garleek, Oyunons, and eek Lekes.'"

1379   As with line 1109, perhaps a foreshadowing of Mankind's death in line 2807.

1381–89   Contrition (sorrow of heart) is one of the canonical requirements for true confession; the others are verbal confession and penance. See also lines 1419 and 1431.

1468–80   This stanza and the next constitute Mankind's oral confession, while lines 1494–1531 represent Confession's absolution (explicit in lines 1507 and 1520).

1496–97   Confession refers to Matthew 16:18–19, "And I say to thee: That thou art Peter; and upon this rock I will build my church, and the gates of hell shall not prevail against it. And I will give to thee the keys of the kingdom of heaven. And whatsoever thou shalt bind upon earth, it shall be bound also in heaven: and, whatsoever thou shalt loose on earth, it shall be loosed also in heaven."

Confession's point is that God has granted the power of absolution to His church and His priesthood.

1601   A leaf is missing from the manuscript following this line. The action of the missing text seems reasonably clear: Mankind enters the Castle of Perseverance accompanied by the seven cardinal virtues. Meekness and Patience, the only two virtues whose introductory speeches are missing, clearly spoke as well, since Mankind answers them in lines 1671–75. Before the virtues introduce themselves, the World, the Flesh, and the Devil and their accompanying sins retreat from Covetousness' scaffold to their own scaffolds.

1621–23   The idea that Adam's sin in eating the apple was gluttony appears in a number of medieval sources. The preachers' manual *Qui bene presunt* of Richard of Wetheringsett (ca. 1220) includes a chapter on gluttony in its fifth Distinction, *De viciis*, in which he notes that it was Adam "qui propter pomum amisit Paradisum" ("who was driven from Paradise because of an apple"). Richard's treatise was very popular in England over the following three centuries. The full text is found in many manuscripts; the quotation here is from London, British Library Ms. Royal 9.A.xiv. I am grateful to Joseph Goering for this reference.

1660   Criticism of estate executors is common through the fourteenth century, since the law gave them considerable control over the distribution of the estate. In Langland's *Piers Plowman*, for example, executors are said to "maken hym murie with oother mennes goodes" (B-text, Passus 20, line 289). E provides several other examples (p. 193).

1668   The lily is commonly a symbol of virginity.

1705b   The hymn *Aeterne Rex altissime* is sung at the service of matins (the first of the day's canonical services) between Ascension (the fortieth day after Easter) and Pentecost (the fiftieth day after Easter).

1711   "Dos" is generally used of an amount of medicine; perhaps a reference to the vinegar and gall given to Christ to slake his thirst.

1731   Not "mothers," but the East Anglian dialect word "moder," "servant or wench" as cited by the *OED* (s.v. "mawther") from the *Promptorium Parvulorum*. The term is intended to be an insult.

1742   St. James the Greater, one of Jesus' apostles, who is reputed to be buried at Compostella in the province of Galicia, Spain.

1744   Backbiter's slanderous activities "both in England and in Wales" are less likely to be a comment on the Welsh than a convenient rhyme for "Galys."

1778–90   One of Backbiter's jobs is informing on his fellows, acting as a "snitch." Thus it is he who advises the three Enemies of the failure of the seven sins to keep Mankind in their clutches. His revelling in their punishment is part of the normal process of backbiting.

1828   *wyth rowtynge rele*. "in riotous tumult" (*MED rele* n.2). The "rele" figure also bears connotations of domesticity apt to the infighting amongst the seven deadly kinsmen that so amuses Backbiter in that "rele" is primarily the reel (*MED rele* n.1) that thread is spun onto from the distaff, which is another domestic tool that often gets mixed up in domestic brawls. The figure ties amusingly back into the metaphors of thread and weaving that the fiends use in hope of ensnaring their victims. Backbiter thrives on pranks against his fiendish buddies as well as anyone else. See lines 1832–35.

1848   "Lake" was a fine grade of linen; Chaucer's Sir Thopas is dressed in "cloth of lake fyn and cleere" (*CT* VII[B^2]858).

1870   Greed accepts no blame for Mankind's change of heart; the loss is the World's, not his.

1884   *bleryn. MED* v.1 "blear over; stream at the eyes"; v.2 "wail." B glosses: "be blinded" (p. 851); E: "stream at the eyes" (p. 233).

1929   Pride swears by Goliath, the Philistine giant killed by David in 1 Kings 50.

1941   Gogmagog was a mythical British giant defeated by Corineus in 1.16 of Geoffrey of Monmouth's *History of the Kings of Britain*.

2022   This line is a puzzle, and it is not at all clear what it might mean. "Parlasent" could be the French phrase "par asent," "voluntarily," which also appears in line 1013, but the rest of the line remains obscure. Happé suggests that the line is addressed to the virtues as primroses, "first flowers," and that the verb, "pleyeth," should be read as *OED* v, "to bestir or busily occupy oneself." Thus the line would mean, "O first flowers, stir yourselves willingly." This reading is not entirely convincing, and it does not explain the ending of the verb, "pleyeth," which should appear as "pleye" (Happé, *Four Morality Plays*, p. 626).

2053   *oure flourys*. This is the first reference to the flowers with which the Virtues defend the castle; later (line 2145) it becomes clear that their weapons are red roses, symbols of the Passion.

2115   *wyld fere*. "Wild fire" was a general term for gunpowder-based stage effects often, as likely here, thrown or "cast." See Butterworth, *Theatre of Fire*, pp. 21–24.

2120   "Motyhole" is clearly an insult, though its meaning is not clear. Furnivall and Pollard, *Macro Plays* (p. 200), took it to mean "moth hole," and E (p. 195) related it to "motty," "containing motes or dust," but neither of these is very convincing. Happé suggests that the first element is more likely derived from "mot" ("loose woman, harlot," *Four Morality Plays*, p. 626), see *OED* s.v. 3/1. But "filthy cunt" perhaps says it best, with *moty* implying "musty" or "dirty," and "hole" being what it is.

2145   *rosys swete and softe*. The anonymous treatise *Vitis Mystica* (attributed both to St. Bernard and St. Bonaventure) describes the roses with which the Virtues defend Mankind as symbols both of Charity and of Christ's Passion (*Patrologia Latina*, vol. 184, cols. 708–15) [Chapters XXXIII–XLI].

2198   *blowe your brode baggys*. Belial's call for bagpipes may simply be a mustering call to war, though, given the obscenity of his and his associates' attitudes toward women, more than military warfare may be implied. Bagpipes were commonly used to signify lechery and the dance of the flesh, which would be in keeping with the fiends and the seven sins' perpetual reducing of the Virtues to whores, sluts, and obscene parts of the anatomy (see note to line 2120). N.b., Eustache Deschamps' reference to the pipes as "instruments des hommes bestiaulx" (*Oeuvres Complètes*, v:127). That the drunken Miller leads Chaucer's pilgrims out of town with his bagpipe (*CT* I[A]565) has been often discussed as a type of concupiscence, lechery, and gluttony. Edward A. Block comments on the bagpipe as a sign of carnal lust, gluttony, avarice, and dissipation in Chaucer, but, especially, in the paintings of Bosch and Pieter Brueghel the Elder ("Chaucer's Millers and Their Bagpipes"). So too Scott, who explores typology linking bagpipes to gluttony and lechery as the piper plays upon pig stomachs and genitalia to make his squeal ("Sow-and-Bagpipe Imagery in the Miller's Portrait"). Scott cites British Library MS Sloane 748, fol. 82v, for an image of a pig playing bagpipes next to a jester holding his genitals (p. 289, n. 1). See also Robertson, on bagpipes as signs of the old sexual dance, in *Preface to Chaucer*, p. 243, and in figures 15, 33, 35, 37, and 42.

2198a   Taking into account the elaborate references to weapons, shields, and banners as the sins prepare for battle, as well as the stage plan's description of the Devil's battle costume, the provision here for an extended battle would form a spectacular climax to the fight for Mankind.

2212   *malaundyr*. Mallender is a form of chronic dermatitis in horses, characterized by sores on the legs.

2239   *wynnyth a scho*. The phrase "to win one's shoes" with the meaning "to prove oneself in battle" appears in several fifteenth-century texts. So in the romance *Sir Perceval of Galles* King Arthur tells Perceval that he will "wynn thi schone" in battle with the sultan (ed. Braswell, line 1595).

2269   *I mene the sacrament*. The sacrament to which Abstinence refers is the Eucharist, in which the "bread" of lines 2267 and 2270 is the body of Christ.

2303a   Anderson notes that Chastity's invocation of the Virgin Mary and her threat to "quenche" Lechery's "fowle hete" may indicate that she throws a bowl of water over her, especially since Lechery later complains that she has been "drenchyd" (see *Drama and Imagery in English Medieval Churches*, pp. 81–82). Conversely, Chastity might engineer Lechery's falling into the ditch, which is filled (for the moment) with the water of grace.

2329   *this dyche I fowe*. Although there is no stage direction to confirm it, it seems likely that the "dyche" from which Sloth empties the "watyr of grace" is the same ditch described in detail on the stage plan. The most significant argument against this conclusion is the stage plan's option of barring the place "strongely . . . al abowt" instead of digging a ditch, since it would not be clear in that case what Sloth would empty. Where the sins have been unsuccessful in their direct assault on the castle, Sloth gains entry by appealing to Mankind's innate laziness, just as Greed will draw him out of the castle by offering him creature comforts.

2335   *Thre mens songys.* A three-men's song would have been in three parts — usually treble, mean, and bass — like the song proposed by the Three Mights in *Wisdom* (lines 613–20); or, perhaps, a catch like those sung by Sir Toby Belch, Sir Andrew Aguecheek, and Feste in *Twelfth Night*. The three-men's song had a long history of association with drama; the two songs which survive with the Coventry Christmas pageant of the Shearmen and Tailors are both three-men's songs, as are many of the theater-related songs published by Thomas Ravenscroft. For the Coventry songs, see *Coventry Corpus Christi Plays*, ed. King and Davidson, pp. 166–73; for Ravenscroft's songs, see *Pammelia* (1609), *Deuteromelia* (1609), and *Melismata* (1611).

2379   *myrth.* The manuscript reads "myth" (might, power). Either word makes sense in the passage, but the rhyme word ("dyrt") suggests that E's emendation to "myrth" is correct.

2385   *cowche qwayl.* This may well have been a game. The character Franticness in John Skelton's anti-Wolsey satire "Speke, Parrot" (a close relation to *Castle*'s Folly) causes men "to play cowche quale" (Skelton, *Complete English Poems*, p. 243, line 426).

2390   *qwene.* There is a pun involved in this line, since Lechery's "qwene" has a double meaning of "queen," as Chastity has already used it in her previous fight with Lechery (line 2315), and "whore, slut," which is clearly the sense in which Lechery is using the word here.

2403–04 *my ballokys bathe / And leykyn.* Perhaps the licking metaphor comes from the behavior of dogs cleansing themselves at rest, though it's hard to imagine Accidia having such dexterity.

2421   As Smart noted ("*Castle of Perseverance*"), the Canwick gallows with which the World threatens his minions stood on Canwick Hill near Lincoln. The site was notorious since in 1255 eighteen Jews were hanged there for the murder of the eight-year-old Hugh of Lincoln. The executions were clearly political in nature, since a young Jewish boy had already confessed to the murder and had been executed.

2435   St. Giles is the patron saint of beggars, cripples, and the insane. Covetousness' offer to Mankind is perhaps not as good as it sounds. Alternatively, the reference might be to a notional "St. Guile," an appropriate name for Greed to swear by.

2445   Greed (Avaricia) is here associated with Cupiditas (also meaning Greed) which, as 1 Timothy 6:10 tells us, is the root of all evil.

2482   *I gynne to waxyn hory and olde.* One of the more troubling tropes of old age is the increase of miserliness (see note to line 91), as if to secure oneself against the crippling fear of loss and disablement that inevitably are on the horizon. Compare the anxieties of Elde in *The Parliament of the Three Ages*. The fearful compulsion is so great that Mankind leaves the castle abruptly with Coveytyse, giving the virtuous ladies no opportunity to try to dissuade him (n.b., stage direction after line 2556).

2488   *arayed in a sloppe.* A "slop" would be loose and practical, though unfashionable, unlike the fine clothes of Mankind's youth (n.b., lines 623–26).

2494   A mark was an amount of money (never minted as a coin) equal to two-thirds of a pound, or 13 s. 4 d.

2513   E (p. 197) suggests that the "Bok of Kendys" refers to *De naturis rerum* of Alexander Neckam (1157–1215), an encyclopedic collection of scientific knowledge.

2537   This sounds like a proverb, but it does not appear in any of the standard sources.

2589   That is, in Heaven.

2644   Generosity apologizes directly to the audience for having lost Mankind to the clutches of Greed.

2649–51 The Bad Angel's misogynist rant is well known as a proverb; see Tilley, W 686–87.

2665–73 Mankind speaks of money as a personification, "Penny-man."

2703   *my castel cage.* The "cage" to which Covetousness takes Mankind may well be the "cupboard" mentioned on the stage plan (see p. 105), situated at the end of Mankind's bed under the castle. The "cupboard" would likely have been portable, perhaps a chest, since Garcio appears to carry it off (around line 2981).

2726   See note to line 2494.

2740   The noble was a gold coin first struck during the reign of Edward III in 1344–46, with a value of 1/3 of a pound, or 6 s. 8 d.

2742   In a world in which banking and investing were only available to the very rich, money was generally stored in a locked chest. Such storage was, of course, vulnerable to theft, and one of the few methods of longer-term secure storage available to all was secret burial.

2745–47 That is, "I would not spend any of it even to save my neighbor from the gallows."

2816   *Thanne was I wel knowe.* Clearly a reference to the Black Death. Although the first wave of this epidemic reached England in 1348–50, outbreaks of plague occurred with some frequency over the next three hundred years. Death's "grete pestelens" likely refers to the first wave, in which as much as 30–40 percent of England's population died, but the later outbreaks would have meant that no one in the audience would have been ignorant of Death's power.

2820   *grete fyschys ete the smale.* Proverbial; see Whiting F232. But here Death's point is that the covetous use their predatory preoccupation mainly as a diversion away from facing the facts of life: in death, they are the ones who will be devoured, regardless of how great they are.

2823   *Hem schal helpyn nothyr mel or mete.* Death's taking the proud and covetous while they are feasting is a favorite trope in medieval drama. See the Death of Herod Play in N-Town, where Death watches the privileged who are unaware of his presence until he slays them all to exit in a dance of death, with admonitions to the audience. Or consider the presentation of Belshazzar's feast in *The Play of Daniel*.

2876   The "outrage" which Mankind has committed against the World is his residency in the Castle of Perseverance and his adherence to the seven Virtues.

2900 The breaking of Mankind's gall bladder would presumably increase the amount of yellow bile (gall) in his body. Since an excess of yellow bile leads to a choleric temperament, Mankind would be provoked to anger at the thought that his goods might go to someone not of his family ("kende").

2979 That is, "things will not go according to my plans, that my estate should go to my wife and children."

2985a It is not clear whether this line should be spoken or not, since the sense of it is given in English in the following lines.

2990 The sin of despair involves the denial of God's mercy, the blasphemous thought that one's own sins are too great for God to forgive. Mankind's prayer against despair is thus important, for were he to give in to this sin his wickedness would be far greater.

3007 At the last moment Mankind opens the door for his possible salvation by rejecting both his sinful life and his thoughts of despair and placing himself in the mercy of God.

3008 According to the stage plan, the Soul (perhaps played by a boy) has been under Mankind's bed for the whole of the play so far, waiting for his entrance. Although it would be a long wait, it would hardly be impossible, and the sudden appearance of the Soul at the moment of Mankind's death would provide a simple but extraordinary theatrical effect.

3012 The Soul addresses the dead body of Mankind, probably positioned on the bed from under which the Soul has just emerged.

3029 A leaf is missing in the manuscript after this line. Given the context, it seems likely that the Good Angel answers the Soul's question of line 3021 with advice concerning its salvation, prompting the Bad Angel's rejoinder in lines 3030–33, appealing to the audience on why such salvation should not be permitted. It is probable that the argument between the Good and Bad Angels, which would have begun in the missing passage, was intended to foreshadow the colloquy of the Four Daughters of God which follows at line 3129. This final discussion puts the question on an entirely new level; while the Good Angel here cannot think of a logical reason ("ryth resun," line 3043) why Mankind should not be damned, the arguments of Peace and Mercy which follow transcend mere logic.

3031 That is, out of the Castle of Perseverance.

3063 *But Mercy pase alle thynge*. Bevington notes an allusion here to Psalm 145:9 (Vulgate Psalm 144:9): "God's compassion is over all that he has made" (B, p. 883).

3096–97 The passage is derived from the line "Quia in inferno nulla est redemptio," from the Office of the Dead.

3101–03 The Bad Angel threatens to slice off the Soul's sinful bits once they get to Hell.

3114–18 *Have this . . . have thou that*. The Bad Angel makes a charade of Mankind's former poor decisions, reenacting them with blows. E.g., compare line 2719.

3115   The Bad Angel's accusation repeats the point made in one of the extra-metrical Latin tags (line 503a), that the man who is given to Greed will never say "enough."

3122   The Bad Angel attaches an accounting ("synful tydynge") of Mankind's sins to the Soul's back.

3124   Psalm 114:9, "Placebo Dominum in regione vivorum" ("I will please the Lord in the land of the living") was sung as the first antiphon in the Office of the Dead.

3135   The colloquy of the Four Daughters of God which ends the play is based on the doctrine that, although the conflicting ideals of Justice and Truth (on the one hand) and Peace and Mercy (on the other) lead to differing conclusions concerning man's salvation, these were reconciled by the Crucifixion. The personification of these four abstract qualities derives, at least in part, from Psalm 84:11–12. The function of the four daughters in establishing the theological foundation in late thirteenth-, fourteenth-, and fifteenth-century literature is noteworthy. In the drama, besides *Castle of Perseverance*, see N-Town Play 11: *The Parliament of Heaven*, where the four daughters of God settle the Justice/Mercy question in favor of humankind prior to the Annunciation and Salutation. The idea likewise appears in *Mankind* as Mercy (here depicted as male) frames the aberrant behavior of Mankind when the protagonist calls for mercy at the end and Mercy, who had earlier been mocked off the stage, returns to help him, citing Jesus' sacrifice to convince Justice of Mankind's worthiness despite all his retrogressive ways. Likewise the idea is alluded to in *Everyman* when, as Everyman and his Good Deeds step into the grave, he, like Humanum Genus, calls for mercy. In other literature, the colloquy provides the hopeful solution to Robert Grosseteste's theologically rich *Chateau d'Amour*, and in Langland's *Piers Plowman* (B-text Passus 18 lines 110 ff.), after Christ on the Cross forgives the one thief, darkness descends and Mercy appears out of the west and Truth from the east to debate with Rihtwisness from the north and Peace from the south the meaning of Christ's sacrifice. See also *Gesta Romanorum* 34 about Agios, a Wise Emperoure; *The Allegory of Mercy, Truth, Justice, and Peace*; and also *The Charter Abbey of the Holy Ghost*.

3147   See also lines 3368–69. Doctor Faustus expresses the same regret in Marlowe's play just before he is dragged off to Hell: "See see where Christs blood streames in the firmament, / One drop would save my soule, halfe a drop, ah my Christ!" (A text, scene 13, lines 74–75).

3207   *us three*. Not the four daughters, but those on the one side of the argument, Peace, Mercy, and Christ, whose sacrifice tipped the balance in their favor.

3215   Unlike the final lines of the other stanzas, this line is not placed to the right of the brackets and thus has not been indented.

3252a   *Quoniam veritatem dilexisti*. I have been unable to identify the source. Eccles identifies it as Psalm 1:8 (E, p. 201), but Psalm 1 has only six verses. Bevington cites Psalm 51:6 (B, p. 888), which accords somewhat with the King James Version ("Behold, thou desirest truth in the inward parts: and in the hidden part thou shalt make me to know wisdom"), but not with the Vulgate ("Thou has loved all the words of ruin, O deceitful tongue"). The Wycliffe Bible reads "Thou lovedist alle wordis of casting doun; with a gileful tunge."

3313a   As with line 2985a, it is not clear whether this line is to be spoken or not.

3342   Mercy speaks simultaneously to God the Father and God the Son.

3368–69 See note to line 3147.

3425   The idea of Death as a dance appears frequently in the literature and iconography of the fifteenth and early sixteenth centuries. See Clark, *Dance of Death*.

3437   *us thre*. See note to line 3207. The adherents to the other side of the argument (as Justice sees it): Justice, Truth, and God.

3547a   This prayer is said liturgically for the benefit of souls in Purgatory.

3591   This is a common alliterative tag, though it may well derive from the intrusive quality of the sound of a bell.

3620   A direct reference to the parable of the talents (Matthew 25:14–30), in which the coins (talents) are a metaphor for the good things God gives to man, which he must use to increase the good things in the world.

3697b   This common medieval sentiment is found in a variety of texts, most influentially in the anonymous *Speculum Christiani* (p. 73). The full text reads "Sicut scintilla ignis in medio maris, sic omnis impietas viri ad misericordiam Dei" ("Like a spark of fire in the middle of the sea is all the wickedness of man compared to the mercy of God").

3628   The seven acts of mercy are feeding the hungry, relieving the thirsty, clothing the naked, offering comfort to the imprisoned, offering hospitality to pilgrims (or sheltering the homeless), caring for the sick, and burying the dead. The first six are drawn from Matthew 25:34–40.

3636a   This line from the Athanasian Creed assumes critical importance in Langland's poem *Piers Plowman*, since it constitutes the text of the pardon given to Piers in Passus 7, line 110 (B-text).

3637   The goods of this world are morally neutral, and can come to man through sin (line 3297) or by God's gift.

3649   The manuscripts of surviving plays, especially those with a liturgical connection, frequently conclude with an indication that those present should sing the hymn *Te Deum laudamus*. It is not clear from the *Castle* text whether the hymn was to be sung, or the character of God (who has in the previous four lines stepped out of his role and addressed the audience directly as an actor) would simply speak the text.

 **TEXTUAL NOTES**

ABBREVIATIONS: **E**: Eccles, *Macro Plays*; **H**: Happé, *Four Morality Plays*; **MS**: Folger Manuscript V.a.354 (the Macro Manuscript)

1	*PRIMUS VEXILLATOR*. MS: *Primus Vexil[. . .].*
4	*mankynde*. MS: *man* is smudged.
5	*our lofly*. MS: *our lo* is smudged.
14	*SECUNDUS VEXILLATOR*. MS: *Secundus Vexil[. . .].*
17	*hys last*. MS: *hys l* smudged.
18	*God*. MS: *god ~~good~~*.
	aungelys. So E. MS: *aungel*. H: *aungel[ys]*.
21	*behende*. So E. MS: *be hende*. II: *be-hende/*
27	*PRIMUS VEXILLATOR*. MS: *Primus Vexilla[. . .].*
28	*thre*. So E. MS, H: *iii*.
32	*meynten*. So E. MS: *meyten*. H: *mey[n]ten*.
42	*lofty*. MS, E, H: *lofly*.
43	*Aungellys*. So E. MS: *Aungell*. H: *Aungell[ys]*.
58	*Flesch, iwys*. So E. MS: *flesch ~~pan~~ i wys*. H: *Flesch i-wys*.
64	*stryvyth*. MS, E, H: *strywyth*.
80	*gan*. MS: written above the line but marked for insertion.
92	MS: From this point on to the end of the banns the speech headings (Primus/Secundus Vexillator) are backwards in the manuscript, and have here been reversed.
99	*ful*. So E. MS, H: *foul*.
114	*whanne he may*. So E. MS: *whanne may*. H: *whanne [he] may*.
124	*Ladi*. MS: written above the rest of the line but marked for insertion.
132	*parcellys*. So E. MS: *parcell*. H: *parcell[ys]*.
after 134	MS: a line is written in the bottom margin of the folio but the page is cropped in such a way that it is illegible. It does not appear to be a part of the play.
144	*oure leve*. MS: another word starting with *l* is cancelled before *leve*. H: *oure lyvys*.
159	*prinse*. MS: added above the rest of the line over what appears to be ~~*pride*~~.
184	The emendation is Eccles' (E, p. 8). MS: *Ther is wythe*.
192	*Werld*. MS, E, H: *werd*.
215	*kene knyth*. MS: *kene ~~kyth~~ knyth*.
258	*Bothe*. So E. MS: *bote*. H: *Bot[h]e*.

262   *dryve to*. MS: *dryweto*. E, H: *drywe to*.
270   MS: *If that w[e may]*, added in right margin above line 269.
301   *To*. So E. MS, H: *ii*.
308   *To*. So E. MS: *do*. H: *[To]*.
             devylys. MS, E, H: *dewylys*.
312   *evyl*. MS, E, H: *ewyl*.
346   *Werld*. MS, E, H: *werd*.
355   *Heveneryche*. MS: *heue ryche*. E: *heueryche*. H: *heve-ryche*.
356   *syttyth*. So E, H. MS: *syttyht*.
367   *bale schal*. MS: ~~*schal*~~ *bale schal*.
378   *And fayn*. MS: written in left margin.
379   MS: line 380 is written above this line in the margin but cancelled.
488   *have*. MS: written above the line but marked for insertion.
523   *Foly ruste*. MS: *foly* ~~*truste*~~ *ruste*.
545   *lyve*. MS, E, H: *lywe*.
553   *of lofte*. MS: *of* ~~*last*~~ *lofte*.
568   *Of God*. This emendation was proposed by Furnivall and Pollard. MS, E,
                H: omit.
580   *be*. MS: written above the line but marked for insertion.
625   *robys ryve*. MS: *robys ryve* ~~*wyth rych*~~.
631–38   MS: written in two lines but marked for breaks into eight.
639–46   MS: written in two lines but marked for breaks into eight.
668   *a*. MS: written above the line but marked for insertion.
713   *al hys*. So E, H. MS: *al hys al hys*.
748   MS: a letter is scratched out at the beginning of this line.
785–86   MS: written in one line but marked for break into two.
787–88   MS: written in one line but marked for break into two.
804   *off*. MS, E, H: *of*.
934   *steryste or staryste*. MS: *stertystys or starystys*. The suggested emendation is
                E's. H: *steryst[e] or staryst[e]*.
945   *chyldryn*. So E. MS: *chyrdryn*. H: *chy[l]dryn*.
984   *soure syth*. MS: *sour* ~~*snow t*~~ *syth*.
985   *iwys*. MS, E, H: *wys*.
1016   *Slawth*. MS: *sslawth*.
1020   *systyr*. So E. MS: *sytyr*. H: *sy[s]tyr*.
1045   *growe glad*. MS: a letter is erased between these words.
1068   *no man*. MS: *no* ~~*ma*~~ *man*.
1084–85   MS: written in one line but marked for break into two.
1086–87   MS: written in one line but marked for break into two.
1094   *be ful*. MS: *be* ~~*feld and flod*~~ *ful*.
1109   MS: line 1110 is written but erased before this one.
1114–15   MS: written in one line but marked for break into two.
1116–17   MS: written in one line but marked for break into two.
1124   *knyve*. MS: the *n* is written over a *y*.

1144–45	MS: written in one line but marked for break into two.
1146–47	MS: written in one line but marked for break into two.
1160	MS: this line is not written in the right margin as other tail rhyme lines.
1166	*I ne rekke.* So E. MS: *I rekke.* H: *I [ne] rekke.*
1172	*lyfe.* MS: written above the line but marked for insertion.
1174–75	MS: written in one line but marked for break into two.
1176–77	MS: written in one line but marked for break into two.
1183	*thou.* So E. MS: *thu.* H: *th[o]u.*
1185	*If thou gyf.* MS: *If ȝyf.* H: *If [thou] gyf.* E: *If þou ȝyf.*
1201	*wyl forsake thee day.* MS: *wyl for sake day.* H: *wyl for-sake [the] day.* E: *wyl forsake þe day.*
1204–05	MS: written in one line but marked for break into two.
1206–07	MS: written in one line but marked for break into two.
1208	*bedde bothe.* MS: *bedde ~~browth~~ bothe.*
1234–35	MS: written in one line but marked for break into two.
1236–37	MS: written in one line but marked for break into two.
1238	The manuscript's repetition of the speech heading is likely just a scribal error.
1248	*gray.* MS, E, H: *gay.*
1250	*sevene.* So E. MS, H: *vii.*
1253	*But of othyr.* So E. MS, H: *of othyr.*
1257	*sevene.* So E. MS, H: *vii.*
1286–97	MS: written in six lines but marked for breaks into twelve.
1298	*CONFESCIO.* MS: *Confessio.*
1304	*For all.* MS: *For ~~olde~~, all* is written in the left margin.
1314	*in.* MS: written above the rest of the line but marked for insertion.
1324	*counfort stronge.* MS: *counfort ~~good~~ stronge.*
1337	*CONFESCIO.* MS: *Confessi[. . .].*
1373	*evyl.* MS, E, H: *ewyl.*
1374	*evyl.* MS, E, H: *ewyl.*
1377	*hym prene.* MS: *hym ~~preue~~ prene.*
1404	*syhe.* So E. MS: *shye.* H: *[syhe].*
1422	*my.* So E. H: *[my].* MS: *I.*
1440	*evyl.* MS, E, H: *ewyl.*
1452	*to.* MS: a letter is cancelled before this word.
1460	*But kepe.* MS: *but h kepe.*
1473	*syttyth.* So E. MS: *syttyh.* H: *sytty[t]h.*
1511	*thee the.* MS, E, H: *þe.*
1513	*fyve.* So E. MS, H: *v.*
1537	*sevene.* So E. MS, H: *vii.*
1551	*werldly.* MS, E, H: *werldyly.*
1552	*Goo to yone.* So E. MS: *goo ȝone.* H: *Goo [to] yone.*
1553	*For it is.* So E. MS: *for is.* H: *For [it] is.*
1581	*the.* MS: written above the line.

after 1601	MS: *Detraccio ad caro* is written in a different hand in the bottom margin of this folio. *Malus angelus* is smudged out above it. A leaf is missing after this one.
1606	*alwey Envye*. MS: *alwey ~~eny~~ envye*.
1629	*maydyn Marye*. MS: *maydyn ~~to~~ Marye*.
1631b	*placere*. So E, H. MS: *plcere*.
1635	*grace*. MS: written in the left margin.
1644	*thowtys wyckke*. MS: *þowtys ~~þy~~ wyckke*.
1648	*but thwyte*. MS: *but ~~tw~~ thwyte*.
1658	MS: this line is written in the right margin but marked for insertion.
1669	*your*. MS: written above ~~*my*~~.
1691	*sevene*. So E. MS, H: *vii*.
1705b	*et dicet*. So E. MS *&[. . .]*. H: *et [dicet]*.
1707	*fro foly*. MS: *fro ħ foly*.
1746–49	MS: written in two lines but marked for break into four.
1750–53	MS: written in two lines but marked for break into four.
1767–68	MS: written in one line but marked for break into two.
1791–94	MS: written in two lines but marked for break into four.
1795–98	MS: written in two lines but marked for break into four.
1812–13	MS: written in one line but marked for break into two.
1821	*Why ne had*. So E. MS: *why had*. H: *Why[ne] had*.
1822b	*verberabit*. So E, H. MS: *verberauit*.
1836–39	MS: written in two lines but marked for break into four.
1844	*goode*. MS: written above the line but marked for insertion.
1853–54	MS: written in one line but marked for break into two.
1855	*Lewde*. MS: *lowde*.
1862	*Therfore a*. MS: *therfor ~~thou~~ a*.
1863b	*verberabit*. So E. MS: *verberauit*. H: *verbera[b]it*.
1889	MS: line 1892 is written after this line but is cancelled.
1921	*woful*. MS: *wowful*.
1940	*Whanne*. So E, H. MS: *Wahanne*.
1958	*cache*. MS, E, H: *chache*.
1969	*herawd*. So E. MS, H: *heyward*.
1970	*damyselys*. So E. MS: *damysely*. H: *damysely[s]*.
1981	*kachyn*. MS: two letters are cancelled before this word.
2000	*To men thei*. So E. MS, H: *to men ben*.
2056	*sevene*. So E. MS, H: *vii*.
before 2112	MS: *Ira* is written in a different hand in the top margin of this folio.
2149	*wreke*. MS: written in right margin after ~~*breke*~~.
2163b	*Vae*. MS, E, H: *ve*.
	venit. So E. MS: *ven[. . .]*. H: *ven[it]*.
2164	*not hys*. MS: *not ~~tame~~ hys*.
2177	*synne had he*. MS: *synne [ink blot] he had he*.
2189	*moderys, all three*. MS: *moderys all ~~at onys~~ þre*.

2203	MS: line 2221 is written but cancelled before this line.
2228	*Yerne*. MS: ~~*be*~~ *yerne*.
2240	*wynne*. So E. MS, H: *wyth*.
2255	*vow*. H: *vowe*. MS, E: *wou*.
2284	*Abstynens*. MS: ~~*a*~~*abstynens*.
2291	MS: this line is also written erroneously to the right with a bracket and then cancelled.
2303b	*concupiscentias*. So E, H. MS: *concupiscen[. . .]*.
2320	*hym wyth synful*. So E. MS: *hym synful*. H: *hym[wyth] synful*.
2332	*Thyrti*. So E. MS, H: *xxxᵗⁱ*.
2335	*Thre*. So E. MS, H: *iii*.
2365	*Belyalys*. So E. MS: *Blyalys*. H: *B[e]lyalys*.
2388	*hathe me dayschyd*. So E, H. MS: *hathe dayschyd*.
2420	*The medys*. MS: *the* ~~*md*~~ *medys*.
before 2431	MS: *covetyse* is written in a different hand in the top margin of this folio.
2448	*gynnyst wende*. MS: *gynnyst* ~~*g*~~ *wende*.
2456	*Coveytyse*. So E, H. MS: *Coveyse*.
after 2482	MS: ~~*luxurya*~~ is written in a different hand in the bottom margin of this folio.
2529	*thou be pore*. MS: *thou* ~~*po r*~~ *be*.
2543	*betyde*. MS: two letters are erased before this word.
2562	*not*. MS: written above the rest of the line but marked for insertion.
before 2587	MS: the bottom of an illegible phrase written in a different hand is apparent in the top margin of the folio. The top of the phrase has been cropped, hence the illegibility.
2598	*thre*. So E. MS, H: *iii*.
2610	*sekatour*. MS: the *at* is blotted and hard to read.
2612b	*relinquent*. So E. MS: *relinquam*. H: *relinqu[ent]*.
before 2648	MS: an illegible word appears in the left margin next to this line.
2667	*Where that evere*. MS: *that* squeezed in between the other two words.
2693	*pounde I*. MS: *pounde* ~~*of golde*~~ *I*.
2745	*neybore*. MS, E, H: *neygbore*.
2757	*be*. MS: written above the line but marked for insertion.
2768	*too*. MS, E, H: *to*.
2805	*blastys*. So E. MS: *bastys*. H: *b[l]astys*.
2855	*hath*. MS, E, H: *hat*.
2878	*Werldys*. MS, E, H: *Werldlys*.
2891	*lott*. MS: *tt* is blotted and hard to read.
2892	*whow*. MS: *whou*.
2920	*wounde*. MS: *wou[. . .]*
before 2930	MS: *This ought to be p. 184* is written in a different hand in the top margin of the folio.
2932	*what*. So E. MS: *wha*. H: *wha[t]*.
2965	*thee*. MS: added above the rest of the line.

after 2977   MS: *othyr* is written in a different hand in the bottom margin of this folio.

2979   *as I thout.* MS, E: *as þout.* H: *as thout.*

after 3029   MS: a leaf is missing at this point in the text.

3040   *hathe he servyd.* MS, E, H: *hathe servyd.*

3059   MS: *he aperith þe sowle* is written in a different hand under this line in the right margin.

3060   *too.* MS, E, H: *to.*

after 3076   MS: *holtys* is written in a different hand in the bottom margin of this folio.

3084   *Thou were.* MS: *thou be were.*

3110   *schalt.* MS: there is a cancelled *s* or *f* before this word.

3127–28   MS: written in one line but marked for break into two.

3187   *goode.* So E. MS, H: *goodys.*

3215   MS: this line should be written in the right margin like all of the rest of the tail rhymed lines, but it is not.

3228b   *Patrem.* MS: *prem.*

3229–32   MS: written in two lines but marked for break into four.

3233–36   MS: written in two lines but marked for break into four.

3237–40   MS: written in two lines but marked for break into four.

3241–44   MS: written in two lines but marked for break into four.

3245–48   MS: written in two lines but marked for break into four.

3285   *ad infernum.* MS: *ad supernum infernum.*

3344   *thyrti.* So E. MS, H: *xxx^{ti}.*

3345   *to-schent.* MS: *schent* is written above *rent.*

3383   *fro.* So E. MS: *ffre.* H: *fre.*

3385   *to be.* MS: *to þe be.*

3389   *And to.* MS: *and do to.*

3404   *Qui.* MS, E, H: *quia.*
              Domini. So E. MS: *deum.* H: *[Domini].*

3408   *space.* MS: written above *grace.*

3411   *Flesch.* MS: *flsch.*

3421   *comberaunce.* MS: written to the right of *governaunce.*

3422   *putte ful.* MS: *putte a wey ful.*

3430   MS: a letter is erased at the beginning of this line.

3440   *dwellys.* So E. MS: *dwell.* H: *dwell[ys].*

3467   *endynge.* So E. MS, H: *begynnynge.*

3495   *cacche.* So E, H. MS: *chache.*

3497   *Ten.* So E. MS, H: *x.*

3541   MS: this line is written in the right margin after a cancelled line 3537.

3542   *all be.* MS, E, H: *be all.*

3547a   *quietas.* So E. MS, H: *quie[. . .].*
              mansiones. So E. MS, H: *mansione[. . .].*

3574–81   MS: written in four lines but marked for break into eight.

3582–85   MS: written in two lines but marked for break into four.

3586–89   MS: written in two lines but marked for break into four.

3590–93	MS: written in two lines but marked for break into four.
3594–97	MS: written in two lines but marked for break into four.
3597c	*scintilla*. MS: *sintill*. E: *sintilla*. H: *sintill[a]*.
3628	*sevene*. So E. MS, H: *vii*.
3638	*schal be heynyd*. So E. MS: *schal heynyd*. H: *shal [be] heynyd*.

BIBLIOGRAPHY

Anderson, Mary Désirée. *Drama and Imagery in English Medieval Churches*. Cambridge: Cambridge University Press, 1963.

Bawcutt, Priscilla. "A Note on the Term 'Morality.'" *Medieval English Theatre* 28 (2006), 171–74.

Belsey, Catherine. "The Stage Plan of *The Castle of Perseverance*." *Theatre Notebook* 28.3 (1974), 124–32.

Bennett, Jacob. "A Linguistic Study of *The Castle of Perseverance*." Unpublished dissertation, Boston University, 1960.

———. "The *Castle of Perseverance*: Redactions, Place, and Date." *Mediaeval Studies* 24 (1962), 141–52.

Bevington, David, ed. *The Macro Plays: A Facsimile Edition with Facing Transcription*. New York: Johnson Reprint, 1972.

———. *Medieval Drama*. Boston: Houghton Mifflin Company, 1975.

———. "'Man Thinke on Thine Endinge Day': Stage Pictures of Just Judgment in *The Castle of Perseverance*." In *Homo, Memento Finis: The Iconography of Just Judgment in Medieval Art and Drama*. Ed. David Bevington. Kalamazoo, MI: Medieval Institute Publications, 1985. Pp. 147–77.

Biggins, D. "Chaucer's Summoner: 'Wel Loved He Garleek, Onyons, and eek Lekes,' C.T. I, 634." *Notes and Queries* n.s. 11 (1964), 48.

Block, Edward A. "Chaucer's Millers and Their Bagpipes." *Speculum* 29 (1954), 239–43.

Bloomfield, Morton W. *The Seven Deadly Sins: An Introduction to the History of a Religious Concept, with Special Reference to Medieval English Literature*. East Lansing: Michigan State University Press, 1952.

Braswell, Mary Flowers, ed. *Sir Perceval of Galles and Ywain and Gawain*. Kalamazoo, MI: Medieval Institute Publications, 1995.

Butterworth, Philip. "Gunnepowdyr, Fyre and Thondyr." *Medieval English Theatre* 7.2 (1985), 68–76.

———. *Theatre of Fire: Special Effects in Early English and Scottish Theatre*. London: Society for Theatre Research, 1998.

The Castle of Perseverance: Full-length Version (1979 production by Poculi Ludique Societas and the Graduate Centre for Study of Drama, directed by David Parry). University of Toronto Medieval Videotape Collection, 1980 (4 hrs. 15 min.).

———: *A Perspective* (1979 production by Poculi Ludique Societas and the Graduate Centre for Study of Drama, directed by David Parry). University of Toronto Medieval Videotape Collection, 1982 (55 min.).

Cauthen, I. B., Jr. "'The Foule Flibbertigibbet,' *King Lear*, III.iv.133; IV.i.60." *Notes and Queries* 203 (1958), 98–99.

Chase, W. J. *The Distichs of Cato*. Madison: University of Wisconsin Press, 1922.

Clark, James Midgley. *The Dance of Death in the Middle Ages and the Renaissance*. Glasgow: Jackson, 1950.

Cornelius, R. *The Figurative Castle: A Study in the Mediaeval Allegory of the Edifice with Especial Reference to Religious Writings*. Bryn Mawr, PA: Bryn Mawr College, 1930.

The Coventry Corpus Christi Plays. Ed. Pamela King and Clifford Davidson. Kalamazoo, MI: Medieval Institute Publications, 2000.

Craik, T. W. *The Tudor Interlude*. Leicester: Leicester University Press, 1958.

Davenport, W. A. *Fifteenth-Century English Drama: The Early Moral Plays and Their Literary Relations*. Cambridge: D. S. Brewer, 1982.

Davidson, Clifford. *Visualizing the Moral Life: Medieval Iconography and the Macro Morality Plays*. New York: AMS Press, 1989.

Dean, James M., ed. *Medieval English Political Writings*. Kalamazoo, MI: Medieval Institute Publications, 1996.

Deschamps, Eustache. *Oeuvres Complètes*. Paris: Firmin Didot, 1887.

Eccles, Mark, ed. *The Macro Plays*. EETS o.s. 262. London: Oxford University Press, 1969.

Elliott, John MacKay. "An Historical Study and Reconstruction of the Fifteenth-Century Play *The Castle of Perseverance*." Unpublished dissertation, City University of New York, 1977.

Fifield, Merle. "The Arena Theatres in Vienna Codices 2535 and 2536." *Comparative Drama* 2.4 (1968–69), 259–82.

Furnivall, F. J., and A. W. Pollard, eds. *The Macro Plays*. EETS e.s. 91. London: Oxford University Press, 1904.

Gower, John. *Vox Clamantis*. In *The Complete Works of John Gower*. Ed. G. C. Macaulay. Vol. 4. Oxford: Clarendon Press, 1902. Pp. 3–313.

Happé, Peter, ed. *Four Morality Plays*. Harmondsworth: Penguin Books, 1979.

Happé, Peter, and Wim Hüsken, eds. *Interludes and Early Modern Society: Studies in Gender, Power and Theatricality*. Ludus ix. Amsterdam: Rodopi, 2007.

Hildahl, Frances E. "Penitence and Parody in *The Castle of Perseverance*." In *Early Drama to 1600*. Ed. Albert H. Tricomi. Binghamton: State University of New York Press, 1987. Pp. 129–41.

Holbrook, S. E. "Covetousness, Contrition, and the Town in the *Castle of Perseverance*." *Fifteenth-Century Studies* 13 (1988), 275–89.

Isbell, Harold, trans. *The Last Poets of Imperial Rome*. Harmondsworth: Penguin Books, 1972.

Johnston, Alexandra F. "Parish Playmaking before the Reformation." In *The Parish in Late Medieval England*. Ed. Cliver Burgess and Eamon Duffy. Donington: Tyas and Watkins, 2006. Pp. 325–41.

Kaiser, Walter J. *Praisers of Folly: Erasmus, Rabelais, Shakespeare*. Cambridge, MA: Harvard University Press, 1963.

Kaske, Robert. "The Summoner's Garleek, Oynons, and Eek Lekes." *Modern Language Notes* 74 (1959), 481–84.

Kelley, Michael R. *Flamboyant Drama: A Study of The Castle of Perseverance, Mankind, and Wisdom*. Carbondale: Southern Illinois University Press, 1979.

King, Pamela. "Morality Plays." In *The Cambridge Companion to Medieval English Theatre*. Ed. Richard Beadle. Cambridge: Cambridge University Press, 1994. Pp. 240–64.

Knight, W. Nicholas. "Equity and Mercy in English Law and Drama (1405–1641)." *Comparative Drama* 6.1 (1972), 51–67.

Langland, William. *Piers Plowman: A Parallel-Text Edition of the A, B, C and Z Versions*. Ed. A. V. C. Schmidt. Vol. I. London: Longman, 1995.

Lydgate, John. *The Minor Poems of John Lydgate*. Ed. Henry Noble MacCracken. 2 vols. EETS e.s. 107 and o.s. 192. Oxford: Oxford University Press, 1911 and 1934.

Mankind. In Eccles, *The Macro Plays*. Pp. 153–84.

Marlowe, Christopher. *Doctor Faustus*. In *The Complete Works of Christopher Marlowe*. Vol. 2. Ed. Roma Gill. Oxford: Clarendon Press, 1990.

McCutchan, J. Wilson. "Covetousness in *The Castle of Perseverance*." *University of Virginia Studies* 4 (1951), 175–91.

Mills, David. "Diagrams for Staging Plays, Early or Middle 15th Century." In *Local Maps and Plans from Medieval England*. Ed. R. A. Skelton and P. D. A. Harvey. Oxford: Clarendon Press, 1986. Pp. 344–45.

The N-Town Plays. Ed. Stephen Spector. EETS s.s. 11 and 12. Oxford: Oxford University Press, 1991.
———. Ed. Douglas Sugano. Kalamazoo, MI: Medieval Institute Publications, 2007.

Owst, G. R. *Preaching in Medieval England*. Cambridge: Cambridge University Press, 1926.
———. *Literature and Pulpit in Medieval England*. Cambridge: Cambridge University Press, 1933.

Patch, H. R. *The Goddess Fortuna in Medieval Literature*. Cambridge, MA: Harvard University Press, 1927.

Parry, David. "*The Castle of Perseverance*: A Critical Edition." Unpublished dissertation, University of Toronto, 1983.

———. "A Margin of Error: The Problems of Marginalia in *The Castle of Perseverance*." In *Editing Early English Drama: Special Problems and New Directions*. Ed. A. F. Johnston. New York: AMS Press, 1987. Pp. 33–64.

Patrologia Latina. Ed. J. P. Migne. Paris: Excudebat Migne, 1844–65.

Pederson, Steven I. "The Staging of *The Castle of Perseverance*: A Re-analysis." *Theatre Notebook* 39.2 (1985), 51–62.

———. "The Staging of *The Castle of Perseverance*: Testing the List Theory." *Theatre Notebook* 39.3 (1985), 104–13.

Pride of Life. In David N. Klausner, ed. *Two Moral Interludes: The Pride of Life and Wisdom*. Kalamazoo, MI: Medieval Institute Publications, 2009. Pp. 9–24.

Proudfoot, Richard. "The Virtue of Perseverance." In *Aspects of Early English Drama*. Ed. Paula Neuss. Cambridge: D. S. Brewer, 1983. Pp. 92–110.

Ralston, Michael E. "The Four Daughters of God in *The Castle of Perseverance*." *Comitatus* 15 (1984), 35–44.

Riggio, Milla Cozart. "The Allegory of Feudal Acquisition in *The Castle of Perseverance*." In *Allegory, Myth, and Symbol*. Ed. Morton W. Bloomfield. Cambridge, MA: Harvard University Press, 1981. Pp. 187–208.

Robertson, D. W., Jr. *Preface to Chaucer*. Princeton, NJ: Princeton University Press, 1963.

Schell, Edgar T. "On the Imitation of Life's Pilgrimage in *The Castle of Perseverance*." *Journal of English and Germanic Philology* 67 (1968), 235–48.

Schell, Edgar T., and J. D. Schuchter, eds. *English Morality Plays and Moral Interludes*. New York: Holt, Rinehart and Winston, 1969.

Schmitt, Natalie Crohn. "Was There a Medieval Theatre in the Round?" *Theatre Notebook* 23.4 (1969), 130–42; 24.1 (1969), 18–25. Both parts reprinted in *Medieval English Drama: Essays Critical and Contextual*. Ed. J. Taylor and Alan Nelson. Chicago: University of Chicago Press, 1972. Pp. 295–315.

Scott, Kathleen L. "Sow-and-Bagpipe Imagery in the Miller's Portrait." *Review of English Studies* 18 (1967), 287–90.

Skelton, John. *The Complete English Poems*. Ed. John Scattergood. New Haven, CT: Yale University Press, 1983.

Smart, Walter K. "The *Castle of Perseverance*: Place, Date, and a Source." *Manly Anniversary Studies in Language and Literature* (1923), 42–53.

Southern, Richard. *The Medieval Theatre in the Round: A Study of the Staging of The Castle of Perseverance and Related Matters*. London: Faber and Faber, 1958.

Speculum Christiani: A Middle English Religious Treatise of the 14th Century. Ed. Gustof Holmstedt. EETS o.s. 182. London: Oxford University Press, 1933.

Tilley, Morris Palmer. *A Dictionary of the Proverbs in England in the Sixteenth and Seventeenth Centuries*. Ann Arbor: University of Michigan Press, 1950.

The Towneley Plays. Ed. Martin Stevens and A. C. Cawley. EETS s.s. 13–14. Oxford: Oxford University Press, 1994.

Traver, Hope. *The Four Daughters of God: A Study of the Versions of This Allegory, with Special Reference to Those in Latin, French, and English*. Philadelphia: J. C. Winston, 1907.

Tydeman, William. *English Medieval Theatre 1400–1500*. London: Routledge and Kegan Paul, 1986. [See especially chapter 3.]

Umphrey, P. J. "*The Castle of Perseverance*, line 695." *Philological Quarterly* 59.1 (1980), 105–07.

Wenzel, Siegfried. "The Three Enemies of Man." *Mediaeval Studies* 29 (1967), 47–66.

Wertz, Dorothy C. "The Theology of Nominalism in the English Morality Plays." *Harvard Theological Review* 62.3 (1969), 371–74.

Westrem, Scott D. *The Hereford Map*. Turnhout: Brepols, 2001.

Whiting, Bartlett Jere, with the collaboration of Helen Wescott Whiting. *Proverbs, Sentences, and Proverbial Phrases: From English Writings Mainly before 1500*. Cambridge, MA: Belknap Press, 1968.

Willis, James. "Stage Directions in *The Castell of Perseverance*." *Modern Language Review* 51 (1956), 404–05.

Withington, Robert. "*The Castle of Perseverance*, line 695." *Philological Quarterly* 14 (1935), 270.

Wood, Chauncey. "Sources of Chaucer's Summoner's 'Garleek, Oyunons, and eek Lekes.'" *Chaucer Review* 5 (1971), 240–44.

🌿 GLOSSARY

abak *back*

abate *cease, stop*

abavyd *amazed, astonished*

abeye, abye, abyn *pay a penalty, suffer
   (for)*

abotyn *about, concerning*

abyde, abydyn *abide, stay*

acompt *account, reckoning*

acord, acorde *agreement*

acordyd *agreed*

adoun, adown, adowne *down*

adred *afraid, terrified*

aforn *before*

afrayed *tormented, harassed*

agryse *be very afraid, shudder with fear*

akale *cold*

aknowe *acknowledge, confess*

almyth, almythy *almighty*

amende, amendyd *change, correct*

anhangyn *hang, be hanged*

anoyed *offended*

a-party *somewhat*

aqueyntawns *familiarity, acquaintance*

aquite *release, acquit*

aray *display, clothing; order; behavior;*
   in aray *in a warlike fashion*

arayed *dressed*

areste *seize, arrest*

aryth *properly, rightly*

asay, asayed *try, test*

asayle, asayleth *attack, assail*

asent *agree*

aslake *diminish, make less*

asoly, asoyle *absolve*

astate *estate, condition, age*

astore *restore*

asynyd *assigned*

asyse *fashion, measure*

atenyde *troubled, saddened*

atwynne *apart, in two*

avale *bring down, defeat*

avaunce, avauncyd *help, assist*

avaunt *boast*

avayle *benefit, aid*

avyse (n.) *advice, orders;* (v.) *consider,
   counsel*

awreke *carry out*

ay *always, ever*

bace *low*

bacheler, bacheleris, bacheleyrs
   young knight, young man

baggys *bags, moneybags; bagpipes*

bakbyte, bakbytynge *slander*

bake *back*

bakyn *bake*

bale, bayle, balys *pain, suffering,
   torment*

ballokys *testicles*

ballyd *bare, bald*

bane, banys *summons, proclamation;
   ruin*

banyour *banner*

barryd *enclosed*

basnetys *helmets*

baston *rod, staff*

bate *strife, conflict*

bede, bedys *beads, rosary*

bede, bedyth (v.) *offer, present*

bedene *immediately; all together*

begrete *regret, grieve for*

begylyd *deceived*

behestys *promises*

behete, behott, behyth, behetyn
　　promise
behove *duty*
beleve, byleve *belief*
beloke *locked up*
belys *bellies*
belyve, blyfe, blyve *quickly*
bemys *trumpets*
bende (n.) *bondage*; (v.) *bow, stoop; obey*
benome *numbed*
berd, berdys *lady*
bere, beryst, beryth *carry, wear,*
　　support; give birth
beryed *buried*
besauntys, besawntys *besants, gold*
　　coins
betauth *taught; revealed*
beteche *teach, reveal*
betydde, betyde *happened, occurred;*
　　current
betyme *early;* **al betyme** *in good time*
bey, beye *buy, redeem; suffer for*
blad *sword, blade*
blase *shine*
ble *complexion, condition*
blendyd, blent *blinded*
bleryn *blear, blind*
bleyke, bleykyn *make pale, turn pale*
blo, bloo *dark; blowing*
blodyr *blubber*
blynne *refrain from, cease*
blythe *happy, joyful*
bobaunce *vanity, pomp*
bobbyd *mocked*
bolne, bolnyd, bolnynge, bolnynnge
　　swell, swollen
bon, bonys *bone*
bone *boon, request*
bord, bordys *table*
bote *remedy, help*
bothyn *both*
boun *ready*
bouth *bought*
bowde *dung beetle, malt worm*
bowe, bowyn *submit, obey; stoop*
bowre, bowrys *bower, chamber, inner*
　　room

boystous, boystously *violent, fierce;*
　　fiercely
bred *roasted*
brede (n.) *breadth*; (v.) *make, cause*
brenne, brennynge, brent *burn,*
　　burning, burnt
brere *briar*
brest, brestyn, brestyth *burst, break*
brethel *rascal*
brew, brewe, brewyn, brewyth,
　　browyn *brew, prepare, make;*
　　brewed
breyd *lift, raise*
breyde, bredynge *breed; breeding,*
　　procreation
broche *pierce*
brod, brode *broad, wide*
brodde *banner*
brothel, brothelys *lecher*
brout, brouth, broutyst *brought*
browe *brow; expression*
brustun-gutte *greedy-guts*
bryth *bright*
bryther *brighter*
bultyn *fornicate*
buske, buskyn, buskyth *hurry;*
　　prepare
buskys *bushes*
byd, bydde, byddynge *command*
byde, bydith *remain, continue*
byggyngys *buildings*
byll, bylle *dwell;* **thi bourys byll** *make*
　　your home
bynne *stall, enclosure*
bysytyth *attacks*

cacche, cache, cachen, cachyn *drive*
cage *prison*
careful, carful *causing sorrow,*
　　harmful; miserable
carpe, carpyd, carpynge *complain, cry*
　　out; complaining
cas, case *subject, matter, theme*
cast, caste, casten, castyn *throw, put;*
　　prepare
cauth, cawth *caught*
caysere *emperor*

caytyf(e), caytyfys, caytyvys *villain, wretch*

certis, certys *certainly*

chace, chase, chasyn *follow; drive, drive out*

chafe *rage, be annoyed*

champe *gnash one's teeth*

chaunce, chauns *luck, situation*

cheke *choke*

chere *behavior*

cherlys *churls, villains*

ches *strife*

chese *choose*

chesun *reason, cause*

cheve *prosper, attain*

chocke *thrust*

chyde, chydynge *complain, complaining*

clappe *stroke*

clappyd *thrust*

claryouns *trumpets*

clateryd *shattered*

clatyr *clatter, rattle*

clay, cley *earth, dirt*

clene *clean, pure, virtuous*

clenner *more pure*

clennesse *virtue, purity*

clere *pure, bright; splendidly*

cleve, clevyn *split*

clokys *cloaks*

clonge *enclosed, buried*

clos *prison, enclosure*

closyd *enclosed, buried*

clott *clod, lump of earth*

clourys, clowrys *sod, earth*

clowte, clowtys *rag*

cloyed *burdened, encumbered*

clyfte *gash*

clynge *waste away*

clyvyn *split, cleave*

colys *coals*

comberaunce *temptation*

comne *come*

comowns *common people*

copbord *container, cupboard, chest*

cope *cope, outer ecclesiastical vestment*

cors *person*

cost *coast, region; habit, manner*

cosyn *relative*

coure *cower*

cowche *crouch, hide*

crachen, crake *crack*

crakows *shoes with pointed toes*

crase *shatter*

crofte *enclosure*

croysyd *crucified*

crulle *crawl*

crysme either *chrism, consecrated oil* or *chrisom, cloth used to cover an infant's head at baptism*

cukke *shit*

cure *care; grief*

cursyn *curse, excommunicate*

cust, cyste *kissed*

dagge *jog*

daggys *pieces, shreds*

dale, dayl, dayle, delle, dalys *valley*

dalyaunce *conversation*

dapyrly *gracefully*

dasche, dayschyd *strike, shatter*

dawe *put to death*

dawnt *tame*

dees, des, desse *dais, platform*

defaute *poverty*

defens, deffens *defense, protection; remedy*

degre, degres *quality, condition*

del, dele *grief, woe*

dele *be concerned; give away; arrange*

delfe, delve, delvyn *pierce, dig*

deme, dempte *judge, condemn; damned*

dene *den*

denne, dennys *valley*

dent *stroke*

denteth *dainty, delicious*

derne *hidden, secluded; stealthy*

derworthly *dearly*

deserviture *deserving; desert*

deseytys *deceits*

deth-drawth *death stroke*

dever, devere *duty*

dew *due, deserved*

dewnesse *rights*

dol, dole *see* **del**

dolven *see* **delfe**

dom, dome *judgment, decision*

domysday *Judgment Day*

don *do; cause*

dote *be or appear witless, silly*

doute, dowt, dowte, dowtys *doubt; danger; fear*

downys *hills*

dowty, dowtyest *brave, worthy, noble; bravest*

draf *filth*

drawe, drawth, drawyn, drawyth *come, go, bring, lead*

drenche, drenchyd *drown*

drenkelyd *drowned*

drepe, drepyn *strike*

drery *dreadful, terrible*

dresse, dressyd (n.) *severity*; (v.) *prepare, arrange*

dreve, drevyn, dryve, dryven, dryvynge, dryvyth drywe *drive, hasten, force to go*

drosse *worthless matter, dirt*

drulle *stagger (?)*

dryfte *force*

duke, dukys *duke, lord, powerful man*

dures *force*

durke *lurk, lie in wait*

dygne, dynge, dyngne *worthy, noble*

dynt, dyntys *see* **dent**

dyr *excrement*

dyrke, dyrknes *black, dark; darkness*

dys *dice*

dyscrye *see, perceive*

dyspyt, dyspyte, dyspyth *malice, hatred, injury*

dystaunce, dystaunsce *conflict, discord, opposition*

dyth *put, place, prepare, perform*

elde *age, old age*

ell, ellys *else*

elmesdede *almsdeeds, charity*

empryse, enprise *power, will, desire*

endewyd *endowed*

endytynge *accusation, accusing*

enforme *inform, explain*

enjoynyd *offered, given*

ensense *consume, arouse*

entayle *settlement of inheritance*

entende *pay attention*

entent *attention, will, purpose*

entysynge *enticing*

erdyn *petition, errand*

erys *heirs*

erytage *heritage, bequest*

eryth *inherit*

ese *comfort, ease*

everychon, everychone *each, everyone*

evyn *exactly, completely*

eysyl *vinegar*

fadde *see* **fede**

fadyn, fadyth *disappear, decline, fade*

faget *bundle of sticks, torch*

fane *banner*

fare, faryst, faryth *come, go, thrive, prosper*

faunt *infant, child*

faute, fawte *fault, defect, default*

fawe *joyful, glad, content*

fay *faith, belief*

fayn *gladly, eagerly*

faytour, faytourys *deceiver*

fede *feed*

feffe, feffen, feffyn, feffyst *endow, give legal possession*

fele *many*

fell, felle, fellyd (v.) *strike down*; (adj.) *fierce*; (adv.) *fiercely*

feller *craftier*

fen, fenne *fen, marsh*

fend, fende, fendys *devil*

fende, fendyd *defend*

ferd, ferdyst *see* **fare**

fere *frighten*

fere, feres *companion*

ferne *distant*

fese *incite, arouse*

fesyl *fart*

feterel *deceiver*

fette *get, cause to come*

flappyn *beat*

flappys *blows*
flapyr *flutter*
flene *flay*
flet *run*
flete *float*
fleterynge *flitting about*
florchyd *adorned, decorated*
florchynge *flourishing*
fo, fon, fone *foe, enemy*
fodyr, fothyr *company*
folde *earth; enclosure*
fond *fail; sink to the ground*
fonde (n.) *fool;* (v.) *tempt; seek; go*
forbete *severely beaten*
forbled *very bloody*
forbrostyn *broken into pieces*
forme-faderys *ancestors, forefathers*
fors *care, regard*
forschent *shamed*
forsothe *truly*
forthi, forthy *therefore*
forthynkyth *repent, cause to repent*
frawt, frawth *equipped, provided*
frayed *bruised*
freelté *frailty*
frele *frail*
frely *nobly, generously*
frere *friar*
fresch, fresche, freschly *bright, brightly dressed; vigorously*
frete, frettyd *gnaw*
freyne *ask, request*
froskys *frogs*
fryke *joyful*
funte-ston *baptismal font*
fyteth, fytyth, fytyn *fight*
fyth *fight*

gadlynge, gadlyngys, gadelyngys, gedelynge *rascals*
gadyr, gadryd *gather, bring together*
gafe *see* **geve**
gale *song, speech*
gamyn *entertainment, sport*
gan, ganne, gannyst *see* **gynne**
gane *overcome*
gard *care*

gast, gastyd *frighten*
gastful *dreadful*
gere, gerys (n.) *equipment, weapons, armor;* (v.) *equip*
gerlys *young women*
geve, gyf, gevyth, gafe, gove, govyn, gyve *give*
geyn-went *return route*
gle *joy, mirth*
glede *live coal, fire*
gobet *morsel*
gonge *privy*
gore *gown; filthy person*
gost, goste *spirit, soul, devil*
gostly (adj.) *spiritual;* (adv.) *devoutly*
gove, govyn *see* **geve**
gramercy *thanks*
grave, gravyn *buried*
graythyd *dressed*
grede, gredyn *shout, call out*
grenne *gnash one's teeth*
gres, grese *grass*
gretynge *weeping*
grevaunce, grevaunse *harm, injury*
greve, grevys *harm*
grocchyn, grochynge, grucche, grucchyn *complain, complaint*
grom, grome *man, person*
grope *grasp*
gryffys *groves*
grylle *fierce*
grym *strife, conflict, agitation*
grype *grasp*
gryse *shudder*
grysly, gryslych *frightful, pitiable*
gun, gunne *see* **gynne**
gyle *deceit*
gylt *guilt*
gylyd *beguiled*
gynne *skill, cunning*
gynne, gynnyst, gynnyth, gunne *begin*
gyrt *dressed*
gyse *custom, use, habit*

hakle *feathers*
hale *hall, mansion*

hals *neck*
han *have*
hap, happe, happys *fortune, success*
harlot, harlotys *evil person*
haryed *harrowed, carried off*
haunte, hauntyth *frequent, keep
     company with*
hawe *hawthorn berry, trifle*
hedyr *hither, to this place*
hele (n.) *health, well being*; (v.) *hide*
helve *handle*
hem *him, himself*
hende *pleasant, gracious*
hendly *graciously*
henge *hang*
hent *taken*
herawd *herald*
herne *corner, nook*
herys *heirs*
hest, heste, hestys *command*
het *promise*
hete *heat*
hethe, hothe *heath, uncultivated land*
hevenerych *heavenly kingdom*
hey, hy, hye, hyye (v.) *hasten*; (adj.)
     high, loud
heynyd *exalted*
hoke, hokys *hook*
holt, holte, holtys *woods, forest*
hore *fornicator*
hore, hory *gray, gray-haired*
hothe *see* **hethe**
houte, howte, howtys, howtyth *shout*
howle *owl*
husbondry *good management*
hydows *hideous*
hyen *exalt*
hyr, hyre *her*
hyth *height*

iche *each*
ichon *each one*
ifounde *found*
iknowe *known, familiar*
ilent *loaned*
ilke *same*
iment *intended*

inow(e) *enough*
ipyth *adorned, decorated*
irchoun *urchin, small child*
irent *torn off, ripped*
irke *grow weary*
ispendyd *spent*
iwys *certainly, truly*

jagge *slash clothing for decoration*
jebet *gibbet, gallows*
jent *elegant, beautiful*
jentyl, jentyll *noble, generous*
jeste *game, entertainment*
jette, jettys (n.) *fashion*; (v.) *strut*
jous *juice*

kachyn *see* **cacche**
kacke *shit*
kakelynge *chattering*
kampyoun *warrior, champion*
karke *injury*
karpyn, karpynge *see* **carpe**
karys *cares*
kawt *caught*
kayser, kayserys *emperor*
kelyn *cool, assuage*
kempys *warriors*
kende, kendys, kynde *manner,
     disposition; family, race*
kendly *naturally*
kene *bold, fierce, might*
kenne *recognize*
kettys *carrion*
kevere *recover*
kewe *mew*
kloye *see* **cloyed**
knappe *blow*
knet, knytte *bind*
knyt, knyth, knytys *knights*
koure *cower*
krake *loud noise*
kyd *famous, renowned*
kylt *killed*
kyn, kynne *relatives, family*
kynnys *kinds*; **al kynnys** *of every kind*;
     no kynnys thynge *nothing*
kynse *wince, shy* (?)

kyrke *church*
kyth, kythe (n.) *close friends*; (v.) *show*
kytte *cut*

lacche, lacchyd, lache, lawth *strike; catch; take; raise*
lace *entwine*
lak *poverty*
lake *pit, grave; fine linen*
lante *see* **lende**
lappe *wrap*
lasche *beat*
lathe *path*
lawnde *glade, grove*
lay *fallow, untilled*
laykys *games, pleasures*
leche *physician*
ledron, ledrouns, lederounnys *rascal*
leene *incline, listen*
lef, lefe, leve *dear*
lege *liege*
lely *truly*
lelys *lilies, maidens*
lemman *lover, mistress*
lende, lene, lent (v.) *lend; pay attention; consent*
lende, lent (v.) *remain, settle*
lende, londys (n.) *loins*; **undyr londys** *stored up*
lenthe *length*
lere, leryth *teach, punish*
lerne *learn*
lernyd *taught*
les *control; falsehood*
lese, lorn *lose*
lesyngys *lies*
let, lete *think, consider; permit; refrain, hinder*
lette, lettyn *refrain, hinder*
lettynge *preventing, obstructing*
leve, lave, lawe, levyn, lyvyn *believe; live, dwell; leave, abandon*
levene *lightning*
lever, levere *prefer, rather*
lewde *uneducated*
leyke, leykyn *play*
lodeyn *rascal*

lofly *beautiful, noble, pleasing, full of love*
loggyth *lodges*
logyd *caused to lie down*
lopys *leaps*
lordeyn, lordeynys *rascal*
lordlyche, lordlyke *lordly, like a lord*
lore *teaching, lesson*
losel, loselys *rascal*
losengerys *flatterer*
loth *reluctant, hateful*
lothly, lotly *horrible*
lout, loute *bow*
lowe (n.) *flame*; (adj.) *low, humble*
lulle, lullyn *put to sleep*
lurkynge *secret*
lust, luste, lustys *pleasure*
lusti *cheerful*
lust-lykyng *pleasure*
lustyly *pleasantly*
ly *stay, remain*
lyche *equal*
lyckely *likely; handsome*
lyckynge, lykyng, lykynge, lykyngys *pleasure, enjoyment*
lynde *linden tree*
lyst *listen; desire*
lyt *little*
lyted, lytyd *descended, alighted*
lyter *brighter*
lyth *light*
lythyr *rascal*
lytly *carelessly*

mad, madde *insane*
malaundyr *see explanatory note for line 2212*
mamerynge *muttering*
marre *destroy, hamper*
maskeryd *confused, bewildered*
masyd *confused*
mat *mate, companion*
mawe *stomach*
mayne *power*
maystry, maystrye *control, dominion*
mede, medys *reward, bribe, recompense*
medelyth *mixes, mingles*

mekyl, mykyl *large, great, much*

mel, mele *meal*

mell, melle *associate*

mend, mende, ment, mendyn, meyndys (n.) *mind, thought; remedy;* (v.) *correct, change*

mendement *reformation, change*

mene (n.) *middle part in music;* (v.) *mean, intend*

menge, mengyth *mix, blend*

menschepe *honor*

mentelys *mantles, cloaks*

merre *see* **marre**

mes-crede *the Creed*

meselynge *diseased, causing disease*

meve, mevyn *move, stir, control*

meynye *followers, retinue, disciples*

mo, moo *more*

mod *mind, anger*

mody *sorrowful*

modyr, modyrs, moderys *mother; wench, bitch*

mold, molde *earth*

mone, monys *lament, moan*

mossel *morsel, small piece*

mote (n.) *speck of dust;* (v.) *must, be obliged to*

motyhole *filthy cunt*

mow, mowe, moun, mown *be able to*

mowle (n.) *ground;* (v.) *whimper*

mucke *wealth*

mustyr *gather, call together*

myche *much*

mydylerd *earth*

mysbede *mistreat*

myschanse, myschaunce, myschaunsse *ill fortune, disaster*

mysdyspent *spent evilly*

mysgotyn *ill-gotten*

myskaryed *led astray*

mysse, myssyd *fail*

myth, mythis, mytys, mytyst *might, power*

ne, nen, nyn *or, nor; neither . . . nor*

nether *lower*

nevene *mention*

ney *approach*

nolde *would not wish*

norche, norysch, norchyst *feed*

nors *nurse*

not *not know*

note (n.) *profit;* (v.) *use*

nout, nouth, nowt, nowth *nothing*

ny, nye *near, close*

nyfte *nephew*

nyth *night*

odyr *others*

offent *break; offend against*

onethys *scarcely*

ony *any*

onys *once*

opresse *overcome*

ordeyn, ordeynyd *appoint, provide, decree*

ore *grace*

orisoun, orysoun *prayer*

os *as*

ost *host, multitude*

othyrwhyle *sometimes*

outewronge *overflow*

ovyrblyve *excessively*

ovyrgoo *overcome*

ovyrlad, ovyrled, ovyrlede, ovyrledde *oppress, overpower*

ovyrlate *too late*

ovyrlyt *too little*

ovyrmekyl *too much, excessive*

ovyrthynke *bother, upset*

owhere *anywhere*

pace, pase, past, pasyt *depart, end*

page *servant*

pall, palle *cloak, gown, rich robe*

parage *allegiance, partnership*

paramoure, paramourys *mistress, lover*

parcellys *parts, roles*

pardé *certainly*

parlasent *willingly*

pate *head*

pelourys *despoilers*

pende *limit*

penne *plume, feather*

penon *banner*
pere *equal, peer*
pertly *quickly*
peyne, peynyns, peynnys, pyne, pyned, pynynge, pynyd *pain, grief, torment*
peyryth *injures*
plyth *pledge*
podys *toads*
pokys *bags*; **pyssynge pokys** *private parts*
pomp *vain display, vanity*
pose *shove*
prefe, preve *demonstrate, prove*
prekyd *adorned with*
prene (n.) *spike*; (v.) *pierce*
pres *pressure, critical situation*
presse *thrust*
prevé, prevy *secret*
processe *legal mandate*
proferyd, profyrth *offer*
prow *profit, advantage*
prycke *torment*
pryckyd *dressed, attired*
prys *worth, value*
pundyr *scales, balance*
putte abak, *set aside*
pycke *pitch*
pylt *turned out*
pynne *pin*
pynyngys *punishment*
pystyl *letter, epistle*
pyth, pytt, pytte *placed, set, adorned*

quayl *quail*
quene, qwene, quenys *queen; whore*
quyte, quyth *pay, reward, pay back*
qwed *evil*
qwell *destroy*
qweynt *ingenious, crafty*
qweyntly *craftily*

rad *quickly*
rafte *see* **reve**
rakle *haste*
rape, rapyn, rapyth *hasten*
rapely *quickly*

rappe, rappyd, rappyth *strike*
rappe, rappys *stroke*
rappokys *rascals*
rasche *haste, hasty*
rave, rawyn *behave madly*
rayed *arrayed, dressed*
reche *reach, stretch out, proceed, give*
recke, recknen, rekke, rowt *care*
recorde *remember, recite*
red *advice*
rede *advise; read*
refeccyon *refreshment*
regystre *written account*
rele *rushing about*
rengne *kingdom*
renne, rennynge, rennyth, ron *run*
rent, rentys *revenue, source of income*
reprefe *reproach*
rere *rough*
res(e) *haste*
respyth *respite*
reve *deprive, take away*
reverense *respect*
rewe *feel sorry, grieve*
rewly *fierce, grievous*
rewme *realm*
rewthe *pity*
Rode *Cross*
rodyr, rothyr *rudder*
rote *root, source*
rouge *treat roughly*
route *run about*
row *harsh, rough*
rowe *rest, repose*
rowte, rowtys *riot; retinue*
rowtynge *beating*
ruble *crush*
ruggynge *destroying, eating away*
rynge *resound, speak loudly*
ryth *right*
rythwys, rytwys *righteous, just*
rythwysnes, rythwysnesse, rytwysnes, rytwysnesse *justice*
ryve (v.) *tear apart*; (adj.) *lavish, ample*

sad, sadde *somber; steadfast, solid*
saggyd *sunk*

sale *hall*

sare *see* **sore**

saun *without*

sawter *Book of Psalms*

sawys *speeches, sayings*

schade *shed, pour out*

schall, schalt, schat *must, be destined to; go*

schamely *shameful*

schape, schapyn, schapyth *direct; fashion, prepare*

schappe *appearance*

schat *see* **schall**

schawe *thicket*

schelde, schyld, scheldys *shield; defend*

schenchepe *disgrace*

schend, schende, schent *disgrace; destroy, overthrow*

schene *bright*

schenful *disgraceful*

schere *cut off*

schet, schete, schetyn *shoot, hit*

schete, schyttyth, schet *shut, confine, secure*

scheve *thrive, attain*

schevere *break, shatter*

scho, schos *shoe*

schonde *disgrace, ruin*

schorn *fashioned, reduced*

schreve, schrevyn *see* **schryve**

schrewdnes *malice*

schrewe, schrewys *villain*

schryffte, schryfte *confession*

schryve, schryvyn, schreve, schrevyn *make confession, hear confession*

schyfte *move*

schylle *shrilly*

schyte, schyttyth, schytyn *shit*

scyfftyd *divided*

se, sene, seste, seth, sy *see*

sed, sede *seed, semen*

sekatour, sekatourys, seketouris, sekkatours *executors*

sekyr *certain, secure*

sel, sele *moment, time*

selkowth *wonderful, marvelous*

sely *wretched; insignificant*

seme, semyn *appear, seem*

semly *handsomely; appropriately*

sen *since*

sendel *fine silk*

sens *incense*

serdyn *have intercourse with*

sertys *certainly*

ses, sese, sesse *stop, cease*

sese, sesyd *seize, give legal possession to*

sesun *season; legal possession*

skallyd *scurvy, scabby*

skape *escape*

skathe *damage, injury*

skerre *frighten, scare*

sklaundrys, sklaundyr, slaundyrs *slander, malicious gossip*

skoute, skoutys, skowte, skowtys *whore, slut*

skyl, skyll, skylle, skyllys *reason, argument*

skylful *reasonable, moderate*

skylfully *reasonably*

slake, slakyth *abate*

slaw, slawe *slow, slothful*

slawth, slawthe, slow, slowe *sloth*

sleyt, sleytys *trick; skill*

sloppe *loose gown*

slugge *laziness*

sly *crafty*

slynge (n.) *sling, noose;* (v.) *throw*

smeke *smoke*

smert, smerte (v.) *suffer;* (adj.) *severe, sharp*

smete *struck*

smodyr *heavy smoke*

snelle *vigorously*

snowre *scowl*

snowte *nose*

sobyrnesse *abstinence, temperance*

socoure *help, aid*

sojet *subject*

sokelys *sweet-smelling flowers*

soloyen, solwyd *sully*

somme *sum*

sompe *swamp*

sonde, sondys *land; messenger*

sore (n.) *misery*; (adj.) *painful, sorrowful*; (adv.) *grievously, painfully*

sotel *wily*

soth, sothe *truth*

sothfastnesse *truth*

sothly *truly*

spede *hasten; thrive, fare, succeed*

spell, spelle *speak, tell*

spense *storeroom*

sperd *enclosed, shut up*

spete *sharp point*

spetously *shamefully*

spetows *shameful*

spew *vomit*

sportaunce *entertainment*

spot *disgrace*

spousebreche *adultery*

spud *knife, dagger*

spyll, spylle, spylt *destroy, spill*

stakyr *stagger*

stat, state, statys *condition, position, estate*

staunche *firm, certain*

stede *stead, service*

steke, stekyd *shut up; slit one's throat*

stere, sterre, steryste *incite, stir up*

sterre *star*

sterve *die*

stevene *voice, cry, petition*

stomlynge *stumbling, unstable*

stonge *pierced*

stounde *moment; time of suffering or danger*

stout, stowte *fierce; sturdy*

strenger *stronger*

stresse *hardship, force*

streyne *restraint*

stronde *shore*

stroyed *destroyed*

stye *path*

styf, styffe *powerful, resolute*

styfly *steadfastly*

stynt *stop*

styrt, styrte *leap, escape, avoid*

stytelerys *crowd marshals*

sureté *safety*

swot, swet *sweating*

swote *precious, gracious*

swyche, syche *such*

swythe *immediately*

sye, syest, syh, syhe *sigh*

syinge *sighing*

symonye *trafficking in church offices and sacraments*

syth, sythen, sythyn *since, because, afterwards*

tale, talys *speech, story*; **holde no tale** *care nothing for*

tappyn *strike*

tapytys *tapestries*

targe *shield*

te, tee *go*

teche, techyn, techyth, tawt, tawth *taught; given*

tene, tenyn, tenynge (n.) *pain, grief, anger*; (v.) *harm*

teneful *harmful, painful*

tente *pay attention*

ter *tar*

terage *land, soil*

tere, torn, tore *tear, rend*

tey, teye *tie, bind*

thane *then*

thé *thrive, prosper*

thedom *prosperity*

thende *prosperous, thriving*

thorwe *throughout, by means of*

thost *turd*

thrall *servant*

throwe *moment, period of time*

thryst *thrust*

thwyte *whittle, carve*

thycke, thykke *abundant, prolific*

to-dayschyd *smashed, shattered*

tol, tole *tool*

to-rase *demolish*

to-schende, to-schent *destroy*

tottys *devils*

towte *backside, genitals*

trace, trasche, trase *course, path*

trat *hag*

travest *opposition*

Tre(e) *Cross*
trebelen *make a loud noise, proclaim*
trecchyn *deceive*
trost *trust, rely on*
trostyly *faithfully*
trotte *move quickly*
trow, trowe *believe, think*
trumpe, trumpys *trumpets*
trussyd *packed, enclosed*
tryst *trust*
turmentry *torments*
tweyne *two*
tyne *lose*
tyre *dress, attire*
tysyd *enticed*
tyth *quickly, immediately*
tytly *quickly*

underne *midmorning; 9:00 a.m. See explanatory note for line 138.*
undyrfonge *undertake*
unhende *inappropriate, ungracious*
unkynd, unkynde *ungrateful, uncharitable, unnatural*
unnethe *scarcely*
unquert *wicked*
unsayd *not spoken*
unslye *foolish, unwise*
unthende *unprosperous, unhealthy, feeble*
unthryfte *decadence*
unwolde *infirm, ill*

vale *valley*
varyaunce *dispute, conflict*
vaunce *lift up, advance*
vaunward, vaward *vanguard*
vayle *benefit, advantage*
velony *disgrace*
verité *truth*
vesture *clothing*
vexillator *herald, standard-bearer*
vyle *vile*
vyre *crossbow bolt*

wagge *move, set in motion*
wane *lacking*

wanne *when*
wappyd *wrapped*
wappyn *strike*
war, ware *careful, wary*
warne *forbid, stop*
wave *wave, waver, move to and fro*
wawe *move, go*
wax, waxit, waxyn, waxyt *grow, become*
waytyth *lie in wait, ambush*
weche *which*
wede, wedys *clothing*
weder, wedyr *whither, to what place*
welde *use; possess; manage*
wele, will (n.) *well-being*; (adj.) *fortunate*; (adv.) *clearly, prosperously, thoroughly*
well(e) *well, fountain*
welny *almost*
weltyr *roll about*
wend, wende, wendyn *go*
wene, wenyth *think; expect*
wenne, wynne *joy*
were *defend*
werke, wirke, wrout, wrouht, wrowt, wyrke *do, make, cause*
werne *forbid; defend; command*
wet, wete, wetyn, wot, wost, woste, wyste, wyt, wytyn *know, find out*
weyen, weyin *measure, weigh*
weytys *scales*
whedyr, whethyr, wedyr, wheydyr *which*
whow *who*
whowso *whoever*
whwtynge *shouting*
wirke *see* **werke**
wod, wode, wood, woode *mad, insane, confused, furious*
wonde, wondys (n.) *wound; rod*
wonde, wounde, wondyn (v.) *wrapped, wound*
wone *wealth*
wonne *dwell*
wonnynge *dwelling*
wonys *place, dwelling*
wost, woste, wot *see* **wet**

wrak, wrake *ruin, destruction, harm, pain*

wreke, wrekyn, wroke, wrokyn *avenge*

wrenchys *tricks, deceits*

wrethe, wretthe, wroth, wrothe *wrath, anger*

wrout, wrouth, wrowt *see* **werke**

wryen *turn away*

wynne (n.) *see* **wenne**; (v.) *entice, capture, regain*

wyste *see* **wet**

wyt, wyte (v.) *see* **wet**

wyt, wyttys, wytys (n.) *mind, senses*

wyth, wythe, wythte *person*

wythly, wytly *quickly*

wythsyt *withstand*

wytty *intelligent, clever*

yare (adj.) *quick*; (adv.) *quickly*

yeld, yelde, yolde *pay, submit, yield*

yelpe *boast*

yene, yone *those*

yep *alert*

yerde *rod; enclosure*

yerne *quickly*

yonge, yynge *young*

yys *yes*

yyt *yet, nevertheless*

Stanzaic Guy of Warwick, edited by Alison Wiggins (2004)

Saints' Lives in Middle English Collections, edited by E. Gordon Whatley, with Anne B. Thompson and Robert K. Upchurch (2004)

Siege of Jerusalem, edited by Michael Livingston (2004)

The Kingis Quair and Other Prison Poems, edited by Linne R. Mooney and Mary-Jo Arn (2005)

The Chaucerian Apocrypha: A Selection, edited by Kathleen Forni (2005)

John Gower, *The Minor Latin Works*, edited and translated by R. F. Yeager, with *In Praise of Peace*, edited by Michael Livingston (2005)

Sentimental and Humorous Romances: Floris and Blancheflour, Sir Degrevant, The Squire of Low Degree, The Tournament of Tottenham, and The Feast of Tottenham, edited by Erik Kooper (2006)

The Dicts and Sayings of the Philosophers, edited by John William Sutton (2006)

Everyman and Its Dutch Original, Elckerlijc, edited by Clifford Davidson, Martin W. Walsh, and Ton J. Broos (2007)

The N-Town Plays, edited by Douglas Sugano, with assistance by Victor I. Scherb (2007)

The Book of John Mandeville, edited by Tamarah Kohanski and C. David Benson (2007)

John Lydgate, *The Temple of Glas*, edited by J. Allan Mitchell (2007)

The Northern Homily Cycle, edited by Anne B. Thompson (2008)

Codex Ashmole 61: A Compilation of Popular Middle English Verse, edited by George Shuffelton (2008)

Chaucer and the Poems of "Ch," edited by James I. Wimsatt (revised edition 2009)

William Caxton, *The Game and Playe of the Chesse*, edited by Jenny Adams (2009)

John the Blind Audelay, *Poems and Carols*, edited by Susanna Fein (2009)

Two Moral Interludes: The Pride of Life and Wisdom, edited by David Klausner (2009)

John Lydgate, *Mummings and Entertainments*, edited by Claire Sponsler (2010)

Mankind, edited by Kathleen M. Ashley and Gerard NeCastro (2010)

COMMENTARY SERIES

Haimo of Auxerre, *Commentary on the Book of Jonah*, translated with an introduction and notes by Deborah Everhart (1993)

Medieval Exegesis in Translation: Commentaries on the Book of Ruth, translated with an introduction and notes by Lesley Smith (1996)

Nicholas of Lyra's Apocalypse Commentary, translated with an introduction and notes by Philip D. W. Krey (1997)

Rabbi Ezra Ben Solomon of Gerona, *Commentary on the Song of Songs and Other Kabbalistic Commentaries*, selected, translated, and annotated by Seth Brody (1999)

John Wyclif, *On the Truth of Holy Scripture*, translated with an introduction and notes by Ian Christopher Levy (2001)

Second Thessalonians: Two Early Medieval Apocalyptic Commentaries, introduced and translated by Steven R. Cartwright and Kevin L. Hughes (2001)

The "Glossa Ordinaria" on the Song of Songs, translated with an introduction and notes by Mary Dove (2004)

The Seven Seals of the Apocalypse: Medieval Texts in Translation, translated with an introduction and notes by Francis X. Gumerlock (2009)

DOCUMENTS OF PRACTICE SERIES

Love and Marriage in Late Medieval London, selected, translated, and introduced by Shannon McSheffrey (1995)

Sources for the History of Medicine in Late Medieval England, selected, introduced, and translated by Carole Rawcliffe (1995)

A Slice of Life: Selected Documents of Medieval English Peasant Experience, edited, translated, and with an introduction by Edwin Brezette DeWindt (1996)

Regular Life: Monastic, Canonical, and Mendicant "Rules," selected and introduced by Douglas J. McMillan and Kathryn Smith Fladenmuller (1997); second edition, selected and introduced by Daniel Marcel La Corte and Douglas J. McMillan (2004)

Women and Monasticism in Medieval Europe: Sisters and Patrons of the Cistercian Reform, selected, translated, and with an introduction by Constance H. Berman (2002)

Medieval Notaries and Their Acts: The 1327–1328 Register of Jean Holanie, introduced, edited, and translated by Kathryn L. Reyerson and Debra A. Salata (2004)

🖉 Medieval German Texts in Bilingual Editions Series

Sovereignty and Salvation in the Vernacular, 1050–1150, introduction, translations, and notes by James A. Schultz (2000)

Ava's New Testament Narratives: "When the Old Law Passed Away," introduction, translation, and notes by James A. Rushing, Jr. (2003)

History as Literature: German World Chronicles of the Thirteenth Century in Verse, introduction, translation, and notes by R. Graeme Dunphy (2003)

Thomasin von Zirclaria, *Der Welsche Gast (The Italian Guest)*, translated by Marion Gibbs and Winder McConnell (2009)

🖉 Varia

The Study of Chivalry: Resources and Approaches, edited by Howell Chickering and Thomas H. Seiler (1988)

Studies in the Harley Manuscript: The Scribes, Contents, and Social Contexts of British Library MS Harley 2253, edited by Susanna Fein (2000)

The Liturgy of the Medieval Church, edited by Thomas J. Heffernan and E. Ann Matter (2001; second edition 2005)

🖉 To Order Please Contact:

Medieval Institute Publications
Western Michigan University
Kalamazoo, MI 49008-5432
Phone (269) 387-8755
FAX (269) 387-8750
http://www.wmich.edu/medieval/mip/index.html

Typeset in 10/13 New Baskerville
and Golden Cockerel Ornaments display
Designed by Linda K. Judy
Manufactured by McNaughton & Gunn, Inc.

Medieval Institute Publications
College of Arts and Sciences
Western Michigan University
1903 W. Michigan Avenue
Kalamazoo, MI 49008-5432
http://www.wmich.edu/medieval/mip

 WESTERN MICHIGAN UNIVERSITY